THREE SCORE AND TEN

A HISTORY OF CHRIST SCHOOL
Arden, North Carolina
1900-1970

David W. McCullough

Publisher: Ralph Roberts

Vice President/Publishing: Pat Hutchison Roberts

Cover Design: **WorldComm®**

Senior Editor: Vivian Terrell

Production Editor: Gayle Graham

Interior Design and Electronic Page Assembly: **WorldComm®**

Printed in the United States of America

10 9 8 7 6 5 4 3 2 1

ISBN 1-56664-104-7 Library of Congress number: 96-61366

WorldComm®—a division of Creativity, Inc.–is a full-service publisher located at 65 Macedonia Road, Alexander NC 28701. Phone (704) 252-9515 or (704) 255-8719 fax.

WorldComm® is distributed to the trade by **Alexander Distributing,** 65 Macedonia Road, Alexander NC 28701. Phone (704) 252-9515 or (704) 255-8719 fax. For orders only: 1-800-472-0438. Visa and MasterCard accepted.

Mr. Dave

To
Joe and Betsy

and to

Ann, Lucy, David, and Jim

Contents

Preface

I love Christ School. That's why I undertook the pleasure of writing this book about Christ School, its first seventy years. It's neither definitive nor exhaustive.

Three Score and Ten is not the usual history. There is some narrative and chronology. There are many anecdotes and much material written or presented by alumni themselves. It is about things common to all Christ School students during a period that was not Camelot. It was better than Camelot: it was real. We can never outlive it nor escape its reach. But then most of us wouldn't want to. It's a story that should leave none untouched and should evoke memories for all.

The preface is a place to thank all who helped in the project. For fear of leaving out the name of a single person, I can only thank all of you.

One last observation. We were blessed with three powerful leaders: Fr. Wetmore, Fr. Harris, and Mr. Dave. For that miracle we must be eternally grateful.

Bill

What wonderful years those were. How grateful I am to have been a part of the lives of so many Christ School boys.

12/11/96

David McCullough

Introduction

Christ School began as a dream in the mind of Fr. Thomas C. Wetmore. The dream was carried on and strengthened by Fr. Ruben Rivers Harris and his son David P. Harris over nearly seven decades.

That dream began on four acres of barren hilltop which was deeded to the School October 10, 1900. It did not appear to be a place where dreams of any kind could take shape. B.F. Shuford, a long time friend of both the Wetmores and the Harrises, described the parcel as the only area of land in Buncombe County that "couldn't even grow thistle." (He was right. Instead it was to become a place where countless numbers of boys grew into men.)

Mr. Dave, who on more than one occasion was caught in the shower all lathered up when the water pressure disappeared, often wondered out loud why the school had not been founded in the valley below, where water pressure would remain high.

During those early days, the school was not a pretty sight, but Fr. Wetmore envisioned a boarding school which would also serve as an industrial training school for surrounding mountain children (who would gladly walk up to ten miles a day or so for an education) and a college preparatory school for those boys who came from across the state or elsewhere. He foresaw a school that would provide sound education and religious training at a minimal cost for those boys and girls who wanted to improve themselves.

During the years 1900-1970, these three leaders never lost sight of their conviction that they could provide an excellent education at a modest cost. When Fr. Harris decided to convert Christ School to a boy's boarding school only in the mid-1920's, he made certain that expenses remained low and that the school was still for those of modest means.

After World War II, when the pressure from colleges demanded even better academic performance, Mr. Dave continued the Christ School dream. When he retired as headmaster in 1967, room, board, and tuition had just risen to $2,000 a year, and the school's strength lay in its ability to accommodate students of solid middle class background whose parents sent their children here from small towns, the countryside, a few major cities (New Orleans, Savannah, Charlotte, Greensboro, and Richmond), and some mid-western and northeastern states. These were parents who often sent their sons here at great personal sacrifice. The tuition through most of those years was an average fee, meaning that parents who could pay more than the average usually did so, thus enabling some boys to attend whose parents could not afford the minimum. In the process, Christ School never wavered in its goal to make men out of boys while providing a college preparatory education.

For most of that time, as the early literature shows and alumni of that period remember, Christ School was for those boys who chose to attend here and were willing to assume the responsibility for their own success; those who were unwilling or unable to measure up to the high academic and moral standards set by Fr. Wetmore and his successors were weeded out.

View from the cloister.

I: 1900-1906

The Seed Is Sown

It was obviously not the physical plant which attracted students to Christ School when its doors officially opened on September 30, 1901, to twenty day students–boys and girls who walked to class from distances up to six miles away. What the campus consisted of was a hastily built three-story red school house sitting on a four acre knoll mostly barren of vegetation and plant life and surrounded by dense woods.[1]

This center of learning, constructed of cedar shingles and torn down in 1914, stood on Yard A where the present linden tree offers comforting shade in the spring.[2] It commanded a knoll which sloped westward and on which was not to be found a single tree. Before that year ended, some eighty-nine mountain children had spent part or all of that time under a staff of four: Mr. Wetmore, the principal; Mrs. Wetmore, John H. Gilreath, and Miss Celestine McCullough, the latter two receiving salaries of $250 and $225 each for a year's labor. The length of school years were uncertain during this period, varying from six to eight months. One year, both Fr. Wetmore and his wife were absent from school from Christmas until Easter because of her illness. Teacher G.H. Wright conducted school business during their absence, with the year ending around Easter.

Even today students have little difficulty in determining where the first two school buildings were located, each constructed on the same site. In the fall and spring, an observer can look out of the windows on the top floor of the Susan A. Wetmore Administration Building and see the outline of the original as the grass will have a slightly yellowish hue.

What brought these children to the Red School House was their and their parents' desire to provide them a better way of life, a way out of hunger and poverty in a mountain area almost totally cut off from the rest of the world and lacking in public schools. They were the willing tools, and a few dedicated teachers did the rest, teaching a mixed group from grade one through ten (the highest grade at that time) and age was no barrier.

---

[1]There were two students in 1900: General George Washington Lyda and Sam Stroup.
[2]Mr. Dave, who had a degree in horticulture from North Carolina State, planted this linden tree there in 1951. He dug it up as a seedling while driving through the Great Smoky National Park. The Georgina White Memorial Hall was dedicated on June 14, 1901.

There was no shame if a fifteen year old was in a third grade class, for he was a victim of circumstances, not choice.

But even as they were setting up a school to teach mountain children craft and industrial arts and practical skills which would improve their economic situation, the Wetmores were from the very beginning laying the foundations of a college preparatory school that would one day supercede the vocational side. By the next fall, Thompson Hall was completed, a boy's dorm which housed twenty-one boarding students. And the catalogue for the 1902-03 school year clearly stated that besides providing a training in industrial and academic studies, Christ School provided "the further advantage of college preparatory classes."

Christ School's first admissions policy did not simply admit anyone and everyone. Primarily it was a school for those who had no money to attend school elsewhere. "To pupils at Christ School," Fr. Wetmore said on many occasions, "it is not a choice between Christ School or some other, it is the only possible opportunity open to them to get an education." Neither rain, sleet, mud, nor snow would keep these children from coming.

The distinguishing point which determined whether a boy or girl was to be admitted to Christ School hinged on whether or not the student truly desired an education. No one was ever turned away for lack of money, but each was expected to carry out the spirit of the school. The catalogue of 1902-03 affirmed this idea: "It is our purpose to place this school within the reach of all who prove themselves worthy . . . . The total cost is put as low as possible ($5 per month for boarders). It is not our desire to make money out of the school, but to make good men and women. No effort do we consider too great to help those who are trying to help themselves, and only this class are we able to take in the school."

In 1902, Mr. Wetmore admitted twenty-one boarders who filled up Thompson Hall, but more than half that number were turned away. Most of the boarders were unable to pay the $5 per month for room, board, and tuition, but some were able to pay in farm produce and all helped keep the costs of school down by doing all work around the place except for the cooking. Even those who could pay were not exempt from the daily chores–making beds, waiting on tables, cutting wood, starting fires, and feeding chickens, for the aim was always to provide practical training for life. The seedbed of what was later called the self-help system was already planted. By the fall of 1905, Fr. Wetmore felt good about what had thus far developed. He said, "Christ School is not an experiment but an established fact." This was to be borne out in August a year later when Mr. Wetmore died suddenly at age thrity-seven, for the roots he labored to plant continued to grow, even amidst some turmoil.

With the arrival of the first boarders, the order of the school day was set which carried over into the transition period that was to follow Mr. Wetmore's death. The schedule focused on work, study, and play–all underscored and strengthened through open expression of thanks to God. Chapel services (an abbreviated form of morning prayer), Bible study, the pledge of allegiance, and announcements marked the first half hour of each school day which began at 9 a.m. From time to time, outside ministers and laymen were brought in to lecture during this opening exercise. Day students arrived for this period.

The day began with first bell at 6:30 and breakfast at 7:30, with room clean-up for boarders in-between. From 8 to 9, there was a combination period of work and study–a long job period if needed and a long study hall if the weather was bad or if academic deficiencies justified it. Classes then ran from 9:30 to noon. Filling in the next hour was noon-day prayer in assembly followed by dinner (the big meal was eaten in the middle of the day) and recreation or rest. The boarding students and faculty ate in the dining room-kitchen area located in the basement of Thompson Hall, which, after St. Dunstan's Hall was built in 1916, was to be converted into a furnace and shower room. Day students ate on the grounds in good weather and inside the school house on bad days.

Classes resumed from 1 to 2:30, followed by work from 2:30 to 4 p.m. There was much to be done–carrying logs to the dormitory for heat, carrying water from nearby springs until the well was dug in 1903, and doing chores on the farm, from shucking corn to feeding chickens. For the next hour, there was a period of recreation, with most of the boys playing baseball and most of the day students, boys and girls, trudging home to do their chores. For the boarders, there was an hour of study at 5 p.m. with supper following.

The evening schedule included a half hour of study (7 to 7:30) while the meal was being digested, with recreation from then until 9 o'clock. The evening was concluded with prayers and roll call in the dormitory at 9 o'clock and lights were out for all a half hour later. When day was done, there was apparently little mischief, for Asheville was far away, there were no night spot attractions in Arden and Fletcher, and the schedule was a long and tiring one. Sound sleep was the reward for hard work.

The curriculum was a genuine mixture of vocational and academic subjects which would provide a student with marketable job and craft skills and a pathway to college, depending upon how far each student wanted to go. Tuition for day students in each of the areas of study ranged from fifty cents to one dollar a month.

Included under academics were English Language and Rhetoric, English Composition, English and American Literature with reading from the best authors. Emphasis was placed upon memorization, acting out, discussion, formal readings and declamation. Other subjects were Latin (grammar, translation, and composition), Higher Arithmetic, Algebra and Geometry, Civics, History, Geography, Chemistry, Physics, Physiology, and Hygiene.

The practical courses provided a wide-range of vocational directions. The business course included bookkeeping, commercial law, typing, and stenography. Boys, in particular, were directed into carpentry and furniture-making. Plain and fancy cooking was taught to the girls in domestic science, and sewing class instructed girls in patching and mending and dressmaking.[3] Music was also a part of the curriculum, and the whole school was taught to sing at no extra charge. Instrumental training was provided for a small fee. A printing press gave students training in this area, and students printed the early catalogues and the *Galax Leaf*, the first school paper.[4] Telegraphy provided another vocational path. But along with these practical courses, each student choosing such direction was also required to take basic academic courses such as reading, writing, spelling, arithmetic, pertinent facts of chemistry and physics, and so on. A student could end up with one of three recognitions: a vocational certificate, a general academic certificate, or a college preparatory diploma.

Considered a most important part of the process of educating both students and boarders was the library and reading room found to the left of the main entrance as you walked into the school house. By 1903, it contained more than one thousand volumes (mostly gifts from friends and philanthropic organizations), magazines, and newspapers. The library was open each evening to day students and boarders alike and provided a place of pleasure for some during the 7:30 to 9 p.m. recreation period. The catalogue of 1902-1903 said that a lecture was given each week on current events and that the reading of students was directed each week to articles of special interest.

To teach here in the early years meant, for practical purposes, taking a monastic vow of poverty. The reward was taking children of all ages and impoverished backgrounds as far as their feet and minds could carry them. It was seeing the eyes of the girls light up when they made their first loaf of bread and the proud smirk of a barefoot boy who had walked five miles to school as he handled a mitre properly or completed the crafting of an end table. Proud because he made it and proud because it helped pay his way. These dedicated people–the majority were women in the early days–were more than teachers of crafts and knowledge; they taught manners and conduct and visited the homes and shared the ups-and-downs of each youngster, and even provided kindly but stern rebukes when necessary. The teachers here during the Wetmore years are now merely names of the past, but their legacy of personal sacrifice is a permanent memorial.

The catalogue of 1902-03 shows the teaching staff had grown from an

[3]"January 17, 1902, will always be one of the more memorable days–The first loaf of bread was made by the girls' cooking class."–*Galax Leaf*

[4]Printing was taught by Adrian Mallory, who reportedly was a great, great, great grandson of Benjamin Franklin, no mean printer himself. Quite talented, Mallory also did oil painting and took orders.

initial two to five. They were Mr. Wetmore, the principal, who taught Bible, Boys' Industrial, Mathematics, and Physics; Mrs. Wetmore, (Bible, Latin, and Higher English); Miss Lilian Eichbaum, (Domestic Science, Singing, Physical Culture, and Lower English); Mr. John Gilreath, (Middle Grade English and Lower Mathematics); and Miss Margaret F. Beale, (Instrumental Music). Other names who also made the long daily walk to teach at Christ School during those years were Miss Celestine McCullough, Mrs. Anna McBee, Mrs. Augusta Justice, Mr. George H. Wright, Miss Lillian Taylor, Mr. Capehart, Miss Florence Schaefer (primary school), Garland A. Thomasson (stenography), Mrs. Mary Bronson (matron), and Mrs. Kate Stark (music).

Though living conditions were primitive then to what we know now, these mountain children did have a good time and found much to be happy about.[5] One had to be content with more simple things, with made-up games and little equipment and not much money to spend. Imagination was a long step toward fun. Just eating an occasional piece of hard penny candy bought at the little store near the grist mill would brighten the long trek to school. An orange, usually to be found in a stocking at Christmas, would cause a face to light up with eager anticipation. And baseball, throwing it up into the air and catching it as though you were a Ty Cobb or tossing it around with several classmates, was an almost year around experience. In fact baseball was Christ School's first sport and was played in both fall and spring. Only the months of December-to-February might be considered too cold.

It was Fr. Wetmore who kept interest high in baseball. He was a rabid fan and would often be found down at Wetmore pasture watching practice or a pick-up game between the boys and the community. In these early days, both students and men who worked for the school played for Christ School, as was the case elsewhere. Two power-hitters Fessor remembered playing for Mr. Wetmore's team were Charlie Whitaker and Ben Shuford, who worked for Mr. Wetmore.[6] That's why some of the early baseball pictures suggest that the teams had some age on them. Christ School had been open three weeks in its first year when the Greenie squad toppled an Arden team at the pasture, 10-8. Four days later the school team beat the same outfit 12-11. The next year, a school group sponsored debates and other programs to raise money to buy red-and-white uniforms, a first for a Christ School athletic team. They trounced Arden 24-14 and went on to play Fruitland and Farm School. The games provided entertainment for the community, with parents coming by foot or wagon to cross Gap Creek to watch their team.

The Greenie pasture was not the easiest field to play on. It was uneven,

[5]A dynamo arrived in January 1903 to bring electricity to the assembly room and to the kitchen in Thompson Hall. Lamps and oil provided most lighting. A water tank and pump were among some immediate needs. They were added two years later but there was no storage tank.

[6]Shuford's two sons, Charlie and Walter, both attended Christ School for many years and were outstanding athletes at North Carolina State.

rough terrain, often flooded in the spring, and visited too frequently by the Wetmores' cows strolling the full length of the meadow. The field, looking west, was situated on what is now the soccer field. At one end, in centerfield, stood two towering water maple trees. Mr. Wetmore made a standing wager that he would give $5 (an amount equal to Christ School's first endowment gift) to anyone who hit a ball over the maples. Batters continued to accept the challenge long after Mr. Wetmore died, until the baseball field was moved up to the main campus (c. 1920) on what is now the football field. No student ever claimed that prize. One account has it that on a night in 1915 someone (perhaps a disgruntled hitter) entered the field and cut down one of those colorful maples.

Several organizations were formed which provided social occasions for the weekends, both for boarders and day students alike. They provided pleasure, they stimulated the mind, and they helped hone individual abilities and talents. Included among them were the Literary Society, the Log Cabin Association and the Girls Friendly Society.

Apparently an effort had been made earlier to form the Christ School Literary Society out of a similar community society that existed before the school was founded, but it got off the ground in January 1904 when about thirty boys and girls drew up a constitution and elected officers. By April, a series of three debates had been held and the Easter issue of the *Galax Leaf* said the members have "shown themselves to be earnest and able arguers and contest every point hotly." The topic to be debated in April was–Resolved: That George Washington was a greater general than Robert E. Lee. That topic was certain to raise some starch. And one of the features to be added to the commencement that year was a debate. The Literary Society held its debates in the library and they involved boys only. The girls were equally involved in the society and displayed their ability by readings and declamation.

An interesting innovation was the Log Cabin Association of Christ School started by the smaller boys in 1902. Membership in this organization was limited to interested boys and Mr. Wetmore. William C. Campbell described the origin in an article he wrote for the *Galax Leaf* in 1904.

> The way we came about to build the cabin was that a few small boys on a Saturday built a little hut out of sacks and took it to the woods, and that night we had a feast and the big boys got interested in it and stole the hut and carried it away.
>
> So when the big boys decided it was the thing to do, they joined with the little ones and built a more substantial cabin with slabs of wood and tin provided by Mr. Wetmore. He also provided them some tin cups and plates to eat out of as well as other utensils.

To become a part of this "feasting" organization, initiation was required. Again Campbell provides a first hand account:

> One mode of initiation is to turn a boy over a barrel and put a curtain behind him, and tell him to say 'Bring forth the royal bumper and let him bump.' When he says that, a boy on the other side of the curtain butts him nearly through the barrel.

The Christ School branch of the Girls Friendly Society was a social and outreach group that involved not only the girl day students who attended Christ School but also others in the community. It provided a social occasion in which the girls could meet to share prayer, light-hearted conversation, and show off some of their examples of sewing, cooking, and embroidery. When the society was organized is not clear, but the first mention of the group appears in the February 1905 issue of the *Galax Leaf.*

Among its annual contributions to the school life was the presenting of a program at school just before Christmas vacation began, with the members being assisted by some members of the Domestic Science class. The program provided occasion for the girls to display the social skills acquired during the year. The entertainment provided on December 17, 1905, included recitations, tableax, and music. One of the highlights of the evening occurred when the young ladies, dressed in the bright costumes of Indian maidens, presented a ritualistic dance in the assembly room. From there the program moved into the library, which had been turned into a wigwam.

The occasion was also a money-making opportunity for the Girls Friendly Society, and they cleared $9.50 that evening, with $8.50 being sent to a missionary hospital in Nanking, China, and a dollar to the Church Periodical Club in New York, which supplied the library with magazines and books. On display in the "wigwam" were articles of needle-work made by the members. Joining in the effort was the Domestic Science class, whose members sold in the science room candy and cake made by that group.

The Girls Friendly Society was a continuously growing organization and the Sunday following the program five new members were admitted, bringing the GFS to twenty-nine medal members and a large class of probationers. The girls were looking forward to Easter and the beginning of spring. They received as a gift eight rolls of crepe paper which the older girls were to make into brightly colored hats for the Easter parade.

One pleasurable occasion could never be erased from the minds of the Christ School boarders enrolled in the year 1902-03. This marked the appearance that fall in Asheville of Theodore Roosevelt, the President of the United States, who was on a tour deep into democratic country. For

Christ School students, the visit of this indomitable spirit was a holiday from the classroom. Thanks to a gift from Mr. E.F. Robbins, a Chicago businessman, transportation was paid for to allow the students to make the journey September 9 to Asheville to join thousands of other anxious to see and hear this most vigorous President, whose face had been cut a week earlier when an automobile ran into the car in which he was riding. The wagon-trip was three-hours each way, preceded and followed by the dusty walk on foot to-and-from Arden.

By 1904, the basics for an education at Christ School had been provided.[6A] With a flurry of dedicated work, service, and money-raising trips to the North, Fr. Wetmore, who continued to hold services in other mission churches, had succeeded in expanding the facilities from the red school house built in 1901. Now the campus also included a boy's dormitory, a two-story carpentry and craft shop, a fifty-four-foot deep well, a bell tower, a 107 acre farm, a garden plot, and a chicken yard. Milk and butter came from the Wetmore farm, as did some ice from the ice-house. Salaries for teachers, scholarships for boarders, and other necessary expenses were being met from contributions of church societies and individual business men from the speaking trips undertaken by both Wetmores. Those trips took them to Chicago, Delaware, Maryland, New York (including the Stock Exchange) Rhode Island, and Pennsylvania.

By 1904-05, Fr. Wetmore was beginning to speak about the key element missing from the school–a chapel which would symbolically point to Christ as the center of what life here was all about. Prayer and religious exercises were offered every class day in a section of the assembly hall separated by a divider. But this was a temporary arrangement in Mr. Wetmore's mind, not suitable for conveying the real feeling and mysticism a church would provide.

The money required to turn the chapel into a reality was $1,000, the cost for the materials. The labor had already been promised by workers and farmers in the surrounding area, and the stone would be quarried from the school farm, in an area slightly southeast of the old dairy barn. The chapel would stand on the knoll, a few feet to the northwest of the school building.

"The chapel is needed more than we can express," Mr. Wetmore said in February 1905, "and will be a power to help us reach higher things not only in the School, but also in the community for miles around." In his heart, the chapel would not only serve the boarders, but also the day students and their parents and others in the community who needed a place of worship. By the end of 1905, half of the money had been raised for a chapel which Mr. Wetmore would design.

In writing about the need for the one thousand dollars in the *Galax Leaf* of February 1905, Mr. Wetmore's remarks seemed prophetic:

[6A]During the summer, some 37 children 4-14 years old attended the school, including two 14 year old boys just learning to read and write.

> What more beautiful memorial could be made to some loved one than the erection of this House of God?

Christ Chapel, as it was to be dedicated in formal ceremony May 7, 1907, was not to be completed until after the death of Mr. Wetmore, whose body rests with that of his wife in twin graves beneath the chancel.[7] A block of granite encased in the original oak wooden floors contains an inscription which established their connection to Christ School. Their real memorial, though, lies in the love of living they so generously shared.

The kind of life that Thomas Cogdell Wetmore lived–and the source of his strength–can best be found in an introduction he wrote in a diary on February 14, 1894:

> Be strong and of good courage and do it: fear not, nor be dismayed; for the Lord God will be with thee; He will not fail thee, nor forsake thee, until thou has finished all the work for the service of the House of the Lord.
>
> I Chronicles XXVIII, 20

Mrs. Myrtle Peacock of Oxford stands on the steps leading into the old school building. She was one of many wonderful teachers who sacrificed for the work of Christ School.

[7]Though it would not bear his name, those who contributed the money for the Chapel considered it a testimony to Fr. Wetmore.

❋ The Breadth of My Love ❋

In the stained glass window above the altar,
the founders of Christ School let it be known whom they would follow.

I:1900-1906

The Rev. Wetmore Years

His ministry was brief–an all too short twelve years, of which only half was spent establishing Christ School. But the Rev. Thomas C. Wetmore was to leave a deeply-rooted Christian legacy which his two major successors were to continue for over sixty years, almost without missing a beat. Christ School 1900-1970 is the remarkable story of how three different men shared and expanded the same dream. The Rev. Wetmore found his strength in a Biblical passage he often repeated: "The joy of the Lord is my strength." Those who mourned at his premature passing (and this would include nearly every mountain household from Hendersonville to Asheville) remembered him as a man who "went about doing good."

During the six years allotted Mr. Wetmore to tend the growth of his beloved school, a goal which stood constantly before him was the need to build a chapel. Necessity required that the initial construction must include a school building, a carpentry shop, and a dormitory if the school was to help the mountain boys and girls, for Christ School had a mission to provide industrial training, college preparation, and Christian teaching built upon daily example. Like Moses, Fr. Wetmore got a glimpse of his promised chapel but did not live to conduct services in it. At age thirty-seven he was struck down by appendicitis as the several hour long trip by wagon to the hospital in Biltmore permitted the poison to spread.

It was as though God's hand was on the shoulder of this youthful and energetic young man to found a mountain school. By the late 1880's Mr. Wetmore was made general missionary under Bishop Junius Horner and was on the Education Committee which by 1900 was running twenty schools in Western North Carolina.[8] He lived with his wife in her family home called Struan, situated about half a mile northeast of where Christ Chapel would be completed on campus in 1907. His dream was to build a school to provide education and hope for mountain children otherwise condemned to a bleak future of poverty. In many ways, he was simply

[8]After getting married in 1893, Fr. Wetmore was ordained a deacon in St. Luke's in Lincolnton, N.C. in 1894 and a priest in 1898.

following the lead of his father, the Rev. William R. Wetmore, who served a pastorate in Lincolnton for forty-two years, was a scholar in mathematics, Greek, and Latin, taught in the male academy in Lincolnton, and was a disciplinarian who tempered justice with love.

Mr. Wetmore carried certain advantages with him in the building of this mountain school. He married into the descendants of the Robertson family, which had purchased 1500 acres at a tax foreclosing before the Civil War and built Struan. From that family was to come the initial four acres that made up the original campus as well as much additional land that was to follow in later years. Besides that, Mr. Wetmore was energetic and a natural salesman who had no trouble selling his dream before church groups North and South to support this enterprise so badly needed in an area where public schools were not to penetrate until the early 1920's. And beside him, in Susan Allen Wetmore, he had a wife totally committed to his dream.

Reality began to set in when Susan Lyman deeded four acres to the Wetmores on October 10, 1900, for the use of the school. Two years later, Mrs. Lyman was to turn over an additional two acres to be used for a garden and chicken yard. Christ School did not officially open in 1900 because it was necessary to build a school building. But several of the children were tutored at Struan where the Wetmores lived with her parents. Thanks to a gift from a New York family, a red school house was completed and dedicated in 1901, and on September 30 Christ School opened its doors to twenty students. Georgina White Hall was a three-story, cedar-shingle building which contained fourteen rooms and a small chapel and an unfinished attic. Not only did the one thousand dollar gift pay for the school building, but it provided enough to hire a teacher.

Before the year was over, some eight-nine day students–boys and girls–attended classes for either the whole or part of the eight month school year. The only break was a sixteen day Christmas holiday. These students walked, rain or snow, two to six miles each way from Arden, Limestone, Fairview, Fletcher, Buena Vista, Roosevelt, and Skyland. Thirteen families provided fifty-five students, including nine Rickmans and five Pressleys. Little Susannah Wetmore, who was later to direct the choir and play the organ in Christ Chapel, was a student in that class. Several students came from afar: Charles and Cora Shaffer from New Jersey and Thomas Westfeldt from New Orleans. They were among the few "boarding" students, except that they did not live at Christ School but in homes off-campus.

Besides teaching Bible, shop classes, mathematics, and physics, Fr. Wetmore, when not involved in raising money for the school, was busy with construction–planning and directing the next stage of building. For one thing, in 1902, the third floor of the school building was completed and plastered so that it could serve as a dormitory to house six or seven boys. The rest of Georgina White Memorial Hall contained an assembly room with an adjoining chapel separated by folding doors, a library, a cooking-sewing room, a printing and telegraph office, a weaving and spinning room, and several classrooms. In addition, he oversaw the building of a carpenter's shop (gift of a friend) on the site of what is now the 38 Dorm, and furnished it with an engine, lathe, saws, and a good set of hand tools. Then, ready for more than twenty boarding students that fall was the newly constructed John I. Thompson Memorial Hall which contained eight rooms, two large dorms, and a deep piazza around two sides of the building. The $1,000 needed was given to the school by Mrs. Thompson of Troy, N.Y, in honor of John I. Thompson, who was warden of St. Paul's Episcopal Church in Troy. She gave another $227 to pay for furniture and three years of fire insurance.

To start a mission school from scratch required courage, nerve, intelligence, and abiding faith, the ingredients with which Mr. Wetmore was well endowed. Though somewhat slight in stature and build, underneath his gentle and kind demeanor was a ruggedness and toughness which enabled him to follow a merciless schedule as he almost single-handedly strove to bring a better life to the children of Appalachia.

One necessary ingredient was money. Obviously the mountain folks at the turn of the century were unable to pay the cost of such an undertaking, so that other sources had to be found. Mr. Wetmore looked to the North and a kind of benefaction that had great appeal to the wealthy and strong support within the umbrella of the Episcopal Church. This was an era in which northern philanthropy was especially involved in the kind of self-help mission that Fr. Wetmore envisioned. It was not to be a hand-out to perpetuate hand-outs but a helping hand, whereby children with a desire to succeed would be able to substitute desire, determination (some would call it pluck), and work for the cash required to provide the much needed schooling. For it was education which would provide the craft and trade skills necessary for better jobs and rigorous academic training for entrance into college.

Never once did Fr. Wetmore shirk that somewhat onerous burden of seeking money. What was "begging" to many was God's response to his dream from others. He did not waste time in starting. In November 1901, Mr. Wetmore rode the train on an extended trip to the North, speaking in New York, Baltimore, Boston, and many smaller towns. The success of the trip speaks for itself: he raised funds sufficient to get a well dug, start construction of a boy's dorm, and build a carpenter's shop. While on that trip, he left the school in the care of Mrs. Wetmore and Miss Eichbaum.

In most instances, the donations came from unexpected sources. The first financial help came from a total stranger–a Mr. H.A. Grosebeak, who heard Mr. Wetmore give a five minute talk in a New York church. The first substantial sum came in early 1901, a thousand dollar gift from Miss White to build a red school house. The building was dedicated to her sister, Georgina White, on June 14, 1901. It was Miss Georgina White who first heard Mr. Wetmore's plans and became committed to helping Christ School.

From the very beginning, the Wetmores envisioned an endowment fund as necessary to the survival and growth of the school. In March 1902 the school received its first endowment gift–a five dollar gold piece from a young boy (Bryan Peters) who heard of the school in a New York Sunday School class. The boy worked and saved the money as his contribution.

The endowment that the Wetmores had in mind was not in terms of what people think of today–massive fund-raising campaigns for capital improvements. Their aim was to realize an endowment of $20,000, with the interest (in the 3-4 per cent range at this time) to provide scholarships, especially for the boarding students who would not have the same work opportunity as did the mountain boys and girls learning their trade skills. The process was slow. In March 1902, the endowment fund reached a total of $31. Six months later the figure had almost doubled to $60.

In his trips north and to churches and meetings around the Asheville Mission District, Mr. Wetmore, by 1904, continued to seek money for endowment, scholarship, teachers' salaries, operating expenses, and so forth but he also began to seek funds with which to build a chapel. Most of the labor had been promised by people in the community, at no charge, but a thousand dollars or more was needed to purchase necessary materials. In January 1905, Mr. Wetmore again trekked north to seek money for many things–the chapel included. He obtained money to complete the third floor of the boys dormitory and some funds for operating expenses. By September, $500 was on hand for constructing the chapel.

Who were these early donors? Unfortunately, there is no formal list of such donations so the names of only a few remain. Besides some individuals, the primary givers were the Women's Auxiliaries in the northern churches who were in tune with the mission movement in the Episcopal Church. For example, it was the Women's Auxiliary of the Pennsylvania district that gave the money in 1902 to dig a well for a permanent water supply. That well was located just to the southeast of what is now the Fr. Harris Memorial Chapel. Several years later, a drought lowered the water table and the Pennsylvania auxiliary contributed funds to deepen this fifty-four-foot water source. Another main contributor was Mrs. John I. Thompson of Troy, N.Y., who gave the thousand dollars to construct the first boys dorm (which opened September

1, 1902) in memory of her husband and gave another $1,000 in 1904 toward the school's purchase of a 107 acre farm containing much rich bottom land, leaving the school with a $2,500 mortgage. As noted in a *Galax Leaf* announcing the purchase, the school was immediately offered $3,900 for the same farm, a profit of $1,400. The offer was turned down for two reasons. The land could provide farm income and profit for the school, and it could provide work for those students who could not pay the $5 a month board or other incidental expenses.

Wetmore Pond covered a much larger area than the present school lake. It provided recreation, ice for the community, and water power for a generator and grist mill.

Christ School Chapel was dedicated in May, 1907. Fr. Hughson (right front) was responsible for bringing Fr. Harris to Christ School as rector and headmaster.

I:1900-1906

3

Struan

History is full of ironies. Man often tries to explain contrasts in terms of unexpected contradiction. It appears most difficult for him to grasp that what appears as a contradiction may be a natural consequence of previous conditions.

From one perspective, Christ School was conceived at Struan, the ancestral home of Susan Allen Wetmore, a plantation site that was for a time a center of the gracious Southern living prevailing in antebellum days. It was in this manorial home that Thomas C. Wetmore and his bride lived, and it was here that the two came to a union of minds about the need for a school to provide industrial and academic training for the lost generations of mountain children. What they established and what was to be continued for the next seven decades was a school whose faith and character was built upon honest simplicity and a total rejection of any pretentiousness.

Perhaps the only serious smudge on the Christ School story during those first seventy years, at least from the standpoint of those who like to conserve the best of the past, was the inability of the school to maintain this visible link to Struan. Unfortunately, money has always been a problem, for other priorities always, and rightly so, came first. Attempts at preservation generated much interest among alumni in times past. In the late 1940's some alumni were talking about restoration of the Wetmore House (Struan) but the $50,000 figure was out of reach. A decade later, when the house and sixty-six acres was given to the school by Mrs. Wetmore's daughter in 1954, talk of restoration into an alumni center with some member of the faculty living in an apartment there generated much interest but not much of the $150,000 estimated cost. By the late 1960's time was running out as considerable deterioration had set in. Then in the 1970's Struan fell victim to vandalism and theft from far and near, with a gutting of the interior. Valuable wide-board wooden flooring planks and other fittings were ripped out, closet doors measuring five feet by twelve were taken, and the priceless and beautiful curved walnut stairway which graced the house to the third floor was removed. All of this was done without the asking. The opportunity for restoration was gone.

At the most, now, people can remember what it was–a piece of antebellum elegance which made life in the South more genteel. This house, which Alexander Robertson, a wealthy rice plantation owner from Charleston, built in 1854, was part of a full-sized, self-contained plantation (an anachronism in the western mountains), with slave cottages and grist mill and a sawmill and a carpenter's and blacksmith's shops and formal garden for flowers, shrubs, and food. When riding up to the house from the main Asheville-to-Charleston highway (the Old Airport Road), a visitor could sense from the beautiful white pines planted on either side of the road that he was following a trail leading to gracious hospitality and conviviality to be found at Struan, a Scottish name meaning "winding stream."[9]

Of all the outbuildings that once sustained life at Struan, only one remains, and it is in a badly declining state. That was the present Rock House then occupied by its owner Thomas Murray, who was being evicted for non-payment of taxes. It appears that Robertson not only bought the hilltop property which looked eastward over a valley through which flowed Gap Creek, but he let Murray remain in the Rock House. That house has fallen on bad times, being turned into a hay loft and shelter for cows, with the once wooden floor replaced by piles of manure and straw, and the rock walls crumbling. This house, which antedates Struan, contains at each end the similar kind of rose window which was placed over the entrance to Christ School Chapel. Gone are all the other buildings including at least five slave cottages of French design, a kitchen which was about seventy feet from the house, and a stone stable which appears to be located where the old ice house used by the school could be found. In addition, the saw and grist mills, which splendidly served the valley, and the dam and blacksmith's shop no longer stand.

Certain legends persist about the house, including the typical Southern ghost. This attracted the interest of school students in the area who, from time to time, were permitted to visit the house after the Wetmore family ceased to live there. A feature story in the *Asheville Citizen* dated September 19, 1926, indicated the presence at Struan of Union soldiers (under Sherman's command). The first intrusion, apparently, was that of the 49th Michigan unit which, in their search for corn liquor, kicked in the glass door, and also scarred the surface of a large mahogany sideboard with heel marks. The other occasion reportedly occurred when the estate was turned over to the entertainment of the Union staffs on duty at the hospitals in Asheville. Struan was a center of refuge for friends and relatives who fled Charleston during the Civil War and found a haven there, where often these transients would have to sleep on the floor. It must be remembered that Robertson built Struan as a summer home to be near neighbors from

[9]In an article in the State Magazine, July 19, 1947, Harry Z. Tucker suggests that Struan was built in 1847. He says "The cornerstone of Struan has carved on it: 'A.R. 1847.'" If so, this probably referred to the date Robertson purchased the property from Thomas Murray.

the Low Country who also came to the mountains to cool off. It was only after the firing at Fort Sumter that Robertson escaped to this region, bringing with him valuable furnishings, silverware, artwork, and a collector's library. If the Union troops did come upon Struan, an out-of-the-way symbol of the hated Southern plantation system, it seems highly probable that the men would have burned it down to the ground, especially after being denied both liquor and the silverware, which were buried somewhere in the grounds outside. Anyway, once the war ended, Robertson did not experience the destitution felt by so many of the Southern gentry. Most of his property remained intact.

With no photographs available to convey the whole picture, the memory of Struan must be left to words, however inadequate and incomplete they may be. Several features added distinction to the rolling lawn, which had been made from sod carried in by the slaves, and to the formal gardens which included much boxwood. In front, on the northeast side was the wishing bench, made of concrete; it promised reward to whoever sat on it and expressed his desire. Toward the front and situated among four huge pines sat a round concrete table, perhaps for tea or for the children. In the center of the garden and directly in front of the house was a sundial, and on either side were two figures, Flora, whose flowers were blackened with age, and Pomora, whose handful of fruit had been broken off, welcoming people to Struan.

The house, which is best described as the Greek Revival type, was built by Ephraim Clayton, a prominent Asheville architect. Demolished in 1987, Struan, had two stories with fourteen foot ceilings plus a finished attic. It contained twelve rooms, some of which measured twenty-five feet by thirty. Closet doors were five feet by twelve, and there was a thirty-six inch wide fireplace in each room to provide heat. Each floor was covered by hand-hewn wide-oak planks and the foundation and first floor walls were made of rough stone, stuccoed over to give a smoother finish. The rest of the house was finished with heavy weatherboarded timber.

Still in place when the house was turned over to Christ School was the original wallpaper bought in France while the house was being built, a gray color overlaid with garlands of pink roses tied with blue ribbons. Mrs. Robertson loved bright and fresh colors and the same theme was to be found in the carpets, chintz, sets of China imported from Paris, and on the English cut glass.

Struan was built at a time when men, upon leaving the dining room, moved to one of the little smoking rooms well lined with books, where they could take their conversation and cigars. In the dining hall, the great mahogany table would seat thirty people comfortably when extended to twelve leaves. Also in the dining area was the large sideboard which the Union soldiers allegedly scarred and a fine collection of silver brought from Charleston.

Struan was also memorable for its collection of fine paintings. According to Harry Z. Tucker in the *State Magazine* (1947) the large English hall leading into the house was a picture gallery. Among the hangings were four Morlands, an original portrait of Marie Antionette by Wertmuller, family portraits painted by well known artists, and many other beautiful works of art. In the *Asheville Citizen* feature, the writer observed that a picture portrait of Rubens by Rembrandt hung to the right of the front door as you entered, over an old commode of walnut, on top of which were two fine silver champagne pitchers.

Probably the most eye-appealing thing in the house was the unsupported winding stairway which led to the attic. The steps and bannister rail were both made of walnut, with the treads at some time having been painted white.

Of particular interest to those who have made a study of style and structure of early homes was the construction of the porch roofs. They were curved in the same manner as a ship's hull. In studying the framework of the house, one would observe that not a nail was to be found. The stone which was used to construct the foundation and first floor was quarried on the south side of Burney Mountain and brought to the site by slaves.

As guests approached the mansion on horseback or in a carriage, wiggling across Wetmore Hill from the Charleston-Asheville Highway, they were impressed by the single bay double-tier portico supported by four massive columns on each tier. "The wide verandas," according to Tucker, "open through French doors out to the lawn and flower garden. Pink roses and honeysuckle climb over them and there is a thick border of ivy at the edge."

Struan was nestled on a hill surrounded by white pines; the home where the Wetmores lived looked over Gap (Robinson) Creek to the main road to Asheville.

I:1900-1906

Christ School, Inc.

Following the death of Fr. Wetmore, the full load of leadership fell upon Susan Wetmore. Out of this circumstance, the first regular meeting of the newly formed advisory board met October 16, 1906, at the home of Bishop Junius Horner to set up an organization to deal with the future of the school and to help share Mrs. Wetmore's burden.[9]

In its sixth year of operation, Christ School was already widely known, at least in Episcopal circles, and represented on the board were such out-of-state locales as New York City, Troy (NY), Chicago, Watertown (Conn.), Montgomery, New Orleans, and Morristown (NJ). Several decisions were made at that meeting. The most important one was to form a corporation under North Carolina law, and an executive committee was instructed to draw up a constitutional charter. In addition, the advisory board adopted methods to receive gifts for an endowment fund.

Eleven days later, five members of the advisory board met at Wachovia Bank in Asheville and adopted the work presented by the constitutional committee.[10] Membership on the board was set at seventeen, with any four constituting a quorum to conduct business. It provided for annual meetings and an executive committee of five members who would be the acting authority between meetings and who could be called into session by notice of one member. Officers and members of the executive committee were to serve a one year term or until a successor was chosen.

More important, though, was the hammering out of the purpose of the newly established Association. It stated that Christ School was an institution intended to "provide educational advantages for white boys and girls of the mountain region of North Carolina."[11] It charged the Association with the responsibility of helping to secure operating funds and endowment.

---

[9]Present at that meeting were Bishop J. M. Horner, president; B. F. Huske, secretary; William B. Williamson, treasurer; Mrs. Wetmore, Dr. Swope, Mr. Westfeldt, Mr. Pelzer, and H.F. Addicks, Jr.
[10]Attending this key meeting were Bishop Horner, Huske, Mrs. Wetmore, Williamson, and Addicks.
[11]The first black student was admitted to Christ School in the 1970's.

The first major step toward building up an endowment was announced by Mrs. Wetmore at a meeting of the executive committee March 13, 1907. Mrs. J. I. Thompson of Troy, N.Y., had given the school twenty-five shares of Illinois Central Lease Line 4 per cent stock. This contribution went into the John I. Thompson Endowment Fund with the income ($100 per annum) to be used for "keeping the John I. Thompson Dorm in proper repair, furniture and fittings, paying for insurance," and similar needs. A further report showed that the school had on hand as endowment $2,010 plus another $800 in the Chapel Fund.

It was in 1908 that Christ School Incorporated had its first meeting with Bishop Horner elected chairman. Three new men were elected to the Association, and one of them was Fr. Ruben Rivers Harris, the new rector and headmaster. This group then elected a seven member board of directors, with Bishop Horner as president.[12] In its first official act, Christ School Incorporated deeded all school property to the Trustees of the Missionary District of Asheville (forerunner of the Diocese of Western North Carolina) under limitations described in the Wetmore-Lyman deed of 1900. Provisions were made to accept ten adjoining acres from Mrs. Wetmore known as the rectory lot on which a house was built at the top of the hill for Fr. and Mrs. Harris and their four children.[13]

The Rock House is the oldest building at Christ School, probably pre-dating the Wetmore house.

[12]Other members of the first board of directors were Gen. Davidson, vice president; Mrs. Wetmore, secretary; R. R. Harris, treasurer; Rev. Swope, Haywood Parker, and H. F. Addicks, Jr.

[13]Don, David, Robert, and Dorothy.

II: 1906-1910

5

Troubled Years

Christ School could easily have closed its doors in the fall of 1906. Such action would have been regrettable but understandable. Mr. Wetmore, who died August 3 of that year, was the man who breathed life into the school, but it appears to be the work of the Holy Spirit which kept it alive. Those who strongly believed answered that call.

At the time, Christ School was one of three church-affiliated boarding schools in the Missionary District of Asheville and one of about forty day schools in Appalachia which had at least nominal Episcopal connection. Church financial support of each was minimal. It seemed quite possible that Christ School would fold or at least the boarding part would come to an end.

Money and leadership were critical concerns. Nearly two-thirds of the cost of operating Christ School was obtained from outside sources–particularly from northern friends from Chicago to New York, including donations from numerous women's church auxiliary groups. But when Mr. Wetmore, then only thirty-seven years of age, died, the mantle of leadership fell upon Mrs. Wetmore at a time when women in general were not established in such leadership roles. While Mr. Wetmore lived, one of them could travel north and leave the operation of the school in the hands of the other. But, now, Mrs. Wetmore could not be two places at the same time. The school must suffer either from absentee leadership or from a decline in philanthropy.

What must have clouded the thought of many was Mrs. Wetmore's ability to cope with the boys who boarded as well as general discipline. She did not live on campus and was not frequently seen by the boys since she also had children of her own to raise–Susannah, a talented musician, and Tom, who was to die as a young man from an incurable respiratory disease. But she was also a woman of much strength. Her faith was bedrock and she shared the dream of her husband. Though small in size (she weighed less than one hundred pounds), she was quick-thinking, quick-moving, and either determined or opinionated, depending upon your point of view. Some see in her a practical, pragmatic mind that balanced nicely with the more romantic outlook of Mr. Wetmore. This image of Mr. Wetmore is challenged somewhat by his practical talents. Not only did he ride a horseback circuit that included numerous church missions and school, he was quite mechanical and taught carpentry and craft at Christ School until his death. In any case, as long as faith was the key ingredient, Mrs. Wetmore was more than adequate to carry on the original dream.

Steps were taken quickly to insure the survival of the school. On October 16, a group of ten people (nine men and Mrs. Wetmore) met at the home of Bishop Horner in Asheville and created an advisory board. Elected officers were Bishop Horner, president; E.F. Robbins of Chicago, vice president, W.B. Williamson, treasurer; and B.F. Huske, secretary.[1] About a dozen other people were then named to the advisory board, including three women contributors (Miss F.M. White of New York City, Mrs. Hobart Thompson of Troy, N.Y., and Mrs. Henry Morgan Jr. of Morristown, N.J.) To meet more pressing concerns, the advisory board voted to incorporate the school under North Carolina law, with said corporation to manage Christ School affairs including endowment. Eleven days later a constitution was adopted which spelled out the purpose of the Association:

> 1. To help Christ School maintain an institution intended to provide educational advantages for white boys and girls of the mountain region of North Carolina.
>
> 2. To help secure operating funds and endowment. At this same meeting, Bishop Horner read a deed which conveyed the lands upon which Christ School stood to the Episcopal District of Asheville.

An answer to the question of day-to-day leadership was equally imperative. The problem was solved for the school year 1906-07 when B.F. Huske delayed his plans to go to seminary for at least a year and accepted the position as assistant to Mrs. Wetmore, who became principal. This arrangement permitted Mrs. Wetmore to continue her periodic trips north to raise money. Since Mr. Wetmore had been rector, that position was also vacant. It was filled for part of the year by Rev. R.N. Wilcox, priest-in-charge of St. James-Hendersonville, and later by J. Norton Atkins, a mission priest who travelled throughout the Asheville District. St. James had been Mr. Wetmore's first appointment, and he continued to serve there for several years while establishing Christ School.

[1]Other members were Mrs. Wetmore, Dr. Swope, Mr. Westfeldt, Mr. Pelzer, Mr. Addicks, and Mr. H.A. Grosebeak.

Solution to the question of a permanent rector (chaplain) appeared to come in January 1908, when Fr. Ruben Rivers Harris of Florence, Ala., accepted the call. Fr. Harris, a self-taught scholar, came to Christ School at the biding of his close friend, Fr. Hughson, who was a member of the Order of Holy Cross at Monteagle, Tenn. As it turned out, Fr. Harris was to leave Christ School some eighteen months later to return to Decatur and then Gadsden, Alabama. A rift occurred over the division of responsibilities. As the new rector understood it, he was to be chaplain and to have full authority as headmaster in the operations of the school. The problem became urgent at the May 13, 1909, meeting of Christ School Incorporated, when Mrs. Wetmore stated that as principal of the school she "insisted upon her right as principal to have general management and control of the school under the terms of the trust."[2] Fr. Harris, who was a member and treasurer of the Christ School board, submitted his resignation August 18, 1909.

Dorothy Thomson, who was the youngest of Fr. Harris' four children, remembers vividly their departure from Christ School.[3] "Two strong wills clashed. Mrs. Wetmore wanted to tell my father how to run the school. My father said, 'I'll leave.' We packed that night and left early the next morning." Some people thought the quarrel was over churchmanship, for Mr.Wetmore had conducted morning prayer while Fr. Harris was of the Anglican tradition. "Actually," Mrs. Thomson said, "Mrs. Wetmore was educated by the Sisters of an Episcopal order and never objected to the services." In an interview in 1940, Mrs. Wetmore said her greatest satisfaction and assurance came from knowing that Christ School had a daily communion service, which Fr. Harris instituted here.

To fill the void, J. Norton Atkins became part-time rector in September 1909, serving also at other missions in the area, while W.P. Grier was made acting headmaster, with real authority apparently remaining in the hands of Mrs. Wetmore.[4] Enrollment that fall had risen to fifty in the boarding division and around seventy-five day students. In October of the next year, Fr. Atkins was still filling in as rector but Grier moved on to Gastonia High School as principal and coach. A number of visiting priests also conducted services here during those years.

One thing was becoming clear. Despite the faithfulness and dedication of the teachers, the school badly needed to settle the line of responsibility and to establish a permanent arrangement to give stability to the future. Working in the background to get Fr. Harris to return to Christ School was Fr. Hughson, and the trustees were also interested in inviting him back. By 1911, Mrs. Wetmore was also convinced of the necessity of recalling Fr. Harris, and she made a recommendation to the

[2]The trust placed the control of the school's lands under the Asheville Missionary District but provided that the buildings should be under the control of the Wetmores until their death.
[3]In the 1920's Mrs. Thomson taught literature here and directed a play for the senior class in 1924.
[4]Grier ran the school when Mrs. Wetmore was off campus raising funds.

board on May 11 that he be appointed as headmaster and rector at a much increased salary of $1000. In addition, he would be able to live in the Rectory rent free. Mrs. Wetmore retained the title of principal but the division of authority was made clear. She would conduct money-raising for the school (both for the current expenses and endowment for scholarships) and Fr. Harris would be in charge of spiritual matters, academics, and the daily details of school life. It proved to be a wise decision. Both of these strong-willed and highly intelligent people were dedicated toward the same end, and their energies were now channeled in parallel directions where each could serve without friction. A troublesome drifting had come to an end.

Helping to keep the school together during this period of uncertainty was the construction of the chapel. For two years before his death, Fr. Wetmore had been proposing and soliciting funds to build a chapel so that services could be moved from the little red school house. The new chapel was the centerpiece of his dream–a place large enough, with a sanctified atmosphere, for boarding students and community to worship together. Before construction was to begin in the Spring of 1906, Fr. Wetmore had raised $500 toward the $1,000 needed to pay for the materials. Most of the money was given by Mrs. Rachael Marie Hustace, a friend of the Wetmores, who died before the structure was completed. The sandstone was to be quarried on the school's property, and men in the community had already promised to provide the labor. To be called Christ Chapel, the structure was to symbolize the faith and work that Christ School was intended to carry into the mountains and into the lives of its students.

Many hands arose to help Mr. Wetmore start the construction of Christ Chapel, the completion of which he would not see. But he provided the vision and direction and helped to supervise the project during its initial phase. People served by the Christ School Mission responded quickly to their promises of free labor. Two men, J.W. Pressley and J.S. Stroup, were instrumental in mining the quarry at a site located just beyond the old dairy and hauling the sandstone to the building site, where an experienced rock mason put his artistry on display. Even before the money had been raised, much of the lumber had already been prepared at the old sawmill and Uncle Van Allen kept his combination ox-mule team busy hauling materials to the campus. Several students, including Will Cathey of Skyland, remained at school and worked on the project during the summer of 1906. In addition, there was a constant flow of other volunteers from the community who worked a day or several days at a time. It was most fitting that volunteer labor built their glory to God out of resources–sandstone and oak–which were native to the school.

Even while the frame, roof, walls (plaster) and sandstone were going up, much attention was being given to the interior. The original altar, which is now in the Fr. Harris Memorial Chapel, was built by Mr. Wetmore from sassafras with the design of pomegranates and grapes carved on the altar by Elsie Beale Hemphill. In addition, Mrs. Hemphill, a friend of the Wetmores who taught carving, craft, and domestic science here for many years, did the cherry and cedar reredos behind the altar, and carved the chancel altar rail.

Completed almost by the time the construction of the chapel was finished was a mural on the wall behind the altar. The oil painting, which appears to have been done as a memorial to Mr. Wetmore, was the work of Mrs. Hemphill with some assistance from her sister, Miss Bertha (Bootie) Beale. It was a scene of lithe angels and trumpets imposed over a background of dark green. Sometime around 1974, the scene was buried under white paint when the Chapel was repainted.[5] The chancel window, a depiction of the Christ-Child with outstretched arms, was the work of a well-known New York artist, J.A. Holzer, who became greatly interested in the school through the influence of the Wetmores. Furniture for the chancel was given by a friend in New Jersey and other items were promised for the future. When the Chapel was dedicated in May 1907, the furnishings of the Chapel were nearly complete with the exception of an organ, which was to be donated and dedicated on All Saints Day. It was a gift of Mrs. E.V. Lane and her brother, Dr. Hustace, both of New York, in memory of Mr. Wetmore and their mother, Mrs. Hustace. The original pews, one of which is still on campus, were made in the school shop and were discarded in the mid-1930's when replaced by new ones made in Hickory.[6]

Fr. Harris stands with the acolytes and choir before entering the chapel for the Sunday morning communion service.

[5]Research has been unable to determine who authorized the mural to be painted over or why.
[6]The pews were donated by the Howland family. Reginald Howland was the last non-resident to be a communicant at Christ School.

(Above) The rectory as viewed from the top of the chapel before 1920.

(Left) The seedling would grow up to be one of the white pines on the terrace in front of Boyd Dorm. In the background are the ruins of the first Old Dorm and St. Mary's Infirmary.

This 1915 scene shows the Chapel (left), the second school building, and the first dorm, forerunner of the Old Dorm.

II:1906-1910

6

Early Life

Just as the Chapel was the center of life at Christ School, it was the Angelus which awakened the school (and the community) to that fact. Actually, the Angelus, as we know it, was not installed until April 1913, according to an issue of *Christ School Magazine*. Prior to that there was a bell tower constructed of wood which stood just north of the original red school house. This bell was used to announce the noon hour or sound the alarm for a fire or some other disturbance. By 1911, the bell tower had grown rickety and a bugle was used to punctuate the schedule. Reveille blew at seven in the morning and taps came at ten that night. The October *Galax Leaf* said that an instructor blew the bugle but that he hoped several boys would learn how. The old chapel bell, overworked, was now used only to announce the hours of service. A writer for the *Galax Leaf* observed that so far the bugle speeds up the movement to and from assembly. "Boys now march two abreast from assembly to the mess hall. It is a long line of boys . . ., the last two in line not having left the school building before the first two are entering the dining hall. It is an impressive sight."

The Angelus was given to the school as a memorial in April 1913 by an unidentified donor. Fr. Harris conducted a special service for school and community to consecrate the Angelus before it was put in place in the new small tower built above the sanctuary. It first broke silence at 5:30 a.m. for the traditional Easter sunrise service, and, according to the *Galax Leaf*, the sound "fell in vain upon the ears of many peaceful dreamers." At 5:45 a.m., the choir assembled on campus and sang a number of hymns as the horizon began to brighten in the east. Fifteen minutes later, the first Holy Communion for that day was celebrated with all boarding students present. There was a second communion celebration at 10:30 a.m. at which twenty-two people (students and community) were confirmed with Bishop Horner laying on hands. With the coming of Fr. Harris, the Angelus rang three times daily, at six in the morning, at 12 noon, and at six in the evening. People in the countryside (the ringing could be heard as far away as Fletcher) could set their watches and clocks by the faithful sound. Its function was to announce worship services and to provide three moments during the day when everyone stood still to meditate and offer prayers of thanksgiving to God.

An asset not to be overlooked or minimized during the period of uncertainty was the dedication of those working at Christ School. It was not the money which attracted teachers, for they were paid only two or three hundred dollars a year. It was not living quarters which did not exist, for most of the teachers, like the students, had to walk to Christ School and their record of trudging through rain or snow was even more impressive. What motivated them was seeing young minds turned on by such simple things as learning their letters and learning to write and learning to think ideas through in higher math and history and science and to be guided in sound moral direction under a practical Christian faith.

A variety of names paraded through those early years, more women than men, but all equally dedicated. Many of the young men who passed through, such as B.F. Huske, turned to this kind of mission work to earn some money to help pay their way through seminary. Others were part of a parade which gained experience and moved on elsewhere. All carried with them an unforgettable experience. Huske illustrated their loyalty. When Fr. Wetmore died, he remained over a year to assist Mrs. Wetmore in the operation of the school. Several ministers served as rector during this period, such as the Revs. J.K. Atkins, Eugene F. deHeald, and R.M. Wilcox, the pastor at St. James Episcopal Church in Hendersonville. They travelled in all kinds of weather on foot or horseback or by wagon to provide the religious services and training the children needed. And none served students and community more ably than did the nurses, who went by horse and cart throughout the countryside, traveling uncharted roads and fording running streams to bring medicine to poverty-stricken neighbors and to deliver babies at a time when doctors and hospitals were not accessible. These were the women who were a cross between Florence Nightingale and Joan of Arc.

Even in that one year (1908-09) when Fr. Harris was first on campus, he showed the kind of qualities that would make him a legend in his own time and would make the trustees anxious to get him back. One of these qualities was his ability to pop up wherever and whenever a student was thinking about heading into trouble. An instance, involving Chauncy Roberts, was recalled by Mrs. Dorothy Harris Thomson.

> My father used to have a habit, nervous or deliberate, of patting his foot to the floor or ground. One night Chauncy and the dorm had gone to bed, but Chauncy decided he would run

over to his house after lights out. He waited until everybody had gone to sleep and then tip-toed, shoes in hand, carefully down the stairs. When he reached the front door, he opened it, stepped outside, and slipped on his shoes. It was then that he heard a familiar patting sound and voice which asked, "Where are you going, Chauncy?" And Chauncy, seldom at a loss for words, quickly responded, "I'm going to bed, Sir."

During that first year, before the Rectory was built on a ten acre plot deeded to the school by the Wetmores, the Harrises lived in the Old Dorm where about thrity students stayed in what was basically a barracks. Their apartment was on the west end of Thompson Hall, with a sitting room and kitchen downstairs and bedrooms upstairs. Two of their sons, David and Don, contracted malarial chills and fever in a building that was both damp and drafty. "When the winds blew," Mrs. Thomson said with a smile, "the rugs fluttered. When Don or Dave had a chill, the whole place shook."

Life on campus remained simple and primitive regardless of other circumstances, and this was accepted good naturedly as the general condition of the time. Christ School was established to help provide a way to an improved life. For water, the school depended upon the well built in 1903 and deepened a couple of years later in the face of a severe drought. In subsequent years, other wells were to be dug which, according to David P. Harris Jr., were located roughly in the areas of the 30 and 38 Dorms. Pitchers and basins stood in the dormitories for morning ablutions. Gas lamps and candles provided the first light and were continued for the most part even after a dynamo was hooked up in 1903, to bring electricity to the school building and the kitchen. The Mill Pond was the source of energy that generated a flickering light until nine each night. Lamps and candles cast a dim glow in the dormitory, and when Fr. Harris came to Christ School for good, he increased visibility in the study hall by placing reflectors behind the gas lamps. Behind Thompson Hall was a bathhouse which occasionally had hot water, and several outhouses rimmed the lower edge of the campus.

This was a period in which some building was going on, mostly from lumber harvested on the farm and cut at the Wetmore sawmill. From the standpoint of construction, Christ School was self-contained. The cost of such construction was unbelievably low, with much of the labor provided by older students and friends in the community. Around 1910 the school hired its first maintenance man, Mr. L.V. Boyd, who taught carpentry and woodworking, sawed the wood used to heat the buildings, and did most of the construction. He was an expert in stonework, which was to become the central unifying architectural theme of the school. He learned his craft as an apprentice working on the construction of the George W. Vanderbilt

House, now one of the nation's most visited landmarks. Buildings other than the chapel which contributed to the growth of the school during this four year period were the St. Mary's Mission House (1908), the Brotherhood of St. Andrew Log Cabin (1909), and an extension of Thompson Hall (1909)).

St. Mary's, a two-story frame structure standing in the area where Fessor's Cottage was later constructed, housed the infirmary, the domestic science course, the nurse, and some women faculty. When the Fayssouxs came to Christ School in 1920, they spent a year there. The women in St. Mary's kept an eye on Thompson Hall and occasionally reported boys for untoward conduct (such as streaking to the dorm from the bathhouse), and for slipping in-and-out of the dormitory after hours. The Brotherhood of St. Andrew was the first organization formed by Fr. Harris. It provided religious outreach to the students and into the community and provided the acolytes for daily communion and other chapel services. The extension to Thompson Hall contained the dining hall, which was connected to the kitchen and dishroom by a dumbwaiter. Not only did food and dishes move up and down on this pulley system, but it occasionally became an elevator for smaller boys. The dining room contained eight or nine large tables which seated eight to ten people each.

The year 1909 was rather typical of the financial and admissions picture at the time. The annual expenses for that year, which did not include the cost of boarding students who where paying their way at $6 a month, was $3,020, as reported by Mrs. Wetmore, the principal. The budget blockbuster was the rector's salary of $800. Four teachers received $300 each, and $200 was spent on traveling expenses for Mrs. Wetmore to raise money for the school. Another $150 was allotted for board for teachers and $100 was set aside for maintenance. The light bill ran $70, the fuel bill $75, and insurance coverage for the buildings was $50, based on a valuation of around $5,000.[7]

Every year, the school grew in numbers, though economic conditions did not permit every child to attend the full six or seven months. A typical year was 1907-08. Some 125 children attended the first term, the largest number ever, and there would be an increase after Christmas, in the primary grades. The reason was that the free schools in the region were closed at Christmas and would not re-open until September. But according to Elizabeth Kennard, Christ School made an imprint on all students–long-term or short. "Being young they are sometimes noisy and restless. But in truthfulness, respect for authority, earnestness–the essential characteristics of upright manly boys–the equals of Christ School pupils would be difficult to find." And growing in numbers also were the boarders, since the dormitory could now sleep thirty-six boys. By 1911, the number of boarders reached sixty.

[7]By 1910, the expenses had grown to $3500, including $2500 in salaries for teachers.

There were many health problems confronting the mountains in this era–whooping cough, measles, ringworm, mumps, chicken pox, things we now dismiss as history. In these early years, Christ School provided a nurse not only for the boarders but for the community. In her January 1908 report, Nurse Mary H. Gillette said that 123 calls had been registered in the dispensary during the previous three months, mostly from the day student population and community. To indicate how dramatic was this number of sick, Nurse Gillette said it represented one-third of the cases registered by all New York state district nurses combined during the same period. "As a result, out-of-door visits (house calls) have been limited to about three-a-day, except for emergencies," she wrote. In addition to caring for the sick, she offered a nursing class every Wednesday which was well attended by mountain girls. It provided the rudiments of health care, and it was hoped that some of the mountain girls would be inspired to enter nursing. "We have a dim visage of a hospital in the future," Nurse Gillette added.

If one's yardstick is material things, the children and their parents in this mountain region were thoroughly deprived. But as a counterbalance they possessed strong family ties, self-reliance, and a strong feeling of independence. They developed the kind of craft skills and love of simple outdoor pleasures that brought their own reward. At Christ School, learning was accompanied by simple recreational pleasures–playing baseball and tennis, swimming, trapping rabbits and other small game, playing tag and chase, and throwing acorns or apples in appropriate seasons. Just plain talking or sewing or reading a book were important diversions. Walking a few miles to school–even in bitterest weather producing noses nipped red by frost–were exciting events when accompanied by others. As a result of such "deprivation," any kind of special happening at Christ School was an occasion, and such occasions were usually centered about the church. The late Allan Brown, a professor of classical literature, recalled that in the mid-1930's, while he was attending Christ School, all holidays were related to the church calendar–Christmas, Easter, All Saints Day, and so on.

One of these special occasions fell on May 7, 1907, when Christ Chapel was consecrated. The night before there was evening prayer and confirmation by Bishop Horner. At seven the next morning there was an early eucharistic service. By ten in the morning, a long line of students, parents, friends, and clergy were already lined up at the school building to process to the new chapel. When Bishop Horner rapped at the Chapel door at 10:30, it was opened by George Pressley, one of the builders who represented the mission, and B.L. Huske, the assistant principal who represented the school. The consecration was followed by morning prayer, a choral eucharist, and a sermon by Fr. Hughson of the Order of

Holy Cross, the priest who introduced Fr. Harris to Christ School. Lunch followed the service and then came graduation exercises for five students–Norvin C. Duncan, class valedictorian, Richard Allison, Theodore S. Bronson, W.L. Burke, and Waterman Deal.[8]

The purpose of Christ School remained unchanged, though each person might describe it differently. In the October 1910 *Galax Leaf*, Headmaster W.P. Grier observed that the school stood for three things: 1. Physical culture, 2. Academic development, and 3. Moral development of young manhood. Physical culture was expanded through sports (playing baseball and tennis, kicking football) and performing the required duties of the industrial department (shop). The aim of academic development was not just to inform but to create within each student an intellectual ideal to encourage inner growth–reflection and thought. The third objective was the development of character through moral growth nourished in a situation in which Bible study and religious services were prerequisite. What Christ School does, the headmaster stated, is "teach the boy or young man to be a man, a gentlemen, a citizen, whose duties are manifold, and he himself is responsible for the discharge of these duties."

Most of the non-boarding students found the daily several mile walk to-and-from Christ School to be more like an adventure. Unlike now, farms were few and woods rather than cleared fields dominated the approaches to the school–from whatever direction.

Ruth Merrill, later to become Ruth Black, began her three mile walk from the Fairview section through what was known as Merrills Cove. As she and her brother began the journey along paths made through the woods, the procession would grow longer as others joined in. As they crossed Mills Gap Road where it is overlooked by the ruins of the old Wetmore house they would pass the Old Mill Pond, whose dam was built to provide the hydro-electric power to generate a flickering light for the school.

During the winter the collection of children coming from Merrills Cove were welcomed into the old Rock House inhabited by John Jenkins, his wife and their four children. Hugh slabs of wood sawed at the nearby mill provided a glow in the big fireplace where the children warmed their half-frozen bodies. From there the trail led up the hill past the Wetmore House and came in by Boyd's Shop located in the area now occupied by the 38 Dorm. Keeping things lively along the journey were some rock fights and apple-throwing, mostly by the boys, and a little fighting.

Mrs. Black remembers Struan as being a "beautiful place with a beautiful view into the valley." The pines were smaller then and did not obstruct the view as was the case thirty or forty years later. Two things frightened her along the way. One was the cows stretched in the valley along Cane Creek. The other was a cemetery along the side of the road

[8]Two of the graduates, Duncan and Burke, were to become priests in the Episcopal Church. Allison was to become a pioneer allergist in South Carolina and was the father of a South Carolina bishop. This was Christ School's third graduating class.

Mr. Wetmore

Mrs. Wetmore

which belonged to the Williams family. "I always ran by it when I was by myself." Walking to school by herself became more frequent as many of the other children dropped out of classes during the nine years she attended Christ School (1907-16)–to marry, go to work, or simply give up on education.

Two other landmarks near the Rock House caught their attention: the grist mill and a small store.[9] The former, where Mr. Jenkins spent some time, ground the grain grown on the neighboring farms as well as meeting the school's needs. The small store provided the children penny candy and bottled ginger ale on the way home in the late afternoon. It was run by the Shuford family (many of whom went to Christ School), whose main store was located in Arden, a short distance from the home on U.S. Highway 25 where Richard and Sarah Shuford Fayssoux lived.

The grist mill at the Wetmore Lake dam served the needs of the school and the neighborhood. Skating was a popular winter pastime.

[9]Although the Rock House, probably older than the Wetmore House, was also of pre-Civil War vintage, it has never been the object of restoration concern. In more recent years, it has served as a place to store hay, the floor has rotted out, and cows have settled in it on hot days to find shade against the sun.

(Above) Susannah Wetmore was organist for a time at Christ Chapel. She is shown with the choir. (Bottom left) David Harris Sr. (far end of diving board) was the leader of this group of staff children swimming at the lake. (Bottom right) Fr. Harris stands next to the chapel with a wooden cross. The cross was decorated following the Lenten period when student pledges were removed.

III:1910-1925

Building A Campus

Upon the return of Fr. Harris to be Rector/Headmaster in 1911, Christ School began a period of feverish building activity, which reflected the growing enrollment both of boarding and day students. The books stayed in the black as expansion was done on a pay-as-you-go basis. The twenty-five or more buildings constructed hardly exceeded a combined cost of $100,000, primarily because most of the timber was cut on school property and the construction was under Mr. Boyd, who used as much local and student labor as possible. In 1970, only three of those buildings were still standing–the Chapel, the Little Rectory (which was built for Mr. and Mrs. Dave in 1923 and now is a faculty home), and St. Dunstan's, the dining hall built in 1916, which was remodeled into a library after St. Thomas Hall opened in 1965.[1] The construction was a unifying force, for it not only showed the optimism with which Christ School faced the future, but it was a way of involving the students so that they were more than a passive force in this energetic enterprise.[2] Even though hardly a year passed without some building under construction and much excitement generated, never for a moment did the major tenets of Christ School lose their position of pre-eminence–religion, academics, and physical development. The new buildings were not what attracted students; they were merely vehicles to enable Christ School better to fulfill its avowed goals.

Each of these buildings, now relegated to the pages of the past, had its own identity and played a vital role in the lives of every student. Each structure was enveloped by memories that, like the ancient phoenix, were to be relived as the physical plant was rebuilt during the years 1930-70. But standing constant and vigilant throughout the successive waves of physical change was The Chapel, its message of the breadth of Christ's love seen each evening in the outstretched arms above the altar, reaching out to each student. If we could walk in the shoes of those who came

[1]The Little Rectory has been remodeled and expanded on several occasions.
[2]In addition, some parents were actively involved, either as hired labor or those making a contribution to help pay their children's way.

before us, we would walk through a period physically more primitive than that which is around us today. But in the process we would learn that growth and love and discovery and faithfulness and determination and happiness and stamina and self-reliance have little to do with physical surroundings but everything to do with what was inside the school. If anything, the first quarter century of Christ School taught that form without substance is nothing. As an early alumnus so aptly expressed it when describing Christ School, "What was, really was!"

The first construction undertaken by Fr. Harris in 1911 was that of a log cabin to house the Brotherhood of St. Andrew and the expansion concluded in 1925 with the building of the Fifth and Sixth Cottages, Fessor's Cottage, and a new infirmary to replace St. Mary's, which was demolished. With the exception of the World War years of 1917-18, at least one major project was undertaken each year. These did not include assorted other necessary structures such as chicken houses, barns, out-houses, and sheds. Just before Fr. Harris was to oversee the constant expansion of facilities, Thompson Hall was enlarged with the addition of the dining hall wing and the Rectory was built on a ten acre lot given to the school by Mrs. Wetmore.

Before the expansion of Thompson Hall, the dining room was in the basement along with the kitchen and dishroom. The new dining room, on the same level as the first floor, contained nine large wooden tables which seated nine or ten people each. You entered the dining hall either from the hallway of the dorm or through a door on the west side of the extension. Since the kitchen and dishroom remained in the basement, food was brought up on a dumbwaiter and returned the same way. Quite often, as Fessor recalled, the rope would break to the general splattering and crashing of food and dishes when the dumbwaiter hit the basement floor. The dumbwaiter was also a source of mischief for smaller boys who tried to use it as an elevator. The appearance of the dumbwaiter, no matter how convenient, was short-lived for some unscrupulous boys began to use it to get into food supplies not intended for them.

The Rectory stood just in front of where the headmaster's house is today. It was two-story frame covered with shingles, much in vogue in the mountains during the first quarter of this century. A large grape arbor built by Fr. Harris covered the walkway leading into the screened porch. Bob Harris remembers the large water tank that was in the attic. "To fill that tank, we'd be down at the well and we would pump and pump for hours. We had to do that about once a week."

It appears that 1911 also saw the construction of St. Mary's, which was to serve a variety of purposes until it was taken down in 1925 to make way for Fessor's Cottage. The back porch of Fessor's house intruded on the front porch of St Mary's. With a growth in student body, St. Mary's, a frame structure southwest of Thompson Hall, served as a dispensary and as quarters for women teachers. Living there when Fessor came to Christ School, was Coach Harold Nichols, who had just gotten married.[3] During the school year 1917-18, a wing was added on the east side to provide infirmary beds in case of sickness among the boarding boys. Dick and Sarah Fayssoux lived in St. Mary's for several years after spending their first year (1920-21) in the three-room Brotherhood of St. Andrew's log cabin. When St. Mary's was torn down, a new and more spacious wood-frame infirmary was constructed on the site of the present one. About 1936, an addition was added to care for an increase in enrollment. This infirmary, which burned down in a spectacular dawn fire on Easter Sunday 1938, provided wards for sick students and some rooms for Mrs. Wetmore and any remaining female teachers.

In 1913, the decision was reached to tear down the Red School House and build a new one on the same site. The Red School House was now inadequate. It was too small to accommodate a growing enrollment and it was in a state of deterioration. Getting the bid for the job was M.E. Holtzclaw of Hendersonville, who submitted an estimate of $5,230 without heat or stonework. That was the first and last Christ School building to be submitted to outside contract until St. Thomas Dining Hall was constructed.[4] It would have been impossible for Mr. Boyd to complete such a large assignment in one summer. The cornerstone of the new school house–to be named the Thomas Wetmore Building–was laid August 6, 1913, which was the Christ School festival day inaugurated by Fr. Harris. The *Galax Leaf* of October 1913 stated that more than 300 mountain people were present for a picnic dinner, games, and other festivities. The girls in the Domestic Science Department served lemonade with the assistance of the young men of the school. It was a happy reunion of old pupils and teachers.

Since work on the Wetmore Building would be going on during the school year, it was necessary to provide new classrooms. To accomplish this, Fr. Harris involved Mr. Boyd in constructing six log cabins along the line of the south end of what is now the Wetmore Building. They provided classrooms during the year 1913-14 and then were converted into cabins to take care of twenty-six additional boarding students for anticipated growth. These cabins would almost double the number of boarders in 1915.

During this period, pupils in North Carolina completed their high school work in the tenth grade. One alumna, Mrs. Ruth Black, who went here for nine years and would have graduated with the Class of 1916, remembers the construction of Thomas Wetmore Building quite well, for

[3]St. Mary's was the site of the domestic science classes for many years. One of the instructors was Mrs. Elsie Hemphill.

[4]Merchant Construction of Asheville built St. Thomas Hall, renovated the old dining hall into a library, and constructed the science wing. Bob Daniel of Brevard was the school architect at the time.

her father was a carpenter on the job.[5] "It was a nice building. That was when I finished Mrs. Lanier's class and we started going from one classroom to another." When September 1914 arrived, Christ School students were stepping into the newest facility in the mountains. A writer in the October *Galax Leaf* was to say:

> The building is even more helpful than we expected. The light and warmth give an atmosphere of love and joy. There is something exultant about the house of stone and cedar, where 'Christ is all and in all.'

What Fr. Harris early saw as a pressing need was a new dining hall. Though the extension to Thompson Hall elevated the dining room to the main level, it still did not provide the best conditions. Most students entered the dining room by walking through the main hall of the dormitory. Abuse of the dumbwaiter caused constant confusion, broken dishes, and splattered food. In response to the need, the trustees approved in 1915 a sum not to exceed $2,000 for the construction of St. Dunstan's Hall. This would be Mr. Boyd's first major undertaking and it was the first building to be framed in sandstone since the chapel had been constructed in 1906. After this, major buildings, beginning with the 1930 Dorm, would follow the same theme.[6] The new facility contained an unfinished basement for storing root crops and had a furnace room as well. The kitchen and dishroom, later torn down, were attached to the lower end of St. Dunstan's, separated by a partition from the rest of the dining room. About 1928, a new dishroom and kitchen were extended in an L-shape along the lower corner of the dining hall and the original ones were torn down. A porch was added during the renovation. In 1938, the stage was added to the dining hall as part of the construction of the 38 Dorm. The interior of St. Dunstan's was paneled in oak and rectangular wooden tables provided seats for eight people. Verification as to when St. Dunstan's was built can be seen on a stone to the left of the main entrance on which is boldly inscribed "1916."

[5]The Great Flood of 1916 wiped out most of the farmers in the valleys of Buncombe County. Mrs. Black's family had to move to Asheville and she did not get to complete her senior year.
[6]The two exceptions were the temporary gym built in the summer of 1922 and Memorial Gymnasium built in 1952-53. When President Truman lifted price controls after the Korean War, the money then available to pay for the gym precluded the use of stone.

III: 1910-1925

Finances And Direction

After the board of directors brought Fr. Harris back as headmaster and chaplain and approved the construction of a new dining hall, all the problems did not simply disappear. Finances and the direction in which the school must go became serious topics of discussion between 1917 and 1925.

At the annual August meeting in 1917, Mrs. Wetmore stressed the need for Christ School to become self-supporting but pointed out that money for a limited number of scholarships and a small endowment "will always be necessary."[6A] The physical endowment would be restricted principally to providing maintenance and some improvement.

It became clear during this period, at least to Fr. Harris, that the expansion of public schools into Buncombe County was going to gradually–perhaps even rapidly–bring an end to day students at Christ School. The expanding public schools were improving their curriculum and were less expensive. The role of the private school was to provide Christian leadership and guidance and to teach the values that could not be fostered in a public school environment. The need for a change in direction became apparent in several meetings. In 1919, the board authorized Fr. Harris and Mrs. Wetmore to make out a survey for the Nationwide Campaign of the Church on the basis of a boarding school population of 120. At the July meeting in 1922, Fr. Harris raised for discussion the question of what role church schools in Western North Carolina should play now that the public schools were "offering so much more than they used to." It was a period of time in which day student enrollment was declining rapidly, especially in the primary schools where children no longer had to walk so far to attend classes. The final answer would come a few years later, for several board members were apparently hard to convince of the need to change, but the writing was clearly on the wall.

World War I and the growing economic crisis which was to spread like cancer across agriculture in the post-war years affected Christ School

[6A] Occasionally, the board met at the time of the annual summer picnic/festival, which also marked the celebration of the Day of Transfiguration.

as well as almost every other segment of the nation's fabric. Much of the debate here in the early 1920's involved the extent of future support of the Episcopal Church at both the local and national level. At its November meeting in 1920, the school's trustees, whose chairman was Bishop Horner, received a budget estimate for 1921 of $10,000, of which $2,100 would come from the interest on endowment. This left a deficit of $8,000 to be covered. The bishop said $6,500 of this sum would come from the National Women's Council Board in New York and that he would recommend to the Missionary Committee a raise in salary to $1,500 for Fr. Harris.

What darkened the horizon further was the December first fire which consumed Thompson Hall and destroyed all the belongings of more than thirty boarding students.[7] At a special meeting of the board two days later, Bishop Horner stated he would make an appropriation of $5,000 for the running of Christ School during 1920 and Mrs. Wetmore made a gift of fifty acres of land adjoining school property. To complicate matters, this was a period of time when the national church was beginning to feel the economic crisis and was searching for ways to reduce its financial commitment to church and church-related schools.

A sense of desperation hung over the trustee meeting on Armistice Day 1921. In discussing the 1922 budget, Bishop Horner saw the financial picture as grim. "I don't see how we are going to make it next year." He underscored this remark by pointing out that the national church's contribution had been cut to $4,500, leaving a deficit of $2,000. Though no decision was made, the trustees seriously discussed using the interest from scholarship endowment for daily operating expenses in 1921. Furthermore, Mrs. Wetmore was instructed to send out a statement of the exact financial condition of the school "if that $2,000 was not restored by January 1, 1922." Because of Mrs. Wetmore's heroic fund-raising efforts and the restoration of that cut, the school finished that year in the black with not a penny to spare. For the next year, the national church agreed to appropriate $6,500 and an additional $1,000 to be paid in monthly installments for one year beginning July 1, 1923.

Two issues were emerging to complicate the picture. One would affect Mrs. Wetmore's ability to raise funds for Christ School and its related mountain mission work. In July 1922, she was informed by Bishop Horner that the national board would "have to consider how far she was at liberty to make appeals for funds." With money becoming tighter, boundaries were being more sharply drawn for those seeking funds. The other issue involved the extent of financial support to be provided in the future by the Diocese (old Missionary District of Asheville). In 1923, of special concern were differences which arose over how the Holt Fund was to be used. At the July 15 meeting of the Christ School trustees, Bishop Horner suggested

[7]It was a day Fessor would never forget. He was to (and did) marry Sarah Shuford in Christ School Chapel. When the dorm burned down, it destroyed the best man's clothes along with everything else.

dividing the Holt legacy into four equal parts, with like sums going to the four church schools in the Diocese: Christ School, Valle Crucis, Appalachian, and Patterson. This position was strongly challenged by Mrs. Wetmore, who pointed out that such action would violate stipulations of the will. This proposal by Bishop Horner, which would have diverted money intended for Christ School to the other institutions, did not go beyond the discussion stage but the struggle of how to allocate funds to church institutions re-emerged in 1925 at a special meeting called by the Bishop. He asked the board to consider the "advisability of Christ School joining in a campaign with the other three Diocesan schools to raise $200,000." It was a catch-22 proposal, for Christ School was the only one of the four institutions to operate in the black and not burdened by indebtedness. After some discussion, the board voted unanimously to stay out of a unified drive for funds. Mrs. Wetmore remained free to seek money for the school. In a sense, Christ School was, by its 25th year, staking out its independence and establishing the framework whereby it would shortly become an Episcopal-related, but not a church-supported, boarding school.

The Gamma Lambda Sigma Fraternity had its origin in October 1914 in this log cabin.

(Above) Fessor (Coach Dick Fayssoux) played on this 1915 championship baseball team. He is third from the left in the middle row.

(Below) Moving earth has a long, honorable history as this early picture shows the worklist getting ready.

III:1910-1925

Boarding Only

With the decline in day enrollment as each new public school came into place in Buncombe County, Fr. Harris was already looking ahead to the transition to a boys only boarding school. For one thing, he decided to take advantage of his son who seemed to be hanging around and unsettled about what he was going to do. By 1921 David Harris was on the staff, following Fessor by one year, and with him came some first hand knowledge of preparatory school life he had acquired during his years at Kent School, a school which had a self-help system of its own and made use of student-run government with seniors and prefects taking the lead.

When the Christ School student body was strongly populated by day students, there was less need for organized athletics, for many of the boys had to return home after class to do a variety of farm chores. Hence athletics on campus consisted primarily of baseball, later football, trapping, hiking, and self-amusement. And there was one tennis court. But the change to a full time boarding school required athletics instead of farm chores and an increase in the number of rooms on campus. The latter was solved in 1922 with the beginning of construction of six cottages to accommodate forty-eight students, twenty-two more than the old log cabins, which were gradually torn down, could accommodate. In addition, a seventh cottage was used for a while to provide space for eight more students. A gymnasium would be required to meet the needs of physical development.

The Old Gym, intended to be a temporary structure, was put up in 1922 when Fr. Harris felt he had some money to spare. What he planned to do in a few years was either to renovate or put up a new one. Evidence of this was his decision to build it of shingle rather than the sandstone used a few year's earlier in St. Dunstan's Hall. The cost was around $3,000 and the work was done by Mr. Boyd. From its inception the roof leaked because of improperly dried timber. Basically the gym was four walls and the only heat was what nature put there or what the boys generated by their own physical efforts.[8] A huge storage box sat at the south end and bleachers on the north. Extending along each side were narrow benches attached to the studs, and boys sitting there during games were close enough to the court to stick a foot out and trip players, if so inclined. In the fall, racks were put up to hang football gear on and in November frozen socks or jocks remained so when a player returned to dress the next day. Most visiting teams dressed to play before coming to Christ School; others changed into uniforms in the basement of the Old Dorm and used the Bathhouse for other functions.

John Dougherty, who was a scrub on the first Greenie basketball team in 1922-23, said the gym had a tin roof. "When it rained, the noise was so great you couldn't hear your teammates. The roof was not sheeted but was simply cross-planked and the tin was nailed to that. There was neither insulation nor heat." He went on to recall that one winter Fessor decided the students should have a calisthenics class in the gym. "Unfortunately," Dr. Dougherty said, "Fr. Harris and Mr. Dave were supportive of this idea. The only excuse for missing calisthenics was being sick, and the sick were visited by one of the Big Three."

Certainly it was the only gym in North Carolina to have games postponed because of rain and ice. The best part of the Old Gym was the floor, which Fessor kept unscarred and shiny for thirty years, simply by exercising his lungs occasionally when anyone dared to step on the floor without taking his shoes off first. That first team, by the way, with not one experienced player on it, was winless in thirteen games. By coincidence, the last Christ School team to practice in the Old Gym (it played all its games on the road in 1952-53) was also without victory.

Making way for an increasing boarding enrollment was the construction of six cottages sometime between 1921-25. The cottages replaced the old log cabins as they deteriorated, and the cost of each new cottage was about $1,500. In addition, in 1925, a cottage was constructed for Fessor and his wife, placing him in a strategic position where he could see all and hear all with regard to the cottages. His presence insured decency. Two years later, another cottage was built near the 38 Dorm and it provided room for students from time to time.

As originally constructed, the cottages had a front porch and a large hall inside which led into four rooms, two on each side. The back porches were to be added later. As Frederick Krauss recalled, the cottages had a central hot-air furnace with a vent in the hall. One student fired it as a separate job. One had to use the Bathhouse for shower and toilet facilities. Later a shower, toilet, and sink were to be installed in a corner of the big hall. Until about World War II, a couple of the cottages were rented during the summer to vacationing friends of the school. David Harris Jr.

[8]Visiting Asheville School basketball coach Hop Arbogast occasionally wore ear muffs and gloves when his basketball team played in the Christ School gym. There were times when a person, if he didn't move about, might suffer frostbite.

recalled that both Bob and Don Harris frequently rented one and that friends of Mother Harris frequently stayed in the cottages. Two of the cottages still exist. The Second Cottage, which was the first to be removed in 1948-49 to make way for the construction of Boyd Dorm, was carried to Frog Level where it became the home of Pete McDaniel's sister, Helen Webb, both of whom worked for the school. Fessor's Cottage, was hauled off in 1965 to become a residence in Brushy Creek. The Fifth Cottage gave way to Harris Dorm.

Six cottages were built on campus during the mid-1920's, housing eight students each. A back porch allowed for outdoor sleeping. Most of the cottages occupied what are now the locations of Boyd and Harris dormitories.

The sawbell was the alarm system until 1942. Students could tell the mood of the headmaster by how it sounded.

Fr. Harris (far right) is shown with the faculty in the mid-1920's. They are (left to right) Zach Alden, an unidentified lady, Mr. Dave, Fessor, and Mac Alden.

III: 1910-1925

Fr. Harris: Man And Legend

Who was Fr. Harris–the man who sustained the ministry and dream of Fr. Wetmore so faithfully and transformed Christ School into a boys boarding school at the critical juncture of 1926. Duncan MacBryde '28, who became a Presbyterian minister and professor, describes Fr. Harris as "a saint waiting to be canonized." That did not mean he was saccharine, for here was a man who could awe boys by chinning himself with one hand on an outdoor horizontal bar when he was in his late fifties. He had an enormous hold over the boys–much like the Pied Piper–except that his tune was directed toward good. How he accomplished this is answered in part by his daughter, Mrs. Dorothy Thomson:

> He had an enormous amount of patience and an enormous amount of love. I never heard Fr. Harris raise his voice. When he told us to do something, no one ever hesitated or asked why.

His background is sketchy, somewhat even in the minds of his children. As Mrs. Thomson so perceptively explained, "When you are growing up, you simply take your father for what he is and do not think about his past. Then, when you grow up and leave, the right moment to ask never again seems to come along." Among those cloudy aspects are the extent of his formal schooling and preparations for the ministry. What is known is that Fr. Harris neither completed high school nor attended college or seminary, but that before he was ordained in 1902 at age thirty-seven, he had read for the law and he had spent fourteen years as a teacher, a principal, and a superintendent in the school system of Decatur, Ala.

A striking likeness of Fr. Harris hangs in St. Dunstan's Library, and on Alumni Weekend, the boys from his era are often seen gazing into his eyes. The portrait, painted in the summer of 1914, was done by a New York artist, Wilford Conrow. He had a long-time interest in Christ School as well as three great-nephews who attended school here–Todd, David, and Pierre Mallett. In painting the likeness, Conrow worked from photographs and snapshots as well as suggestions from the Harris family and faculty. The *Christ School News* of November 1941 carried this commentary about the painting:

> The likeness is an excellent one, and the picture very beautiful. It shows Fr. Harris in his cossack, a silver cross hung about his neck, with his left hand grasping his belt–an attitude characteristic of him. The background colors of blue and green–representing a somewhat fanciful sky–were chosen by Conrow to set off the figure. To one side is a bit of landscaping, suggesting a broad valley rising to a mountain peak.

To those who knew him, Fr. Harris was one of those peaks and many alumni recall vividly several of his mannerisms. One was a little half-whistle and another was a tapping of his foot, both of which were ways in which he thwarted some misadventure before it began or which served as a warning to the students to stop what they were doing. Many recall that during his Chapel talks, Fr. Harris would take out his watch and hold it in his hand as he stood in the aisle to make clear a simple, important, and frequently emotional point. He would glance at the watch from time to time to make certain that his talk did not exceed ten minutes. At other times, his hand would clutch the cloth belt which encircled his waist and his words would be punctuated by a gentle swirling motion, almost like the pendulum swing of a clock.

Unfortunately, a portrait of Mr. Dave which hangs next to that of his father draws from alumni mostly a reaction of chagrin, discomfort, and disbelief. It was as though the artist at the last moment smoothed plaster across the face, removing at once the strength and vitality embedded so deeply. Gone were the earth-tone tan and the deep lines and wrinkles. In an age before the Adonis-look, most boys at school desired to look something like Mr. Dave. Many wondered how this could be done and not a few pinched their foreheads and went about frowning in hopes of acquiring that look. It did not then dawn upon any of us that the deep lines and wrinkles came naturally to someone who had the task of looking after us. Hopefully, some day an artist (who already knows and loves Christ School or will take the time to learn its past) will do another portrait of Mr. Dave. He could well take as his model the black-and-white picture taken in 1954 by the late alumnus Hamilton Millard, who was a photographer for such publications as the original *Life* magazine and *National Geographic*. It captures strikingly the lines, the wrinkles, the smile, the informality of Mr. Dave posed in an open-neck shirt. Even in black-and-white, alumni who see this picture know once again that this is The Man.

A third portrait which hangs in the school building–one of the founder–was disliked by Mrs. Wetmore. As reported in the *Christ School News* in November 1941, she requested that the picture, which had hung in the old school building, not be placed in the new one for it was "so poor a likeness." At that time, the school expressed the hope of obtaining a new portrait of Mr. Wetmore in the near future.

Though Fr. Harris did not come to Christ School permanently until he was around forty-five years of age, he was an energetic, stimulating person who inspired others to do their best. He never stopped and his schedule ran from daily early morning communion until about midnight when he would make a last round to bank the furnaces. His youngest son, Bob Harris, never recalled his father sitting down during the day. Margaret Brumbeloe, who lived in a house directly west of Boyd Dorn, commented on his ceaseless activity:

> At night, we could see through the woods across to the campus. At late hours and early in the morning, you could see the lantern flickering as Fr. Harris moved briskly about, looking after his boys, tending the furnaces, ringing the Angelus, or feeding the chickens.

While leading boys was his speciality, Fr. Harris lived his commitment to God in an exemplary fashion that was admired by school and community. Not only was his black cossack seen in Chapel and the classroom but also in many mountain homes where he brought prayer and comfort and advice to the sick and needy. It was Fr. Harris who replaced morning prayer with an Anglican service that included robes and incense and regular communion. This service was not converted to a sung mass until Fr. Boynton arrived in 1933, for Fr. Harris did not have a strong enough voice to sing the eucharist. He introduced the daily early morning communion service which he seldom missed, even while conducting it in an unheated Chapel where the elements were sometimes frozen and bare hands turned numb. One of his most popular innovations–especially among the community members–followed the regular Sunday evening service. For those who wished to stay, a forty-five minute song fest followed with the people selecting their favorite songs from the hymnal.

Even though Fr. Harris did not finish high school or attend college or seminary, he was a self-taught scholar who was a master teacher of Latin and mathematics and literature. Respect for him in the classroom was so strong that students stood whenever he entered the room. This respect carried over into the lives of the boys who also stood whenever a girl entered the room. The students in the 1920's described Fr. Harris as their "best teacher."

Among the many jobs Fr. Harris performed during his never-ending-day was that of keeping night study hall. Even when he left study hall to slip across to his office under the stairways, things remained quiet. According to Clair Thain, "students respected Fr. Harris too much to want to let him down, even if he wasn't looking." While keeping a strict study hall, Fr. Harris was always prepared for the occasional sleepy head. Before making his appearance, he would stop at the well outside the school building and fill a glass with cold water from the dipper. He would place the glass on his desk and when a boy dozed off, he would pour a little of the cold water down the boy's neck. "So badly did everyone want to do right by Fr. Harris," said Fessor, "that even when the unsuspecting boy jumped up, no one in study hall would laugh–except inside."

Fr. Harris had a deep faith in private education, more so as public education expanded and became more secular. His daughter believes Fr. Harris went to a Roman Catholic boarding school somewhere near his home in Union, Kentucky, but did not graduate. When his father died, he became the head of the family and in the years that followed he became a self-educated man. Helping in this respect was the fact that Fr. Harris came from an educated family: all his sisters were teachers. His father, again according to Mrs. Thomson, was a kind of Daniel Boone, a man of the woods. As a young man, Fr. Harris migrated to Alabama, bringing with him a mule team to start a freight line. That didn't do too well and he ended up teaching school in Decatur, where he was later principal and superintendent. In a lighter vein, Bob Harris recalls how important Fr. Harris felt boarding schools to be in preparing young people for life. According to this account, Fr. Harris told his wife that she was to raise each of the children until they reached the age of 12, then he would take charge. At that point, Fr. Harris took charge and sent all the children off to school. "I didn't know of such an arrangement, at least not first hand," Mrs. Thomson said, "but it explains to me what happened. I went off to school when I was twelve. My father really believed in boarding schools. No one asked us if we wanted to go or where we wanted to go." The three sons attended Kent and Mrs. Thomson went to St. Mary's on the Poughkeepsie.

Trapping and taking Fr. Harris' chickens had to rank high on the entertainment list of boys in this period before vending machines and organized sports. By Thanksgiving 1930, Dillon Cobb and Edgar Robinson were acknowledged as the hunting team which had set a new record for catches. At that point, they had captured forty-eight rabbits and eight opossums.[9] The old record was held by Warren Redd and Dutch Eason in 1928, when they had landed twenty-eight rabbits by Thanksgiving but no opossums. Other game included beaver, and from time to time enterprising young boys at school sold the rabbit and beaver skins to bring some cash to otherwise empty pockets. One year Mr. Dave joined his

[9]By the end of the year, the record-breaking duo caught over sixty rabbits. The numbers caught the next year dropped dramatically.

brother Bob in the trapping business at Christ School. The two boys caught quite a few rabbits and then sold them to the boarding students for ten cents each. "The students would take them down into the woods and roast them," Bob Harris said with a laugh.

Kidnapping Fr. Harris's chickens or stealing some eggs was motivated from time to time primarily by a desire to appease the appetite. But it was sport also and a couple of the participants indicated that the fun lay not so much in the thrill of getting away with something but the predictable results. Fr. Harris, ever shrewd and refusing to be outwitted, would snare the culprits and deal out the expected punishment. This provided a security to boys which cannot be gained in any other way–like the ending of a familiar story which one likes to hear over and over. Fr. Harris never let the culprits down.

Fessor was the source of two such incidents. One night, Howard Hall, better known as Gutsy because of his eating propensities, went out with a razor and was going to whack a chicken's head off without making any noise. When he swung the blade, he missed the head and cut off the toe of a chicken instead. When Fr. Harris came down to feed his chickens the next morning, he observed the one with the missing toe. Eventually he found out the culprit–mainly by waiting for the boy to expose himself through gloating, and appropriate action was taken.

Another chicken incident followed an afternoon forest fire on Mrs. Wetmore's property along the south side of the Christ School road. The boys were called out from class to help fight it, along with many other people from the countryside. As the fire began to be brought under control, some of the boys disappeared. The next morning an old dominicker rooster, likened to Abraham in age, was missing when Fr. Harris came to the chicken house. He didn't say anything about it, but bided his time and waited for the grapevine to learn what happened. The boys who disappeared had caught the old rooster and took it down to Gap (Robinson) Creek and built a fire. They cut the rooster up and put each piece in a quart can. The boys involved later said they boiled the thing for about two hours but that the rooster never became tender enough to eat. Some days afterwards, Fessor was standing in the hall of the school building by the door when a boy walked in. Fr. Harris was standing on the side of the hall opposite Fessor. As the boy passed by, Fr. Harris reach out and caught his hand. There was a good, deep scratch across the back of the boy's hand. Fr. Harris said, "What? The old rooster had pretty sharp spurs, didn't he?" That was the end of the episode. Fr. Harris let the boy know that he was on the ball and the disappearances ended for some time.

Fr. Harris was wise in the way of boys and he knew how to deal with them before the word interact became so commonplace. Another incident, some years later, displayed this wisdom. He had been missing some eggs from the hen house and he wanted to put a stop to it. One day at assembly after lunch, he came down to study hall dressed as if he were going to Asheville. At assembly, he announced that his classes would not meet that afternoon. Then he walked across the campus and toward Arden as though he were going to catch the 1:30 train. After Fr. Harris had gone into the woods, he changed direction and doubled back. He picked up a can of overripe eggs which he had hidden behind a big white pine and slipped behind one of the buildings near the chicken house to see what would happen. This building had an opening large enough for the chickens to get in and out and it was large enough for a boy to squirm through. Fr. Harris must have remained there for about half an hour before a boy came and squirmed in; then he moved closer to the house to await the boy's exit. When the boy had almost crawled out, Fr. Harris started pelting him over the head with those overripe eggs. In the process, Fr. Harris pelted two of the boy's accomplices who were supposed to be standing guard. No more punishment was required. Discipline had been tempered by the humor and irony involved in justice meted out.

Fr. Harris and Mother Harris stand under the grape arbor at the rectory. The year was 1915.

III: 1910-1925

Living Conditions

It would be easy to dismiss living conditions in the first quarter of the century as being primitive and to infer that primitive environment produces inferior life. Such thinking would have swept most of our early forbearers into the dust bin. The early years of Christ School certainly were primitive if one's measure was solely material things. They did lack the ease and convenience and gadgets which surround us today. But they were not lacking the important things–dignity and pride and independence and determination and a willingness to learn and work hard and earnestly to improve their lot. It was not the environment which taught right and wrong and the distinction between truth and honesty and how Christ taught love and sharing: it was the teachers.

The log cabins, which had been used as classrooms in 1913, became living quarters for boarders in 1914, nearly doubling the number of such students. Primitive, yes, but nice to live in, according to Fessor, who spent a year and a half living in one. Lighting was by kerosene lamp, heating by a sheet metal stove sitting in the middle of the one room which slept four boys, and there was no plumbing. Instead, each boy had a wash basin and pitcher, and water brought by pail from the old well. Frequently, the ice had to be broken to wash one's face. To bathe, one walked a couple of hundred feet due west to the Bathhouse and its shower and toilets. It was up to the boys in each cabin to gather the firewood for the stove. They cut it on a saw at Mr. Boyd's carpentry shop and brought logs down by the armfuls.[10] Late, during winter nights, Fr. Harris could be seen darting in and out of the log cabins, making sure the fires were properly banked.

One benefit of having these stoves was that the boys could cook on them. Being made of metal, they would quickly turn red hot. With pangs of hunger the natural state for young men, they engaged in a lot of rabbit trapping which led to extra nourishment. The cabins were equipped by the boys with frying pans and boilers of some sort for cooking purposes. As Fessor described it, "They would skin the rabbit, clean it, and put it in

[10]For many years these logs were hauled to the shop by Uncle Van Allen and Uncle Joe Brown. The wood was cut on the Wetmore property and paid for by the school.

the boiler and parboil it for some time. Then they would put the rabbit into a frying pan and turn it brown. On a bleak afternoon or blustery winter night, with nothing else to do, cooking a rabbit led to an enjoyable feast and a lot of storytelling." In addition, fishing at Wetmore Pond was a common activity and the boys would clean and cook their fish for a culinary delight. One need remember that this was a time when there was little refrigeration (a few ice-boxes) and certainly no walk-ins and it was difficult out of season to provide fresh meat and vegetables for the dining hall. This made "cabin-cooking" even tastier. In the 1920's, Ma Pressley, the cook, would sometimes prepare a rabbit for a few trappers, and Elizabeth Edgerton used to do the same for some of the fishermen during her twenty-five years in the kitchen. In the fall, one of the delightful sources of supplementary nutrients were the apple and peach orchards in the neighborhood. Sunday afternoons, many boys hiked to the top of Burney Mountain to get apples from the orchard of Mr. Clayton, whose children attended Christ School as day students. Sometimes a parent would arrive on campus with a wagon-load of apples for the boys, a payment-in-kind for his children's education. And occasionally students made unauthorized excursion into nearby orchards to ease the plight of overburdened trees. Such apples were excellent to eat and the cores were fine ammunition. Until the emergence on campus in recent years of vending machines filled with a variety of sweets, apples, oranges, and other fruits were generously available on the back porch of the kitchen in St. Dunstan's or in the cold storage cellar below and later in the new dining hall.

As Christ School moved closer toward becoming a college preparatory boarding school for boys only, it required a continuing adjustment concerning the role of athletics. The condition was disappearing in which most of the students returned home in the afternoon to do family chores. The boarding students were on campus all day for nine months, with a three-week break at Christmas. Baseball had been the main sport from the beginning, with Mr. Wetmore and Fr. Harris giving it a firm endorsement. Baseball was played both in the fall and the spring, with a regular schedule drawn up for the spring season. In the fall, games were arranged on an ad hoc basis. Until the 1920's, Christ School ended its year around the first week in May with the result that baseball games were played in the more wintry cold of March and April, with perhaps an early game in late February. Fall baseball was more of an intramural thing, and might involve community and alumni pick-up teams. Stirrings of football began around 1912 with the first organized team playing a couple of games in the fall of 1914. Echoes have it that one of the Christ School pick-up football teams lost a game to an organized Asheville School team at this time by the outlandish score of 90-0. Early on the school had a hard-surface clay court which provided tennis on a recreational basis. It would not be until 1934 that a student would organize the first varsity tennis team. Frank Zimmerman '36 went on to become a ranked high school tennis player whose ability drew the attention of Bill Tilden, the first great professional tennis star. Jimmy Ewin '36, who quarterbacked the football team and played tennis and taught the fifth and sixth grades while a student here, recalls going to the Grove Park Inn with Zimmerman when Tilden was playing a match there. The legendary tennis great also came to Christ School at least twice to observe Zimmerman and hit around with him some. At this juncture, Tilden was conducting a one-man campaign to renew the nation's interest in tennis and to build it into a professional sport. But, to return to earlier years, other recreation consisted principally of hiking and running through the woods and mountains, some overnight camping out, trapping rabbits, squirrels, and beaver, and inventing assorted homemade games. During winter months, recreation was drastically curtailed because there was no gymnasium available until the winter of 1922-23 and no other organized sports except baseball and then football. But before the public schools began to expand into Buncombe, this minimal athletic program did not pose a serious problem since the larger day population got more than enough exercise in walking five to ten miles a day to classes and doing whatever farming jobs remained to be done at home.

Some excellent baseball, football, and basketball teams developed during this era, especially during the 1920's when athletics came under the strong, determined leadership of Dick Fayssoux. He played football in 1915 (no victories) and on the baseball teams of 1915-16, under the direction of Coach Harold Nichols, the man who started the boys on digging away Stump Alley in order to build an athletic field. If Coach Nichols returned in later years, he must have been proud of the work his protege did in turning the Christ School field into one of the area's best for football and baseball. As *Asheville Citizen* sports writers commented frequently in the 1950-60's, there was "no better field in Western North Carolina than the one maintained by Dick Fayssoux." Certainly hundreds of Christ School boys whose minds were then untouched by weather conditions remember Fessor's constant, rather sharp urging to "keep off the gol dern infield." It was because of such vigilance that the field remained ready to play, remained a source of beauty for parents as they drove on campus, and served to embed in the mind of impressionable youth that the responsibility of preservation belongs to all of us. This was a lesson most carried over into their own lives.

One of those great baseball teams played in the spring of 1919 when Christ School, like other institutions, benefited from the return of some older boys whose education had been interrupted by the war. That year the Greenies (the first time they ever wore green uniforms) went on to claim the championship in this region by virtue of a 2-1 victory over Bingham Military Academy, whose roster was often loaded with post-graduate athletes. The spring of 1917 was another good year as the baseball team was led by Harvey Lance, an all-state athlete at Furman University, the pitching of Ingram Cox, and the coaching and play of first baseman Preston (Dad) Warf, who entered the fifth grade here when he was in his late teens. Dad Warf was to return to Christ School after World War I to complete his education and he played for Coach Fayssoux on the undefeated team of 1922. Fessor's description of this championship squad as "one of the best ever in Western North Carolina" may have been an understatement. It contained a gold mine of Christ School athletes. Manley Whisnant, who played sports here for about seven years, became a stellar student-athlete at the University of North Carolina, where he was a member of the Order of Golden Fleece and captain of the football team.[11] He played center. Walter and Charlie Shuford moved on to become track and football stars at North Carolina State, and Bill Corn (pitcher-outfielder) played professional baseball for Baltimore in the old International League. Providing the home run punch along with Corn were Paul Rickman, who became a rural postal mail carrier in Arden, and J.A. Martin, who became a priest.

Graduating classes were small in number during those early years. The first class to have more than ten graduates was that of 1925, which contained fifteen. There were no graduates in the Class of 1921. Because of general economic distress and hardships, not all graduates went to college after completing their Christ School education. But many did and all went back into their communities determined to live the kind of lives they saw in Fr. Harris, Mr. Wetmore, and the other dedicated teachers who served the school so well.

Records show that three boys from the Class of 1916 went on to lives of long service and dedication. Horace Butt, who attended school here 1910-12 (then dropped out for economic hardship) and returned in 1915-16 was one of these. He earned two degrees at the University of North Carolina and became a geologist, traveling all over the world for a major petroleum company.[12] Dick Fayssoux, who needs no introduction, graduated after two years. He played football (quarterback) in 1915 and baseball in 1915-16 at a time when letters were not awarded. He also found time to strike up a courtship with Sarah Shuford by walking the mail pouch to-and-from Arden. Bryan Warren, who entered in 1913, was a prefect for two years, played football and baseball, and was offered a football scholarship to St. Stephens College in New York. Instead he attended Duke, the University of North Carolina, and Maryland before becoming a physician.

[11]Whisnant became superintendent of Thompson Orphanage in Charlotte, N.C., where he served for more than 40 years.

[12]His sister Olivia married Fr. Duncan in the first wedding at Christ School Chapel.

Many of these early graduates, deeply influenced by the spiritual life at Christ School, became ministers. One of the two boys known to graduate in the first commencement exercise in 1905 was Samuel Stroup, who became a priest in the Episcopal Church and a member of the school's board of directors. The other graduate–Robert Sumner, attended Harvard and became an attorney. From the class of 1907, Norvin C. Duncan, who was valedictorian and won the elocution medal, became an Episcopal minister and author. Perry Carter, who attended here only in 1915, became a Baptist minister after finishing at Carson-Newman. He was an avid baseball player. J. Mitchell Taylor (his son and grandson were to graduate from Christ School) entered in 1914 and graduated in 1919, but missed a couple of years because of World War I. He may have been responsible for Christ Schools' athletic teams becoming known as the "Greenies." For a long time there was no consistent nickname though the term "Warriors" was used occasionally. In 1917, Christ School defeated Bingham Military Academy 2-1 to win the Western North Carolina baseball championship–unofficially, at least. As a reward, the team earned new uniforms and Taylor, who was a player/manager, got to pick out the ones to replace the mismatched uniforms worn during the season. "I ordered them green," Taylor said. "I think that's how Christ School became known as the 'Greenies'." Prior to that, the team had frequently been called the "dishwashers,' alluding to the necessary work which each boy had to do.

Medicine and education also attracted a number of these graduates. From the second graduating class (1906), T. Woodfin Sumner received his medical degree from the University of Pennsylvania after completing four years at the University of North Carolina. He practiced in Fletcher and became the school doctor. Boyce Grier, who finished here in 1912 after three years, got degrees from Erskine (AB), Georgia (MA), and Peabody (PhD) and became president of Lander College. He was quarterback of the Erskine football team. Harvey Lance of the Class of 1917 got two degrees from Furman University and became a teacher and coach for forty years. At Furman he was all-State guard in football and honorable mention in the Southern Conference, which then included the likes of Tennessee, Alabama, and Auburn. He played on the Christ School baseball team that year which featured the pitching of Ingram Cox and was coached by student Dad Warf, who was a towering first baseman. Another member of the class of 1907, Richard Allison of Columbia, became the pioneer dermatologist in South Carolina. He was nationally known for his innovation and expertise in this field.

Two of the more feisty early graduates were Sam Cathey '09 and Bill Cathey '11. Sam, who was blinded by an explosion in a roadwork accident, attended the University of North Carolina for five years, earning an AB degree and a doctor of jurisprudence. In 1955, he was honored by President Eisenhower as the handicapped man of the year. Cathey was a judge on the Asheville municipal court. He brother Bill, a fixture at nearly every Christ School reunion, attended Stetson one year before becoming an engineer for the Southern Railroad.

There were others. Fred Kizer–one of several brothers to attend Christ School–finished in 1914 after four years. Like many early graduates, he returned to the campus to work for a year to help save some money for college. As a student, he played football, baseball, and tennis. During that extra year he was assistant coach of football and baseball and in charge of the work crew. Rhea Fayssoux (1915-18), Fessor's brother, studied physical education at the University of Illinois and served in the Navy during World War I and the Air Force in World War II. He played baseball and football as a student and went on to own an automobile dealership and become an amateur magician. He often entertained the Christ School student body with his magic show.

As a boy, David Harris Sr. (second from the left) looks over the dam he and his friends built frequently near the Rock House

III: 1910-1925

Etcetera

Swimming has provided a source of pleasure for Christ School students from the earliest times, though swimming was not something every boy experienced. The major swimming hole was the Old Mill Pond where a dynamo was located to operate the saw mill and the grist house, and to provide electricity for the Wetmores and Christ School until Carolina Power and Light took over the service around 1926. Dugouts were maintained there and the Wetmore, Harris, and Shuford children used the lake constantly. It was here that Dave Harris taught Charlie Shuford '22 how to swim.

> When I was little, I used to dive off the west end of the dam. Mr. Dave would dive in and retrieve me, for all I could do was thrash around. Then one day, after I had done this four or five times, he said he was not coming after me the next time. I didn't believe him and I dived in anyway. Mr. Dave didn't come in. I learned to swim.

The Mill Pond was also the source of ice for the school until the appearance of CP&L. The ice-cutting also provided for the needs of the Wetmores and many other people in the community. Students apparently were never involved in the ice-cutting process, but they used the lake to skate on and play hockey and have snowball fights and were frequent spectators of those who were involved in ice-cutting. The lake would freeze six to eight inches deep and the men would cut out squares and haul them to the ice-house in the woods northwest of the Wetmore House. There they would store the ice, between layers of sawdust, in a pit six to eight feet deep over which was built a rock house. The men would cut out an area of the lake and then float the ice down to a wagon. They left a "walking bridge of ice" across the lake. The grist mill, the saw mill, and the store were on the east side of Gap Creek at the dam. There was a three or four foot deep flume in which the water poured to turn the generator. When the flume was closed at night, more water flowed over the dam. There was a huge heavy gate to lift when the pond was to be drained. The Mill Pond was located to the northeast of the Rock House (manager's house), occupied in the early 1920's by John Jenkins (father of Clarence Jenkins). The lake easily covered several acres and was twenty to thirty feet deep in parts. A figure familiar to students and community was Johnny DeMean, a Finn who was brought in by Mrs. Wetmore to look after the dynamo after the death of Fr. Wetmore. Where he lived at first is a matter of conjecture, but later he is pictured in a rocking chair on the front porch of the old Clarence Jenkins House, a two story frame house close to and on the west side of Struan. DeMean would close off the flume about nine each night, ending the flow of electricity which lit part of the campus. Oil and kerosene lamps and candles did the rest. Uncle Johnny was a kind of student pet and he attended school, graduating with each class.

The Mill Pond, which was fed by Gap Creek, was the scene of both humorous and tragic events. On one occasion, Fr. Harris honored a student request and baptized him by immersion under rather chilly circumstances. Occasionally someone tumbled into the pond during the winter. Charlie Shuford recalls that Gus Pressley fell in and "turned to icicles." He ran up to Wetmore House where Agnes Pressley (the cook at Struan) ministered to him. He had been cutting ice and lost his balance. The most tragic event came in 1924 with the drowning of Roy Wingate, who is memorialized in a stained glass window in Christ School Chapel. Wingate went out into a mucky area to save a student who could not swim and had panicked in shallow water. In fright, the "drowning boy" threw his legs across Wingate's shoulders and Wingate slipped into the muck. While several other boys were pulling the frightened boy into shore, they were not aware that Wingate had been shoved under. It was some hours later before Mr. Dave, who was not at the pond at the time, retrieved the body after many diving attempts.

Since the little pond on the Christ School road was not to be built until after Fr. Boynton arrived on campus (he was a four-letter man at Williams College in swimming, basketball, track, and football), the other places where the students went to swim were Cane Creek (toward the Old Airport), and a lime hole reportedly used by Fr. Wetmore somewhere beyond the Jervey Farm House, and Grove Lake. In 1930, the owners of Grove Lake had it posted and swimming was no longer permissible. Prior to that time, many Christ School students made the two mile walk, not only to swim, but to camp out at the beautiful site. In 1909 another dam was built by Mr. Dave and other children near the Spring House, where dairy products were stored. The dam was built on the stream which takes the overflow from the present lake. Mrs. Dorothy Thomson said the boys used to have to repair it every day or two.

One of the most interesting developments was the publication in 1913 of the *Christ School Magazine*. Whether it continued beyond that one year can not at present be verified. It was an ambitious undertaking and the publication was a cross between a newspaper and a magazine, somewhat like a gazette. Like the *Galax Leaf* it was printed in the school's press shop but was an in-house publication rather than one reaching out to Christ School patrons. At a time when patriotism ran high, an article in the March/April issue described a spirited flag-raising scene Friday, February 21, to honor George Washington with Professor E.S. Clark of the faculty the much applauded speaker.

Interspersed in the magazine were brief quips and tongue-in-cheek statements designed to bring a chuckle to the reader. The January 1913 issue contained the following comment: "Several new boys have come in since Christmas, and are taking hold weekly, especially in the dining room."

The magazine was established by the Galax Society, which had been organized during the Wetmore years to provide a forum for debate, declamation, and discussion–a common forum that broadened the horizon and thinking of students and outsiders alike. The publication was self-supporting through the sale of advertising and fees. It first appeared in January 1913 under the editorship of Alex Kizer '13 who remained after graduation to work here for a couple of years. In the opening issue he wrote about the work involved in getting the magazine started:

> We have spent many sleepless nights and consumed much midnight oil, as well as many cans of Prince Albert, but we have finally appeared before you.

Among the advertisers in the April 1913 *Christ School Magazine* was the Asheville Steam Laundry at 43 West College Street. The message accompanying their display read: "A clean mind in a clean body is the greatest thing on earth. Your teachers, boys, will do the first, and we offer our services to help perfect the latter, by seeing that your wearing apparel is neat and clean."

Several issues brought news of organizations active on campus. The April issue revealed that the Galax Society had engaged in debates over such topics as women's suffrage, international peace, and Saturday school. The latter debate was spurred by Fr. Harris' decision to change the day-in-town from Saturday to Monday. That December the Galax Society held a debate just before Christmas on whether independence should be granted to the Philippine Islands. The affirmative won. In this same issue, it was recorded that the Dramatics Club had presented a play on

December 14, 1912. "The younger players displayed unexpected talent. All give credit to Mrs. (Elsie) Hemphill and Mother Harris for their excellent training." Profits from ticket sales went to the Athletic Association. A Glee Club existed, at least according to the January 1913 issue of the magazine. It was under the direction of Mrs. Clark. Whether this was the first such organization is not clear. It is known that in September 1911, a musical society was formed by Boston Lackey (president) and Boyce Grier (secretary/treasurer). Try-outs were expected to provide a glee club, a male quartet, and instrumental groups. An article in the October 1911 issue of the *Galax Leaf* said: "During the cold winter months, when outdoor recreation is more or less suspended, this organization will undoubtedly prove of both interest and pleasure to the students."

Sports were not neglected in the magazine. The April 1913 issue pointed to a 5-2 baseball record through March, with Bland striking out eighteen batters in a 2-1 victory over Asheville School. The magazine urged its readers not to despair in defeat, a 9-5 loss to the old rival at Riverside Park ten days later. "Though the banners for victory fluttered boldly in the cool breeze, urging each player to do his best, they had to be taken down in defeat at the close of the contest." Three days later (March 28), the baseball team "journeyed (by wagon) over roads of rut and mire, through the rain and snow to Mars Hill, where they split two games with that team."

The highlight of the year for the Galaxy Society arrived April 21, 1913, with the annual banquet. Faculty and ladies on the hill were invited to "enjoy themselves eating, drinking, and conversing." The toastmaster was the Rev. J.P. Burke, and the speakers were Fr. Harris, Professor E.S. Clark, and Mrs. Wetmore. Responses were delivered by Harvey A. Cox, Claude Miller, and Alex Kizer–all members of the society. It was written of Mr. Clark that "his remarks revealed his familiarity with boys." In her talk, Mrs. Wetmore spoke of the benefit of social gatherings and said the Lord had "made women silly to match the men."

Getting to Christ School was never an easy task. For most boys coming from more distant parts, the trip was the first stage in the process of growing up. A fourteen year old traveling from Raleigh or Durham to Asheville would spend nearly twenty hours on the train. He would pass through Greensboro and Charlotte and a hundred other whistle-stops before reaching Arden. Others traveling through Gastonia or Columbia enjoyed a similar experience, except that those arriving from the south often wondered if the train could puff up the Saluda grade.

When these boys, mostly in the age range of twelve to sixteen, reached Arden, the new ones had a feeling of being lost, for the town consisted of a depot, a post office, and a general store. To make things more unsettling, most of them had never seen Christ School before their arrival.

There was only one way to travel to the campus through the 1920's and that was by foot. Uncertain where to go, some new boys would call the school (the only telephone, an old fashioned ringer type that required three longs and two shorts, was in Mrs. Wetmore's house) and they would be given directions how to walk there. Others might wait a couple of hours until another train pulled in, hoping an old boy might get off and lead them on their journey. In any case, they would walk south on Highway 25 to Brown's Pottery, turn left and cross the railroad track, and follow a path which ran parallel to what is now Pensacola Avenue.[13] The first landmark, about a mile from the depot, was the residence of Willie Mae Fletcher, who served the school for many years. It is the only house remaining on the Christ School Road from the early days. From there, the boarders walked along the school road to the top of the Big Hill.[14] From this hill they would cut through the woods, entering the domain about where the front all-weather tennis courts are.

Baggage was always a problem for there were no red caps at the depot. Each student carried his own suitcase and small belongings. A wagon would come over from school later to pick up any trunks or other bulky items unloaded during the day. Occasionally, students would find someone waiting at the depot with a truck or wagon who would haul baggage for ten or fifteen cents each.

Beginning in the fall of 1907, the first building that all arriving students saw was the Chapel. For those students entering after 1917, the Chapel stood as the only major building surviving from the original campus. A student would not see the beautiful terraces that now mark the west approach. Instead he saw a sloping hill which was patched sparsely by weeds, crabgrass, and thistle and scarred by gullies. But what calmed the sinking sensation in the stomach was the sight of some boys on the slope shagging fly balls hit to them by someone standing at the top of the hill. It wasn't long before most new boys would be checked in and join the group at play. Whatever orientation there was consisted primarily of Fr. Harris (and later Mr. Dave) standing on the porch of the dormitory greeting students, handing out room assignments and a broom, and providing the names of roommates. The few things new students needed to know would be announced in the opening assembly that evening.

Sometimes a different greeting awaited the new students. Tradition has it that new boys might encounter a moment of terror as they emerged from the woods after their two mile hike from Arden. On such occasions, the first thing they heard as they stepped into the clearing were terrible crashing sounds in the dorm and a voice screaming "Fresh Meat." The noise came from some old boy beating the wall with a paddle and screaming his greeting, a fearsome sound that made some smaller boys think of home. Then other boys would rush to the windows in the top story

[13]Allegedly this path was formed by Indians. Certainly, Christ School students left many imprints there.
[14]Mrs. Fayssoux remembered this as being called "Cottage Hill." Two cottages belonging to Mrs. Wetmore stood there.

of the dorm to shout greetings. This was all a part of the ritual of arriving, of the walk into the unknown.

The biggest change to come about at Christ School in 1925 occurred without fanfare. It seemed so natural that David P. Harris, should be named to be assistant headmaster in his fourth year here. Fr. Harris was by this time in failing health. He had literally worked himself to the point of exhaustion. He never missed an early morning communion service. He never failed to stoke the furnaces at midnight during the winter. He continued his ministry of off-campus outreach, and brought solace to many of the mountain families. He could never say no to duty. His son promised to be a strong shoulder to lean on. In addition, Dave Harris had a first hand knowledge of Kent School, like Christ School a boarding school with self-help system. The ideas of both schools found a common meeting place in Mr. Dave's practical and pragmatic mind. He knew how to make the system work.

For the boys in school the transition was such an easy one that few were aware when authority moved more completely into Mr. Dave's hands. One sign was that Fr. Harris appeared less frequently in assemblies, but he was always there on occasions to make important announcements or remarks. He was always on the scene to temper any justice that may have been too strong, but in such a way that there was no friction about how the school should be run. In addition, he no longer chinned himself with one hand but the students took it as gospel that he could still do it fifty times. As Mrs. Thomson recalls it, and numerous students from the 1920's agree, the two men never differed on policy or what needed to be done, or certainly not in public. It appears that Mr. Dave was as much in awe of Fr. Harris as any student. The main difference which those students of the 1920's recall between Fr. Harris and Mr. Dave was that Mr. Dave was more serious, more demanding, and a bit rougher on the edges. According to Albert Dougherty '23, he seemed to have soaked up some ideas from the military. "He inspected our rooms twice a day. There could be no wrinkle in the blankets and the shoes must be in a straight line, just poking their shiny nose out from under the bed." But they felt the same love for Mr. Dave as they did for Fr. Harris and Fessor, and recalled above all else that Mr. Dave was absolutely fair.

Money was scarce and Fessor's athletic budget amounted to something like two or three hundred dollars. Of course, he had no fuel bills to pay for the gymnasium was heated by bodies only. At the same time, he did not use new equipment as an inducement to play. Before World War II neither the school nor the boys had money to buy any new uniforms. What they wore were old uniforms stretched to longevity by the diligent care of Coach Fayssoux. What was often called new were some pants or shoulder pads of shoes cast off by the University of North Carolina or

North Carolina State or Clemson. You can imagine how well they fit. More often than not, few boys on the football team would be dressed exactly alike. Often one knee would be poking out of one's pants and a shirt might not have a number on it or be of a different color. If lack of new stuff hurt the pride or feelings of the Greenie players, it was not shown on the field, where opposing teams found that Fessor's players hit with a vengeance but always with fairness and sportsmanship in mind. To Fessor's way of thinking, if a boy did not have the determination to play and to give his best for Christ School, he was not worthy of a uniform anyway. Hence, Fessor made do with what he had, and by judicious buying, a process of hand-me-downs, and constant mending and sewing, he kept Christ School respectably clothed and repaired. He believed there could be no satisfaction in not giving one's best–even if his helmet was not bright and shiny.[15]

Since the day school no longer existed and there was not a large number of students returning home immediately after school, Fessor had to expand the athletic program to include all the students. The building of the gym in 1922 had been a start in that direction for it provided indoor facilities for athletics when conditions were wet outside. But not all boys could participate in varsity sports (football, basketball, and baseball) and there was neither money nor sufficient coaching skills among the staff to add other varsity sports which might utilize other students. The February 1930 issue of *The Warrior* described a new physical education program launched in the fall which involved all the students. It "provided for physical welfare, encouraged healthy competitive spirit, and it developed moral character." In addition, it permitted students who did not go out for the three sports an opportunity to earn a physical education unit also. During the fall, football captain Earl Pressly volunteered to conduct a class from 9:15-9:45 a.m. The program consisted of calisthenics, corrective exercises, and competitive contests, such as relays, potato races, walking contests, and so on. When weather conditions were suitable, the class met outside for tag football, 100 yard dashes, and similar events. During the winter, Fessor coached varsity basketball, ran intramural basketball in the evening, taught five periods, and led two physical education classes of forty-five minutes each between 1:30 and 3 p.m. It was apparently at this juncture that formal intramural basketball was organized with all students divided among ten teams and the faculty joining in the play from time to time. Those first captains were John Orr, Jesse and Orville Rumfeldt (Canadians who seem to be the first students to sleep year round on the back porch of the cottages), Dunk Sullivan, Carl Simpson, one of the Sloan brothers (William, George, or Robert), Sam Northcross, and Henry Russell.[16] This intramural league was to be a regular feature of the athletic

[15]In fact, most of the helmets–form-fitting leather with no padding–were handed down from generation to generation.

[16]Orr's team won the first intramural championship, defeating Sullivan 13-8. Each team had an 8-1 record to that point. In the Junior League competition, Russell slipped past Northcross 15-13.

program until the late 1950's. By then the introduction of other sports cut into the numbers available for this often highly exciting and competitive activity which boosted morale during the severe winter months.

By 1930, thoughts about adding sports to the athletic program were surfacing, but it would be several years later before anything materialized. That spring, R B Edwards, the new math teacher and Wofford graduate, planned to organize a tennis team to utilize the three clay courts that existed then. He spoke of his plans frequently and said there were some "pretty good prospects" on campus. The court next to the school building had an excellent clay surface, but one of the other two had fallen into disuse and badly needed to be weeded, rolled, and the fence repaired. The other courts were located behind the first two cottages. Although the tennis team was not formed then–such an undertaking would be student-led four years later–there was much recreational play. Conversation also involved the starting of a track team but no action was taken until 1933, when Fessor directed a few boys interested in track while also working with baseball. He would coach the track group for thirty minutes following baseball practice. The group was involved in one meet late in May, losing by a lop-sided score to Asheville School. It would be the following spring when track was formerly organized under the direction of Fr. Boynton, the new chaplain, who was an All-American athlete at Williams College.

After World War I, transportation for athletic trips shifted from foot, wagon, and train to travel by truck–at first a Model-T Ford. Until 1928, home games were played on Wetmore Field (pasture) and not infrequently a runner would trip over some roots of large white pine trees. On trips to Mars Hill, Blue Ridge, Swannanoa, and elsewhere (where the fields weren't much better), the boys went dressed in uniforms. They would sit in the open bed on boards cut by Mr. Boyd. They would take army blankets to wrap up in and made the trip even in rain or snow. "We'd come back frozen–victorious or not," said Dr. John Dougherty of his experiences. Coming back was always an exciting part of the adventure for generally the truck would stop to get gas at a country store and the players would store up on some hard candy. After the truck reached the Shuford House (until the route was changed somewhat in 1936) and turned into the Christ School Road, the team would pass a house where the last two girls who attended Christ School lived. "They would always wave to us," Dr. Dougherty recalled with a smile.

IV: 1925-1933

13

A Pivotal Year

The Class of 1928 was leading Christ School into a new epoch without the students themselves being aware of their role. A conscious decision by Fr. Harris and Mr. Dave ended the admission of day students, both boys and girls. Several factors entered into the decision, including less financial support from the national Episcopal Church and the opening in 1925 of a public school system in nearby Valley Springs.

But the mission idea was not terminated. The purpose now envisioned was to provide a church institution and college preparatory education for boys who could not afford to attend more expensive schools. The mountain children flocked to the new public schools in the region. Now the mission was to provide boarding students only the same common sense Christian education at a fee that middle class families, with some sacrifice, could afford. It was to combine continued excellence in education with a continuation of the work system to enable boys to keep down the costs of operating a school, to teach the dignity of work, and to inculcate a sense of responsibility.

For such reasons Christ School began its first all boarding college preparatory year with a 100 students and one hold-over day student (Frances Garren) who was permitted to continue his schooling. But the same system remained; there were no hired workmen, waiters, woodcutters, laborers, and other employees. Only kitchen and laundry help was hired.

Every boy had to take his turn in all the work around a school which had grown from a couple of log cabins in 1900 to twenty-two buildings, several of which were constructed of stone hewn from the hillsides on which the school is located. The boys performed a variety of tasks–washing dishes, digging post holes, chopping wood, sweeping the dining hall, cleaning the buildings, making the beds, and doing landscaping. The catalogue reminded each applicant to make certain he brought with him "a pair of overalls and a pair of workshoes."

Whereas the day students who had been coming to Christ School since 1900 either worked in the workshop to pay their tuition or returned home to do afternoon chores, the athletic-recreational program was expanded in 1928 to meet the needs of an all-boarding campus. So just as each boy was required to work there were no exceptions–so each one was required to spend a certain amount of time in the gymnasium and in some form of athletics outdoors.

The study hall which Fr. Harris kept for so many years was continued and strengthened at this time, with each boarder required to go to study hall from 7 to 9 every night with the exception of Saturday and Sunday. The former was a day to walk to Arden or Fletcher or other nearby points of interest. But there was in 1928 another interesting study period–the one help between 6 and 7 Monday morning to enable students to get a fresh look at their Monday assignments. Whether this study hall increased the number attending early morning communion, there are no records to tell.

And the Chapel, a small sandstone building surrounded by evergreens, Normandy poplars and a Magnolia tree, remained the center of school life. Three times a day Fr. Harris rang the Angelus. Three times daily everyone at Christ School stopped his work to bow his head for prayer or meditation. It was a tolling that reminded the neighbors as far as Arden and Fletcher that Christ School was about His business.

One other major change was taking place then. Fr. Harris, who experienced frail health from time to time from sheer overwork and exhaustion, turned over more and more of the duties of headmastering to his son David Page Harris. He continued his role as rector and provided a ballast as his son began to assume more responsibility. Thus, when Fr. Harris died in New Orleans in January 1933, the board of directors quickly confirmed what Fr. Harris had prepared them for–the Mr. Dave years.

IV: 1925-1933

A New Transition

From Mr. Wetmore's death in 1906 until Fr. Harris came to stay in September 1911, Christ School went through some troublesome years–years of searching for stability and the strength to continue the Wetmore dream. Between 1925-33, Christ School moved through a different kind of transition. Church financial support was rapidly dwindling. Public schools were opening in the mountain region to drain away children who had been a strong source of pupils for Christ School. Fr. Harris was wrestling with the problem of going to boy boarders only at a time when his physical health was being undermined by overwork and a new generation of buildings would be needed to provide permanence. On a campus there is always some trepidation among the students when a transfer of authority is occurring. They were looking for the security of a single allegiance at a time when Fr. Harris and his son were beginning to share leadership. Depressed economic conditions also created uncertainty. Though the Great Depression would not be officially ushered in until the big stock market crash in October 1929, farms and rural areas had been in a depression for a decade. This meant that more Christ School boarding students were able to pay even less room and board, so that additional scholarship and operating funds were needed. In effect, the school was even more dependent upon the efforts of Mrs. Wetmore to raise money each year to bridge the gap between revenues and expenditures. Her tireless energy never failed, even when her beloved son, Thomas Badger Wetmore, twenty-six, died at Struan of diabetes on August 30, 1927. This was the second great loss in her life, but as she had done earlier, she simply renewed her vow to help the school in what were certainly difficult circumstances. In a letter she wrote for the *Galax Leaf* of Christmas 1927, Mrs. Wetmore said:

> For the rest of my life, I expect to devote myself entirely to the work of Christ School on the field, and in interesting those who do not know of it. I ask your prayers and your help.

The credentials of the teachers and their abilities continued to be impressive during this period even though pay was low and hours long. Hardships and endurance came with the job and teaching here required deep dedication and a strong desire to serve. Some came for a year; others longer, but all seemed to be infused with the spirit of what Christ School was. By the late 1920's a number of alumni were beginning to return to join Mr. Dave and Fessor on the staff. They provided a unity, cohesion, rapport, and unified sense of direction necessary to a college preparatory boarding school whose defined goal was to make men out of boys. Teaching here meant financial sacrifice for many since the school was also dedicated to providing educational excellence for able children whose parents lacked the means to pay for an expensive up-east prep school. As the school's goals became defined and word-of-mouth spread of its success in developing academics and molding character, applications, especially after World War II, began to increase dramatically. In 1929, Fr. Harris was rejecting twenty-five to fifty students each year for lack of room. This impelled him to build the 30 Dorm. In the early 1960's, Mr. Dave was informing the board at its annual June meeting that over 100 boys had already applied for admission to a third form class which had fewer than twenty openings.

When Christ School opened in the fall of 1929, there were 110 boarders and board and tuition was $200. This year saw the construction of St. Edmund's Dorm (1930). Because of the depression and unemployment, any man who came by was hired to work on it, as many as forty or fifty at a time. The United Women's Auxiliary provided $10,000 for the sandstone structure. Mr. Boyd supervised the work of his three sons, two sons-in law, Mr. Elmo Stroup, and Dick Fayssoux, who did the carpentry. Three or four others got rock from the quarry.

While the nation was suffering a depression, Fr. Harris and those who surrounded him refused to be depressed. They continued the task of teaching with a zeal that led one alumnus of this era to exclaim that Christ School's success was easy to explain: "Each teacher did the work of two." He might have added that Fr. Harris continued to do the work and worrying of four. Despite a relative continuing outflow of younger teachers during the rugged years, there remained a constant core which could transmit the Christ School ideals and tradition. Fr. Harris (until his death in January 1933) continued to teach Bible and Latin as he had done without interruption since 1911. His son, Dave, had been teaching science and math since 1921. And Fessor had made his impact felt in the lower forms and athletics since 1920. What was more important, these three vital positions (Headmaster, Chaplain, Athletic Director) were all filled by dedicated Episcopalians, strong disciplinarians, demanding teachers, and men who required you to give your best. Since these three were the only leaders on campus directly involved on a daily basis with the lives of each and every student, weakness in any area of this leadership would have been detrimental to the school. Two graduates–fresh out of Chapel Hill–came to the school in 1931 to teach French, English, history, and, upon occasion, math. Zach and Mac Alden would continue to teach here until Zach was called into the military in 1942. They, too, knew what Christ School was about.

From what colleges were the faculty coming–now men, as women teaches faded out with the ending of day enrollment. From 1930-33, they were graduates of the University of South Carolina, Wofford, William and Mary, North Carolina State, the University of North Carolina, Lenoir College, Harvard, and Columbia. Credentials alone did not determine success. Some had minimal college work and others several degrees. Their success was determined by that indefinable inner resource that makes one man teach and another show up. The missionary pull of Christ School was still evident in 1932 as shown by the appearance on the staff of Paul F. Stout, who was brought in by Mr. Dave to assist Mac Alden with the upper form English classes by providing for more personal attention and composition work. Stout, a graduate of Exeter Academy, received a bachelor's and master's degree from Harvard. After leaving Harvard, he worked for a year in Labrador and Newfoundland under Dr. Winfred Grenfell, the world famous English medical missionary.

With one man doing the work of two, Christ School did not require a large staff. In 1933, *The Warrior* listed thirteen people on the payroll to look after 110 students. Only seven of those were teachers and three of them doubled as administrators while teaching a full load of five or six periods a day. The other six were support and one of these, Mrs. Dave, served as school secretary and bookkeeper without pay. Others in the support group were W.B. Troy (librarian and manager of the school bank and Jigger Shop), Mrs. Sula Pearce (organist, nurse, and patron of the dining hall), and Mrs. A. Pressley and Miss E. Pressley (Ma and Etta–the cooks), and Mr. Boyd (the school carpenter). The administrator/teachers were Fr. Harris (Rector, mathematics), David P. Harris (Headmaster, science), and Richard Fayssoux (director of athletics, lower school). The remaining teachers were R.C. Glenn (German, Spanish, Latin), the Rev. J.A. Martin (assistant priest, math), Mac Alden (history, English), and Zach Alden (English, French). Foreign languages were deeply and extensively covered.

On November 16, 1929, Christ School entered a new stage of communication with its alumni and friends. Up to this point, the *Galax Leaf* was the school's only publication and its main function was to interest outsiders in contributing to the work that Christ School was doing for the mountain people. After this, the *Galax Leaf* was to be published less frequently until it went out of existence in the early 1940's.

With Christ School now a college preparatory school without day students, a new audience had to be served–students and alumni as well as the outside audience of parents and friends. As stated by Woodrow Studdert, the first editor-in-chief and an honor student, the purpose of *The Warrior* was "to serve as a medium to stimulate lively interest in school activities, and to keep alive in the students a keen spirit of school life." It was to be a monthly publication put out by interested upper formers and would cover the school scene (academics, athletics, other activities) and include some timely essays and poems by contributing students. There would be an editorial section and faculty would contribute articles from time to time. As the editor-in-chief also stated, the paper would keep parents informed about school life and help alumni keep track of the school and their friends and "keep alive in their minds the memory of their days at Christ School."

The paper quickly moved into its role of providing information to parents and alumni so that they could get a picture of daily life and a perspective of how things were changing and what traditions were being preserved or redirected. In part, the paper was history duly recorded and it had an editorial bite which encouraged improvement and better effort. It pointed out that the 1929 fall enrollment brought in a record 100 boarders. There were no more day students. Three faculty returned: Percy Wise, a University of South Carolina graduate who taught French and English, and was advisor to *The Warrior*; R.B. Edwards, a graduate of Wofford who taught mathematics; and Fessor, who taught the lower forms. New faculty were R.E. Hinman of William and Mary College, who replaced Fr. Harris in Latin and was also librarian; W.H. Dawson of North Carolina State, history; and Mrs. M.C. James of Asheville, a graduate of Philadelphia's Leefson Hill Conservatory of Music, organist and nurse. Fr. Harris taught Bible and Mr. Dave taught mathematics and science.

A later issue was to signal a change in schedule after Christmas when chapel was pushed back thirty minutes to 6 p.m., supper to 6:30 and evening study hall ran from 7:30 to 8:30. The change was necessitated to accommodate the large number of boys who wanted to play basketball. A six-team intramural league was formed with seven players on each team and their games were played each night after study hall. It was reported that spring football was to be conducted for three weeks in March for the second time but under a different format. The previous year, baseball practice was conducted for an hour and this was followed by spring football practice, a pretty tough regimen for those who played both sports. In March 1930, spring football and baseball practice took place at the same time. Interestingly enough, a number of the football players graduating in 1930 went out for that spring practice.

The newspaper recorded many other happenings: Grove Lake was posted against swimming and fishing . . . Christ School belts (black with a nickle plated buckle about 1½ inches wide with Christ School in raised letters) became popular again . . . Betsy and David Harris Jr. had scarlet fever . . . library fines were two cents a day . . . four students from the Boy Scout Patrol (Andrew Johnson, J.D. Perry, W.M. Fields, and E.O. Ledbetter) marched in the Asheville Armistice Day Parade . . . the second stage of terracing on the lower side of the campus also began on Armistice Day with Mr. Dave presiding over the worklist . . . Fr. Harris returned from a ten-day vacation in Ohio, the second time he had left campus since 1907 . . . Women's Auxiliary of the Episcopal Church donated $10,000 for construction of a new dormitory . . . While Fr. Harris was in Winter Park, Fla., during January and February, evening Chapel services were conducted by Mr. Dave and Fessor. Mr Dave also conducted morning prayer at the one Sunday service not covered by a priest . . . Horseshoe pitching was popular at the courts built behind the gym. Last year's champion was Joe Simmons . . . Heavy snow fell in February.

Nothing could add to the excitement of the students (and faculty too) more than the announcement of an unexpected holiday. Usually the students could expect a half holiday on All Saints Day, an occasion which Fr. Harris considered to be one of the most important on the church calendar. There would be a mid-morning Holy Eucharist with procession, after which the boys were free for the rest of the day. As Allan Brown remembered, most Christ School holidays–except for the unexpected ones–coincided with religious events. The unexpected ones came when Mr. Dave, who was a master of timing, felt the boys needed a boost in morale to get them back on the track. Or he might announce one as a reward for some achievement–in victory or defeat. A typical performance came Saturday night, October 29, 1932, at the end of a rather quiet meal after Christ School had lost earlier in the day to Asheville High School 13-12. Down 13-0, the Greenies made an heroic comeback which fell short. After ringing the bell to end the meal, Mr. Dave claimed a Christ School victory where it counted: determination, grit, hard work, a 100 percent effort. His pride in their performance was obvious. "So Monday there will be no school." Pandemonium broke loose as three cheers for Mr. Dave echoed in St. Dunstan's for the next few minutes. On other occasions, Mr. Dave would begin a stern announcement to chew the students out, especially about their school work. "Now I know that a lot of you have brain cramps. For that reason, tomorrow will be a holiday." Many students used such occasions to rest, sleep, catch up on their work, or walk over to the Old Airport and watch the planes come in.

The November 1932 issue of the *Warrior* describes how the students reacted to the surprise Asheville High game day off:

> Everyone was exceedingly pleased at being allowed to sleep until 8:30, but when we awoke in the morning (Monday), great

> was our disgust at finding the heavens gloomy and giving fruitful promise of rain. We stilled these thoughts though and donned raincoats and went to breakfast. Then all did their jobs (or should have done them) and then to assembly.

While all the students did not go to Asheville (for a variety of reasons, including economic), *The Warrior* article goes on to describe what the day was like.

> Fathers and mothers' cars, old Fords and what not, were used for conveyance into town. After assembly a stream of cars and stragglers on foot could be seen coming down the Christ School road (unpaved) in the pouring rain. We are afraid that many a good motorist's temper was ruined for the day by the appearance of hordes upon hordes of thumbs on the Asheville-Hendersonville road. But eventually everyone who started for town reached his destination, some early, some late, but theaters, cafes, drugstores and girls' school received them with open arms, and despite the rain all realized their special plans to perfection.
>
> Some started back to school early and some late. They straggled in at all hours of the afternoon, some wet but all filled and happy. (Several, who extended their happiness beyond the time of return, went into the real estate business, claiming an area of the unfinished athletic field as their domain.)

With three weeks of vacation at Christmas the only time the boys were at home from September until the first of June, and with very little in the way of organized activities available other than sports, both students and faculty depended upon imagination, innovation, and each other for fun and amusement. Two centers of recreation for the upper three forms were the Gamba Lambda Sigma Fraternity and the Carolina Club. The former was established in 1914 and membership was by invitation only. To meet the social needs of the students, the Carolina Club was founded in 1926 and was expanded and renovated in 1932. The GLS had its origin in the Brotherhood Cabin and moved into the Sixth Cottage in 1932 while its present sandstone structure was being completed. Both clubs provided outlets for those students who had permission to smoke and became centers for discussion and debates and provided recreation like radio and bridge. The Frat pioneered the Smoker, a social at which music was provided by records, faculty members were invited, refreshments were provided, and everyone was permitted to smoke. Faculty were often invited to participate in bridge games and tournaments. During this period, the school did not sponsor any dances per se for the student body but both the Frat and the Carolina Club sponsored separate end-of-the-year dances. On at least one occasion (May 25, 1933), the two Fraternities sponsored a joint dance at which Algie Bass and his orchestra from Hendersonville/Asheville played. The gym was decorated, four seniors served as masters-of-ceremonies, and most of the faculty were present.

The old victrola was the musical instrument for dances held at the clubhouses. There appeared to be some competition between the two groups, as each held rushing periods and parties and each had initiations. Some of the Frat members recall "pretty good whacks which penetrated even the thickest padding." In an article in the December 1932 *Warrior*, the writer concluded that "A boy getting into either fraternity should feel honored as they have to be agreed upon by each old member." A few years later, when preliminary work was being done on the Susan Wetmore School Building, the Carolina Club was razed. As years passed, Mr. Dave became more and more disillusioned with the Frat as being "too exclusive and a center of illegal smoking."

In his second year back on the staff, Zach Alden, who with his brother Mac led many interested students on hikes all about the area, attempted to get dramatics started on an organized basis to help boys expand their interests and develop their inner talents. The effort was handicapped by the absence of an extra curricular program in general and a lack of any money to be earmarked in that direction. It was an area which had to be subsidized if Christ School was to become an outstanding college preparatory school. In the spring of 1932, what might be called the pre-Drama Club organization came into existence. Mr. Alden put together an impromptu dramatics class to stage some sort of performance as a part of commencement activities. What emerged was a minstrel show called "Parody Warblers Minstrels and Other Attractions." The minstrel show idea was to spread throughout the next few years. The program consisted of five parts:

1. Two Stygian chorus girls (Jeffrey and Northcross sing.)
2. Skit by Hurst, Stinnette, and Whitlock 16,000 years ago.
3. Ed Leon tap dances.
4. Main feature: Minstrel–semi-circle–spicy jokes, lively gags, and gay repartee. (Hurst, Martin, Cobb, Caughman Wright [interlocutor], Orr, Jarrett [alias Allbright], Carter, Emmitt, Bones, Pete, Tamboo, Dennis, and Bender.
5. Lots of blackface comedians; songs: "When Nobody Else is Around" and "Neath the Cotton Pickin' Moon."

It was billed as an all-black performance. "The dusky girls disclosed their subtle charms to the public eye more than once." The grand finale was "We've Got to Put the Sun Back in the Sky."

Innovation was not limited to any one area of school life. To help renew what appeared to be flagging religious interest, Fr. Harris organized the student congregation on the basis of a parish with a vestry in

1931. The purpose was to provide boys insight into parish life. The program encouraged both faculty and students to make a deeper commitment to the Chapel. How well it worked is perhaps seen in an editorial comment in *The Warrior*:

> We want to compliment the boys upon the hearty services they render in Chapel. It is an inspiration to hear the Mass sung each Sunday morning by 120 boys and men.

The vestry–a first– consisted of ten boys. They were Warner Briggs, Senior Warden; Ralph Morgan, Junior Warden; Robert Jarrett, treasurer; Herbert Carstarphen, secretary; Chapin McKenzie, Harry McConnell, Samuel Northcross, John Orr, Harry Stiller, and Charles Stinnette.

Coupled with this was the organization of a new youth and faith movement, a modified form of the Brotherhood of St. Andrew. The purpose was to instill deeper faith into the vestry, which joined Fr. Harris and the Rev. Martin in services held every night after study hall. Being a member of the vestry not only required regular attendance but the duty to persuade other confirmed boys of the church to join the Order of St. Andrew in order to promote attendance at early morning communion and to assist at the altar. Two other changes greeted the students in the fall of 1932. New Sacred Studies classes would replace Sunday School classes that had preceded the Eucharist at 10 a.m. They would be taught during the school week. In addition, all the seniors would serve as acolytes rather than just a few. They would rotate in reading the evening lesson. Fr. Martin was to train the acolytes and help train the readers.

Dorothy Thomson (Mr. Dave's sister) directed the senior play in 1924. She is second from the left on the back row.

IV: 1925-1933

Warren Redd Remembers

It was fun to talk to Warren Redd about Christ School. He was a student here at a time when Fr. Harris was still boss but when Mr. Dave was breaking in. At the time, the students loved both men. They had a respect for Fr. Harris which transcended that shown to most mortals. This respect did not keep them from seeking out mischief but caused them to straighten up the moment Fr. Harris came into sight. "When he approached you," one alumnus said, "mischief just disappeared."[1]

Now Mr. Dave was learning the ropes and he had a bit of temper and he carried some of the military with him. (He served in the Air Force during World War I.) When inspecting rooms, he required shoes to be lined up perfectly straight in a row, sticking out one inch from beneath the cot. And the beds had to be tucked so tight that a quarter would bounce back into your hand if dropped onto the covers. In the process of learning how to be headmaster, his toughness was tempered somewhat by Fr. Harris's experience.

But most important of all, both men knew boys. Both understood a good joke or funny happening and each could bring home his point without a lecture. They were both men who seemed to be anywhere and everywhere and frequently cropped up in unexpected places to head off trouble even before students could think up the trouble they were going to get into. And if you got into trouble, you could expect to be treated fairly. There were no exceptions: wrong doing produced its own reward. Justice might come in varying forms but it was certain and quick and evenhanded.

Warren Redd was fortunate in that he saw Fr. Harris at his best and saw Mr. Dave beginning to develop his strengths. What was fun is that Warren carried with him memories of Christ School that he loved to recall, and the stories evoked in him a warm laughter and a twinkle in the corner of his eyes. He was like so many of the boys who came to Christ School prior to World War II: Fr. Harris and Mr. Dave were their fathers and Christ School their home.

It's the anecdotes that Warren remembered best. They give insight into

[1]When **Mr. Dave** approached mischief, you disappeared.

the character and make-up of both men who, along with Fr. Wetmore, molded Christ School boys during the first seven decades. It's best to let Warren relate these happenings in his own words.

TROUBLE WAS BREWING

Trouble was brewing one Monday and I didn't even know it. Mr. Dave lived in the little house in front of the Chapel and it had a full-length basement. This Monday, Mr. Boyd was sawing wood and was in charge of the worklist. He had a group of boys carrying the logs from the woodshed to Mr. Dave's basement, where they were stacked up. Naturally inquisitive, some of the boys started looking behind the chimney and found that Mr. Dave had been making some brew, which was just ready to take off. They got into his home brew and each time one carried an armload of wood to the basement, he would have another sample. Whether Mr. Boyd knew what was happening or not, he must have been surprised that a bunch of boys had such a good time carrying armloads of wood. Obviously, Mr. Dave learned what had happened, but this was one time when he didn't say a word.

ONCE IS ENOUGH

I will never forget the night Fr. Harris came upon several of us in the act of mischief. Gene Johnston was in charge of the Supply House which was located in a big cellar beneath the kitchen and dining hall. It was a combination root cellar and storage bin. This particular instance happened during basketball season. Mr. Dave had agreed to let a certain number of boys rent taxis and go to the basketball game in Asheville. Christ School was playing Asheville High. A group of us went to Mr. Dave to seek permission to go but he turned us down, saying that there were too many off campus already. We then began to look for something to do, and you know the old saying about "an idle mind is the devil's workshop." Gene Johnston and I and old Red Barber and several others agreed that we were hungry. So we decided to go over to the Supply House and get us a can of cherries or something and have a feast. We walked up to the Rectory at the top of the hill and saw Fr. Harris in his living room in a big chair, sitting there reading. So we walked back down to the dorm, got a flashlight, and entered the Supply House. Gene handed me a can of cherries and he saw a can of peaches–both gallon size. At that moment we saw an image in the doorway. It was dark and this image was just standing there. All of a sudden we heard something going "Whoop, whoop, whoop, whoop, what's going on here?" And there I was when he flashed the light on me, standing with a can of cherries and Gene holding on to the can of peaches. That was the last time I ever visited the Supply House.

That incident resulted in two punishments, one of which was much harder than the other. The easy one, Warren said, was the weeks the two of them put into digging up an area of the athletic field. It was a big claim. The strip was about three feet wide, fifteen feet long, and four to six feet deep. Neither of them felt they were treated unfairly and both were beneficiaries of the Tom Sawyer system. That is, late on some nights friends would join them for a social hour and some digging to help move the claim along. The real punishment, though, was in having to face Fr. Harris. He didn't say another word. His "whoop, whoop, whoop, whoop, what's going on here?" was all he needed to say. "We knew we were guilty and just disappointing him was punishment of the severest kind."

SOME FIREWORKS

One night we created a ruckus for which we never got caught, but we never did it again either. Because of the quarrying that went on, Mr. Boyd kept plenty of dynamite and caps in the shop. The dynamite was used sometimes to break up huge pieces of the mica shist. This then became the stone which was hand-shaped and used in buildings on the campus. Though the boys knew the dynamite was there, no one ever sneaked any off to use to dynamite stumps on his claim. That night, a bunch of boys was off campus with Mr. Dave but Fr. Harris remained. A few of us wanted to have some fun so we slipped into the shop and got some caps. We didn't fool with the dynamite, we weren't that dumb. We just got the little metal caps and a small roll of fuses. There were about six or eight of us in on it. We cut the fuses all the same length, a few perhaps a little longer. We'd stick them in the caps and then we just circled the school. At a given signal, everybody lit those fuses and took off like scared dogs. All of a sudden those things started going off, and you thought the whole place was going to be blown up. But there was no damage because the caps exploded just like a firecracker would. Of course, the noise brought Fr. Harris out of his house but we made ourselves mighty scarce. In fact, for the next few weeks, everybody walked a mighty straight line.

THE BLUE FLAME

In 1926 I brought one of the few radios to be found on campus. I lived in the Fourth Cottage and we put up an aerial to operate this little battery-operated RCA. All we could get was KDKA (Pittsburgh) and WSB in Atlanta. After I got hold of four sets of earphones, we strung wires under the cottage to each room so that you could lie in bed and listen to one of the stations. Every night we'd turn the thing on and the prefect would come and shut the thing off. We'd all go to sleep listening to WSB. One day the other boys in the cottage decided to try a little experiment. They removed some fine wire (coils) from a Model-A Ford at the shop, wire which was as fine as silk thread. They took this fine wire and threaded it through a needle and then threaded my bottom sheet with that stuff. They drilled a hole into the floor and led the wire into the back room where they took some batteries and several of the coils and put them together. When I went to bed that night, they threw the switch and my bed turned into blue flame. In an instant, I was out of the bed and in came Mr. Dave, making a check. All the time, this wired sheet was making a sound like "zmumpp, zmumpp, zmumeepp." Mr. Dave just stood there laughing. There was no punishment. Mr. Dave just laughed the incident away.

AND ONE NOT QUITE SO FUNNY

Then there was the time they locked the door on me. I don't know why–they were just determined to get something on me. I think it was because I had made up my mind that I wasn't going to get any more hours (worklists) and I was doing everything the way it was supposed to be done and they decided to mess things up. So this particular morning I got up and got dressed and everybody had gone out and my door was locked from the outside. Someone had stuck a stick through the latch and the door wouldn't budge. Thus I was missing assembly. Mr. Dave came down to the room and released me from captivity. As I went into assembly, everybody was sitting there, just dying with laughter. Things suddenly turned quiet when Mr. Dave asked: "All right, who put the stick in the door?" Nobody said a word. Silence reigned. Then he said, "All right, I'm going to ask you for the second time, and that's going to be it: who put the stick in the door?" Nobody said a word. He said, "All right, from now on until somebody owns up, the whole school is on bounds. Nobody shall leave the campus for anything. Now someone did it, and someone's going to tell who did it." Nobody said a word. For two or three days no one said anything. Finally it got to the point where boys who knew who did it got onto the ones who did it, and they finally came up and admitted to Mr. Dave that they did it. He then took everybody off bounds.

V: 1933-1939

16

Fr. Boynton Arrives

Herbert Hoover would not be re-inaugurated President in 1933, but happy days were not yet across the land either. In fact, the New Deal would have only fitful success in dealing with the economic crisis and it would take Adolph Hitler's plunge into war to purge the Great Depression of the millions who remained unemployed. At Christ School, the year 1933 was comparable to that of 1906, when Mr. Wetmore died and the school's six years of existence was in jeopardy. Many dark clouds covered the horizon as the trustees named Mr. Dave to succeed his father as headmaster.

For one thing, Fr. Harris's death left the campus grief stricken, even though Mr. Dave had been headmaster in everything but name only for at least five years. To students and alumni, though, Fr. Harris continued to be the boss. The grief was shown openly–red eyes and tears were common–as hundreds crowded into and around the Chapel for the funeral service and burial on the grounds only a few feet north of the altar where he had committed his life to serve Christ and labored to bring spiritual unity and direction to school and community alike. Among the many bowed and bared heads were those people who experienced first hand Fr. Harris's ministry. In those early years, he would hitch up Old Bess and travel, often with Mrs. Harris in his company, to the cabins and homes in the valley to bring succor and comfort to families in distress. An alumnus who remembers the funeral is Art Armstrong, one of the honor guard (composed of the senior class) who stood watch in the Chapel at two hour intervals from Thursday afternoon until the service Friday morning. At seven that morning, Fr. James Sill, former rector of Calvary Episcopal Church in Fletcher and close friend, conducted a requiem mass for Fr. Harris. "It seems to me," Armstrong recalled, "that the school was pretty much in shock. He had been headmaster for a great number of years and he was much loved both by faculty and students. Mr. Dave was quite upset (his eyes visibly red) as he was quite close to his father."

The senior honor guard also made up the choir for the service, and the six prefects were pall bearers.

Though Fr. Harris had been in declining health for five or six years the boys knew that he could chin himself with one arm (but they had not seen him do so in several years), his death when it came January 11 was unexpected, at least according to his daughter whom he was visiting in New Orleans.

Fr. Harris had no heart trouble as far as anyone knew. He did have terrible attacks of angina, though he did not smoke. (Mr. Dave, who did smoke, also experienced severe angina). While visiting New Orleans, Fr. Harris went to the hospital for a kidney problem. He reached the operating table but the surgeon refused to operate because of the angina which accompanied the kidney suffering. It was the kidney problem that led to his death.

Other things were to complicate the year. By naming Mr. Dave headmaster, the trustees broke with the general tradition by which church schools were run by priests. This made it even more imperative that the school find a man who could bring the same kind of vigor and dedication to the Chapel that Fr. Harris had. The Rev. J.A. Martin, who had been assistant chaplain and teacher for a couple of years, would complete the term as chaplain but he was not being considered for the post. Filling Fr. Harris' shoes was considered an impossible task. To find a man who could carry on the Christ School tradition might require something of a miracle. But belief in miracles–renewable each year–was the bedrock Christ School foundation.

Four days before Fr. Harris's death, the school received what was very distressing news. The National Church Council discontinued its financial support, which would have amounted to $3,500. This cut-off, defended by the Church on economic necessity, meant that thirty boys would lack the scholarship help necessary to go to Christ School. Of the 110 boarders at this time, forty were unable to pay anything. Ten scholarships had been given and the other thirty were to be supported by funds from the National Church. Through the *Galax Leaf*, Mrs. Wetmore appealed to friends of the school to take up this slack: "Many of the boys have no home life except Christ School. Salaries have been cut but (we) still require help from friends." Contributions of any size were earnestly sought. Mrs. Wetmore added, "Little is much if God is in it." During the depression, bank closings created great hardship for millions of Americans as savings were wiped out. As Armstrong recalled, President Roosevelt's closing of the national banks on March 6, 1933, created a new wave of anxiety and uncertainty. "At this time I do remember that the school was without funds (except for the $7.50 Mr. Dave had in his pocket). Really, I don't remember too much about the economic distress because we were kids at the time, and it didn't really affect us that badly, being away from home and dependent upon someone else for our food and care." That someone else was the new headmaster.

The death of Fr. Harris forged a new unity at Christ School, out of which grew a modern college preparatory school gaining notable academic respect during the next thirty-seven years. 1933 was the beginning of a metamorphosis. Christ School was to shed all of its buildings during the next thirty years, except for the Chapel, the 30 Dorm, and two faculty homes. What emerged was a school with new, permanent buildings but one whose philosophy remained the same. The admissions policy remained the same, though now students were enrolled from 15 to 18 states rather than just Appalachia. When the 1938 Dorm was completed and the school had quarters to board 130 students, Mr. Dave commented in the *Galax Leaf* that "our days of expansion in numbers is over, and we look now toward permanence in material things." He considered The Chapel to be the determining, though not the sole factor, in how large the enrollment should be. He thought it an almost impossible task to enlarge The Chapel and appeared to give little credence to the idea of building a new one. The centerpiece which served so well deserved permanence. The Chapel of 1906 was central to the life and spirit of the campus. Mr. Dave had no intention of destroying the special quality it gave to Christ School life. That metamorphosis showed itself in other ways also. The Chapel services took on new life with musical settings. The athletic program was expanded by the addition of new varsity sports and intramurals. A new emphasis was given to extra-curricular activities, with old ones being renewed and new ones brought into a more organized schedule.

Much of what was accomplished during this period was carried out on a hit-or-miss basis. Mr. Dave was pragmatic in actions which would carry Christ School forward. Before school opened in the fall of 1933, the miracle occurred which the more faithful believed in. Christ School found a new chaplain who had energy, imagination, talent, and charisma. He was to become an instant confidant to Mr. Dave, and out of their daily conversations (especially the second breakfast at Mr. Dave's house) emerged ideas which were to make Christ School a modern college preparatory one without changing its approach. For much that happened over the next six years, Fr. Charles Francis Boynton, later to become Bishop of Puerto Rico and Suffragan Bishop of New York, was the catalyst. The seeds were scattered which became the traditions alumni of the next four decades best remember.

No one could hope to replace Fr. Harris. It is perhaps well that Fr. Boynton did not know the man whom he was asked to replace. It was perhaps well that he was a young man, athletic, talented in music and art, rich in humor, confident in the way that youth doesn't look back until it tries to catch up breathlessly with where it's been. In two words, Pop Boynton was brash and dynamic.

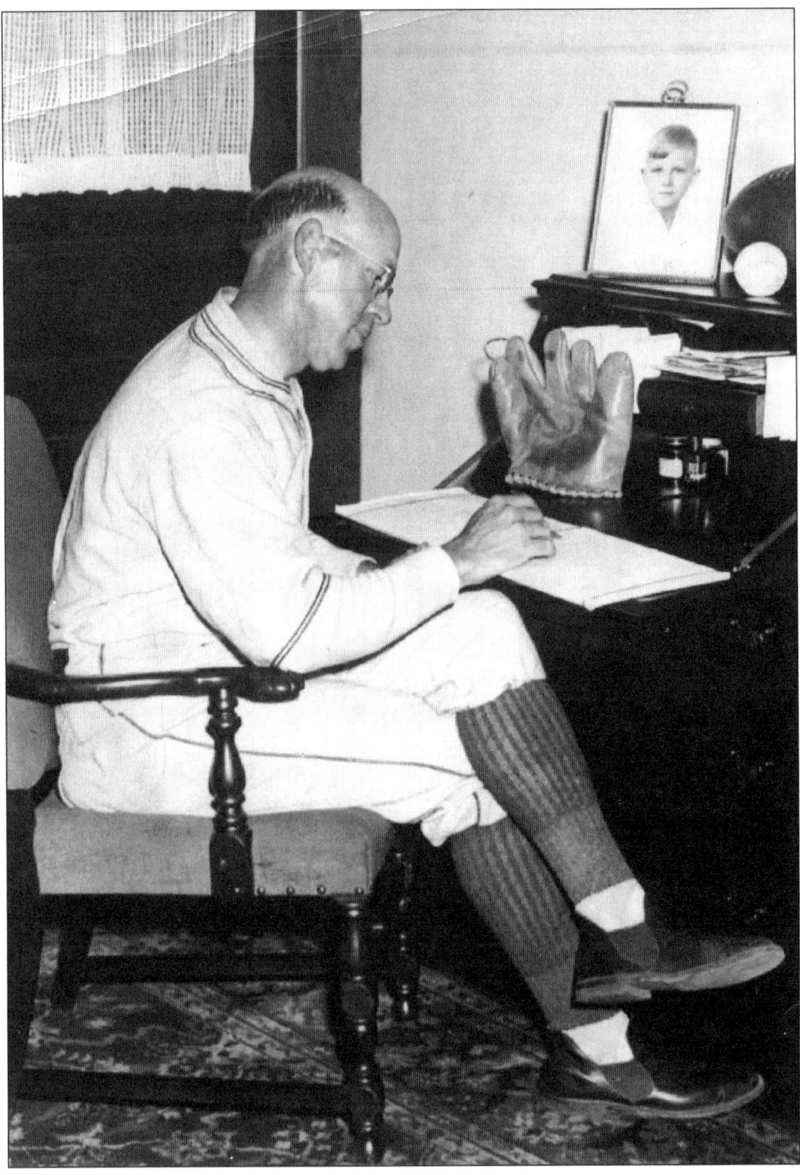

Fessor was Christ School athletic drector and head coach for over 50 years. His basketball shots though the rafters of the Old Gym (built 1922) are legendary.

V: 1933-1939

17

Never A Farm School

Christ School was never a farm school. Not that there is anything wrong with farming. Certainly Mr. Wetmore, Fr. Harris, and Mr. Dave (whose degree from North Carolina State was in horticulture) didn't think so, and many of Christ School's finest came from the farms and hills of the region. Christ School boys were close to the soil and were related to the farm in a way that taught some invaluable lessons of life. In a real sense, Christ School was a Jeffersonian hothouse.

The Christ School that was founded on a scrubby, burnt-over, bare four acres was in time to expand to over 800 acres, including some rich bottom land that followed the old Airport Highway from the bubbling springs to Meadows Store and ended at Cane Creek. In the early 1930's, with the Mill Pond no longer in existence, many students in spring and fall wandered down to Cane Creek to swim and fish. This was especially true after Grove Lake was closed down. The land was acquired in parcels large and small, some given by Mrs. Wetmore, some purchased from Mrs. Wetmore, and some obtained from other sources. When Fr. Harris came to Christ School, the farm included the Old Dairy Barn site and the Jervey House below.[1] A couple of hundred acres were ultimately sold, in part to help pay for some of the large medical expenses incurred by Mrs. Wetmore in the later years of her life.

Since the Rock House was still part of the Wetmore property, the Jervey House was the only farm house belonging to Christ School. It was built by a doctor who came here from Charleston. He lived there for a few years and abandoned it. The house, which remained occupied until the early 1950's, was the only building on school property which never had running water. It was served by a well and several springs lying due west. Next to the house was a barn painted green and it was here that the school's

[1]Christ School possessed about 113 acres by the time Fr. Harris arrived. The original four acres was deeded to the school on Oct. 10, 1900. In 1902, Mrs Lyman donated two more acres to be used as a chicken yard. Then in June 1904, the school paid $3500 for 107 acres of bottom land, with the farm being rented out. When payments were completed on the land in 1907, the title was transferred from the Wetmores to Christ School. All the property was conveyed to the Missionary District of Asheville on September 8, 1908. Years later Christ School was incorporated as a separate entity. Even then, the ground upon which Christ Chapel stands remained a part of the Diocese.

few cows were quartered before Mr. Dave built a modern dairy barn and silo in 1934.

The later occupants of the house were the Mallory family and the Laz Allen family. The Mallorys lived there during the 1920's before moving to the Rock House. Jimmy Ewin '36 remembered the family well:

> I got to know the Mallorys in the late 1920's when my family rented a senior cottage one summer and rented both cottages on Cottage Hill another summer. We would buy cold milk from them. Later when I was a student, I discovered Mr. Mallory had two good-looking daughters–Hazel and Ruby. I remember that I never saw enough of them.

Ewin admitted to having an easy life at Christ School, beginning in the fall of 1934. "If the truth were known, I was on a gravy train. I enjoyed every minute of it." Since he was part student and part teacher, he had a great deal of time to himself and he spent much of it just wandering around and getting acquainted with many people–including the Mallorys, Laz Allen (who occupied the Jervey house), some of Laz's children who worked for the school, and Mr. Boyd ("that jack-of-all trades who could do almost anything"). Besides attending some classes, Ewin ran the Jigger Shop, quarterbacked the football team, turned the Gamma Lambda Sigma Fraternity into a respected center of social activity, and taught the sixth graders (first form). He taught English and arithmetic to six youngsters, with Fessor doing the rest.

> Those sixth graders kept you hopping, especially Tommy Turner and Gene Woody. They were bright. There was also a big plump boy from Hendersonville who was kind of soft. (Carlyle Ingle was to become a starting lineman in the eighth grade and was an All Conference player at Duke University). Mr. Dave turned me loose in that class with no experience, just handing me a text book and wishing me "good luck." I just wrote in the margin of the text and studied enough to teach the next day. That left time for football, basketball, and tennis.

When Fr. Harris arrived, there was no school farm but Mr. Wetmore's successor brought with him a love of animals and the outdoors. With him came chickens, cows, turkeys, and ducks. "If it could fly," his daughter said, "he tried it." Fr. Harris began the school dairy with a cow; Mr. Dave was to expand it into a Holstein herd. This herd of one would expand to four or five cows by the 1920's and the fresh milk was used in the dining hall for cooking and cereal and the cream to make butter. In those early years, the milking and feeding the flocks were part of the many caretaking duties that Fr. Harris carried out himself. Before the modern dairy barn was built, the cows and chickens were kept in a barn behind the old dining hall (St. Dunstan's) and staked out to pasture at several other locations, including Wetmore football field. For a few years, the cows were located at the green barn next to the Jervey House. This barn and fenced in area became the site for raising pigs for twenty-five years, beginning in the late 1930's. In addition to milk for the dining hall, the hens (which were Fr. Harris' favorites) provided eggs for breakfast. Both items were supplemented by generous portions of powdered eggs and milk.

From time to time, Fr. Harris not only had to deal with exuberant youngsters who swiped his eggs or chickens, but he had to deal with those who were trying to be helpful but who simply proved to be trying. David Harris Jr., recalls one such episode:

> One day a boy came running excitedly up to Fr. Harris. He was obviously pleased with the message he brought and expected a pat on the back.
>
> "Fr. Harris! Fr. Harris!" he shouted. "I just killed a huge blacksnake that's been eating your chickens. I found him in the henhouse."
>
> Fr. Harris turned red, his temples popped out, and he almost couldn't speak. It was the closest, I understand, that Fr. Harris ever came to smacking a boy. What the boy didn't know was that Fr. Harris had put the blacksnake in the henhouse to keep the rats away from the eggs.

The dairy operation began in 1934-35. Mr. Dave went with his son and Darby Lance to an auction in Tennessee, where the headmaster purchased a Holstein herd including a bull. To accommodate them, he built what was up to then the most modern dairy barn in this area, with milk stanchions and silo. Until then, the school had a farm operation on the shares with Laz Allen, who raised pigs (on the slop he picked up at the dining hall) and grain. One of the real treats for the younger boys every day was to ride on the garbage wagon to the Jervey house and help slop the pigs. For some, it was even worth the risk of getting a worklist for being late to assembly. To operate the dairy, Mr. Dave hired Thurman Lance as the original herdsman. Lance remained until the mid-1940's and then returned for a few years in the early 1950's. The last herdsman was Zeb Barnwell. After Barnwell left, two faculty members were to oversee the operation of the farm and dairy until it was phased out in the 1970's. They were science teachers Richie Meech '50 and David Fortney. The timber for the barn was sawed and the frame put up by the father of Tom Baldwin '43.

For some years in the 1920's, a few students had job assignments milking the cows. John Freas '27 milked the three cows in the barn behind the dining hall, sometimes assisted by J. Wilson Cuningham, later president of the Christ School board of directors and a leading Winston-Salem furniture merchant. Some students still remember the dairy which the Wetmores had and going over to the spring house and drinking fresh, cold milk. The small stone house used to store milk and butter in was located at a spring at the foot of the hill just as you cross the stream to go to the Rock House. Once Mr. Dave acquired the eighteen-cow herd and continued to enlarge and improve it, the students had an endless flow of fresh milk in the dining hall three meals a day. It was not until the early 1960's that health regulations (requiring all milk to be pasteurized) that Christ School and Warren Wilson College (old Farm School) went out of the dairy business. For some years afterwards, the school continued the dairy operation, selling the raw milk to Arcadia Dairy and purchasing its needs from them at a wholesale price.

Although the boys did not do the milking when Mr. Dave expanded the dairy operation, there were occasions when some of the students did milk the herd. The first dairy herdsman was subject to periodic bouts of drinking and was not available for a few days at a time. It was then that a select group of proud boys would take over the chore–at four in the morning and again in the afternoon. By tradition, at least one naive or near-sighted boy was included in the group to milk one cow better known as a kicking specialist. Students in 1944 remember the eighteen inch snow that blanketed the campus and created five to six foot snow drifts between the football field and the dairy. Crews of students dug a long trench to the barn to keep the milk flowing to the dining hall, carrying five and ten gallon containers on freezing shoulders.

One of the more humorous yet frightening moments at the dairy occurred in 1940. Sometime during the afternoon, the three year old son of Chaplain Reid Hammond slipped away from his home. After chapel, Fr. Hammond walked over to the dining hall where his wife came up to him agitated and distraught. Immediately the faculty and students began scouring the area in search of Ralph. While this was going on, the dairyman came up on campus with the child in hand. Thurman Lance had been eating his supper when he happened to look up and see Ralph in the bullpen, his tiny fists drumbeating on the nose of a very mean bull. In a drowsy manner, according to Lance, the bull simply swished its tail, winked its eye, and stared quizzically in gentle disbelief.

As the dairy grew, this meant an added bonus for the teachers who lived on campus during the summer. Since cows continued to give generously while the students were at home on vacation, the faculty enjoyed the surplus–plenty of milk to drink and plenty of cream to make butter and ice cream. During the war years, surplus grain was stored in bags in the Old Gym and made available for faculty who wanted to have it ground up for making bread. As Fr. Gale Webbe remembers, this was an important benefit for a chaplain whose salary then was $1500 a year. "You weren't paid a salary based on what you did," Fr. Webbe smiled. "You were paid a stipend which enabled you to do what you did." Faculty supplemented the good life by raising a garden or, as Fr. Webbe did, by buying a few chickens for eggs and Sunday dinner. "That first year I saved a dollar a month and bought a dozen chickens."

Gardening was always a part of the Christ School life, although not all teachers became so involved. The Wetmore's had a garden at Struan but the one at school appeared after Fr. Harris became headmaster. Both he and other faculty members planted crops in a big plot located where the present school building stands. At the top of the garden (where the sunken areaways were situated in front of the school building), the Alden brothers raised prized dahlias. Their efforts at beautification were to continue across the campus while they remained on the faculty. Also a string of rhubarb grew across the front. When Julius and Elizabeth Edgerton became the school's cooks around 1940, rhubarb pie was a frequent dessert speciality. As garden-growing interest among many teachers died out, Julius continued to "suffocate the students with rhubarb, turnips, and sweet potatoes," according to Joe McCullough '42. In addition, Julius padded his income with similar produce he raised on his farm in Lake Lure and which he kindly sold to the school. Underneath the dishroom was a root cellar to store crops, including apples, which in the fall drew millions of yellow jackets to the backporch. When construction began on the school building in 1939, the garden site had to be moved and ended up in a small field east of the water tower. Mr. Dave and other members of the faculty continued their horticultural skills there.

The 1940 Student Council met in the library of the old school building.

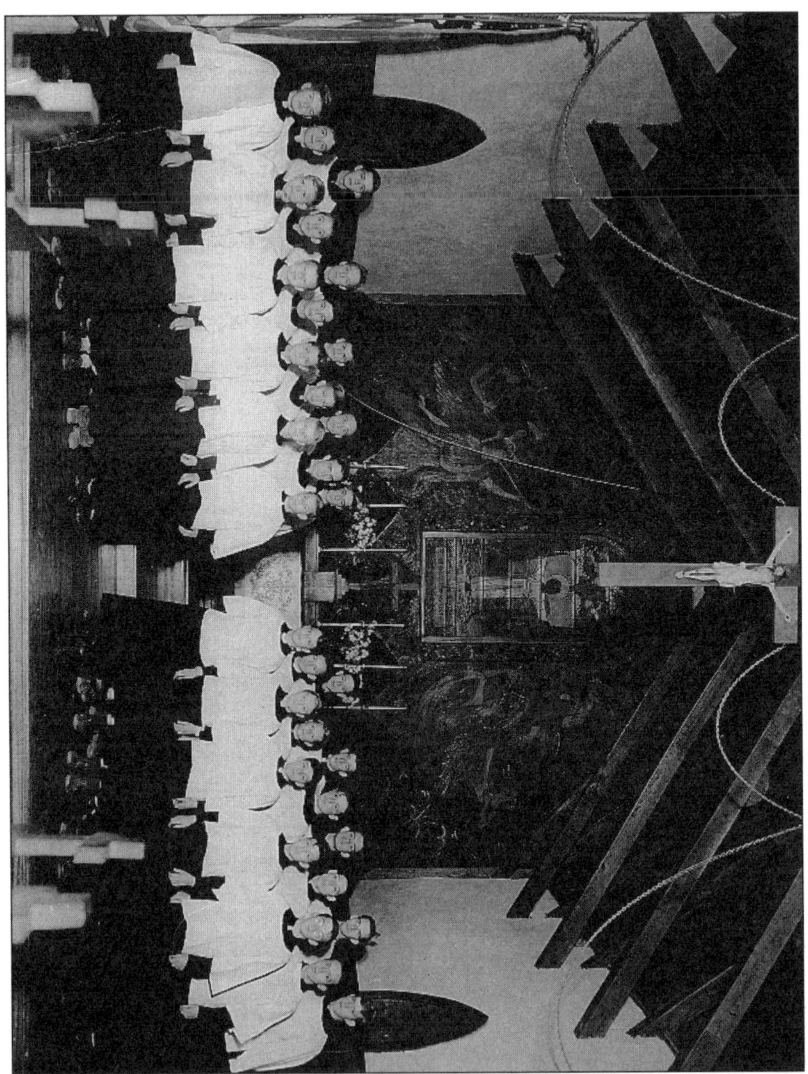

The 1940-41 choir stands in the chapel. In the background is the stained glass window done by the New York artist, J. A. Holzer. The mural was the work of Mrs. Hemphill.

CHRIST SCHOOL FIDELITATE SUCCESSUS

V: 1933-1939

18

A Unanimous Choice

Was Mr. Dave destined to be headmaster? One can approach the subject from two different directions. When Mr. Dave was about ten years old, he received a letter of encouragement from Fr. Hughson (the man who talked Fr. Harris into going to Christ School) in which Fr. Hughson reminded him that God had a great destiny for him in the future. Certainly his role at Christ School fulfilled this prophecy.

Bob Harris, Mr. Dave's younger brother, injects a different perspective: "After finishing at North Carolina State, Dave held several jobs. He worked for Heywood Lumber Company (Old North State) for a while with his friend Harvey Heywood.[1] Then he got a job as a tractor salesman, traveling around to neighboring farms. If I remember correctly, this is when he was fired (punched his boss in the nose) and began to hang around school. He did some pick-up jobs and helped with the worklist occasionally. But mostly he was just hanging around. The amazing thing is that Dave didn't appear to have a chance at succeeding at anything. And yet he was so successful as a headmaster."

It was while he was at Kent that Mr. Dave apparently learned many things about boys and about how Fr. Sill handled them–things which contributed to his own understanding of adolescents. For one thing, Mr. Dave was so homesick at Kent his first year that he kept threatening to go home. Finally Fr. Harris had to send his oldest son, Don, a Kent graduate, to settle him down. Then, again, according to Bob Harris, there was the time Mr. Dave tried to run Kent School. "In his fifth form year, Dave formed a gang of six or seven boys who were disciplining the younger boys. If the younger ones were toadying up to a teacher, they'd take them out and give them a paddling. Finally, Fr. Sill acted and made the group disband and had Dave apologize before the student body."

As far as being destined to return to Christ School, neither Bob Harris

---

[1]Harvey had a car and both dated Elizabeth Merrimon of Asheville. Dave used to double-date with Harvey in the latter's car, but Dave won Elizabeth's hand in marriage.

or his sister, Mrs. Dorothy Thomson, recall any such mandate. "He slipped into teaching and became Fr. Harris's right-hand man. He graduated in agriculture and was interested in the outdoors. Farming and the outdoor side of Christ School, then and later, had a strong appeal to him. While he was hanging around in 1920, he restarted the claim field–clearing up the athletic area even before he was established here. When Fr. Harris died, there was apparently no question in the minds of the trustees that Dave (age 36) was the man for the job."

In 1940, Mr. Dave faced perhaps his greatest career temptation: he was offered the headmastership at Kent. His ties there were strong (all three Harris brothers and Mr. Dave's son graduated from Kent) and his love for Fr. Sill, founder and headmaster, was towering. That respect was mutual. When Mr. Dave graduated, Fr. Sill, his eyes moist, handed him a diploma and added in a whisper, "my dear son." According to Mrs. Thomson, Mr. Dave did not hesitate long in turning down the offer. "Christ School was his and had a long way to go. He could guide it along the path set forth by his father and Fr. Wetmore. And Kent was somebody else's."

When the board convened in a special meeting Jan. 20, 1933, to deal with the problems created by the sudden death of Fr. Harris, five members were present–Mrs. Wetmore, Haywood Parker, Harvey Heywood, Reginald Howland, and Judge Merrimon. They quickly passed a resolution as a memorial to Fr. Harris and then turned to the matter of naming a successor. In 1926, Mr. Dave had been appointed assistant headmaster and in 1928, Fr. Harris had apparently turned over to him the duty of running the school. Fr. Harris continued his duties as chaplain.[2] No one questioned Mr. Dave's ability to take over from his father, and the only area of discussion seemed to hinge on whether there should be a layman or a clergyman running the school. Traditionally, Episcopal boys schools to this time were headed by priests. In the ensuing discussion, it was pointed out that the idea of having a separate chaplain and a separate headmaster was being discussed and applied in some northern private schools. Hence there was little argument to the comment made by Parker, filling in for the chairman, Bishop Horner, who was to die in April:

> Right now, under existing conditions, with the training that he has had, and the service he has rendered, the only person in sight that meets the requirements that we have is Mr. David Harris . . . .

With that in mind, the board unanimously approved Mr. Dave's nomination and gave him full authority to manage and conduct the affairs

[2]It appears that Mr. Dave was now headmaster in everything except name only.

of the school. "It is thoroughly understood what we are doing," Parker added. "That is, we are putting him (Mr. Dave) in charge of the business, the teaching and morals of the school–looking after the boys and seeing that everything is conducted properly." As Harvey Heywood was to clarify still further, "He has the same position that Fr. Harris had, shorn of his clerical powers." Confirmation of this was underscored when Fr. Martin, who had filled in briefly as rector during the troublesome period after the death of Fr. Wetmore, agreed to serve temporarily as chaplain. In addition the board named Fr. Preston Burke, a Christ School graduate, to fill Fr. Harris's vacancy on the board. The first sign of trouble that lay ahead for the new headmaster came at this meeting when Mrs. Wetmore announced the National Council of the Church had withdrawn its 1933 appropriation to Christ School. The Council said it was pruning from the budget schools "capable of taking care of themselves." This coincided with the view expressed by Fr. Harris for several years: that Christ School must be self-sufficient. To his son fell the hurdle of turning that into permanent reality.

Knickers were in style when this picture was taken of Mr. Dave and his wife, the former Elizabeth Merrimon of Asheville.

The Fr. Harris Memorial Chapel was built in 1936-37; a cloister was added to connect it to the main chapel.

V: 1933-1939

19

Plan Of The Campus

It is not known with absolute certainty whether the growth of the Christ School campus followed a pre-determined logic or rather a pragmatism that evolved its own natural evolutionary logic. The story goes (and it may be true) that Mr. Dave planned buildings on the back of envelopes as he drank his pre-dawn cup of blackness called coffee in St. Dunstan's Hall. (It was in this manner that he planned meals daily for the students.) If so, none of the envelopes remain.[3]

But certain conclusions are inevitable. When he completed the 1938 Dormitory, Mr. Dave announced that the school had reached the maximum size in numbers–around 140 boys. To expand much beyond this number would be to overtax the chapel, dining hall, and athletic facilities. This figure was extended into the 150s when the Boyd and Harris dormitories replaced the six cottages, thus providing a few additional rooms. Even with the increase in numbers the chapel remained adequate in size with five students sitting in each pew and twenty-five to thirty boys in the choir, and the dining hall was not overcrowded because food was sent to the faculty homes for wives and children, and non-faculty staff who lived off campus did not eat there.[4]

Design seemed to follow the founder's dream–the chapel would forever be the center and heartbeat of the school, with all other facilities clustered in sight nearby. As the design followed this line of logic, the lower formers (younger boys) were housed in quarters close to the watchful eye of the headmaster at the top of the hill. Equally close were the dining hall, the school building, and the chapel. In addition, these younger boys were separated from too much contact with and influence of the older boys, who lived across the campus. With Christ School working from the beginning on a tight schedule, efficient use of time was imperative. Hence the boys were clustered in dormitories close to all of

[3]Dorothy Thomson, Mr. Dave's sister, recalls that Mr. Dave sketched building designs on envelopes. "He was pragmatic. The first architect hired was probably for the dining hall (1965)." Actually Earl Stillwell of Hendersonville sketched the gymnasium that wasn't built as designed. He also provided, gratis, other plans for Mr. Dave.

[4]With five to a pew, 170 people would fit comfortably (if snugly) into daily evensong.

their activities: the chapel, dining hall, school building, and athletic field. Boys lost little time in moving from classroom to ball field or from gymnasium to room and job periods.

Aesthetics were included in the design as attested to by the clean, simple, straight architectural lines unified by a theme of sandstone, the terracing added in the 1930's, the endless planting of white pines, shrubs and boxwoods, and the clear view across the football field (Old Stump Garden) to Burney Mountain. In time, as more and more married faculty came aboard, houses were to be arranged in a manner which enabled the masters to have easy access to the various areas of school life without intruding upon the natural beauty.

And, finally, the arrangement provided both Fr. Harris and Mr. Dave an opportunity to be all about the campus at any time–acquiring in the process that ability to appear from nowhere into the shadow of a cottage doorway or clump of shrubs to head off trouble before it had an opportunity to take shape. Fr. Harris' low whistle and Mr. Dave's quiet cough were instant deterrents.

In the late 1960's, Christ School drifted from this plan and for several years admitted 165 to 185 students. The result was, as Mr. Dave had foreseen in 1938, overcrowding, congestion, and a rapid increase in disciplinary problems. Such conditions could only lead to tremendous increases in capital expenditures, including the building of an additional dormitory and the rebuilding of Christ Chapel, a controversial matter at best. Not too long before he died, Mr. Dave, in conversation with the late Bill Justice '38, explained why he wanted to keep enrollment in the 150s . "That's the number," Mr. Dave said, "which permits a headmaster to guide, control, and exercise a direct influence on every boy in the school."

The Class of 1933 marched out into the Great Depression. Charlie Hurst (front row, far right) returned to become an outstanding math teacher.

V: 1933-1939

20

The Little Chapel

As Christ School continued its transformation into a second decade as a boys boarding school only, attempts were under way to retain and strengthen the interest and support of alumni. At the center of this activity was the proposal in 1936 to build a small Memorial Chapel in honor of Fr. R.R. Harris, who brought the daily communion service to the campus in 1908 and made it into a tradition to be carried forward by subsequent chaplains. The project had strong appeal among alumni who remembered Fr. Harris's steadfastness even when the zero temperature outside was matched by a temperature only a few degrees higher inside the main chapel, where he conducted these services. Because of the school's tight budget, Fr. Harris never once fired the chapel furnace up to provide heat at this service, yet never once did he fail to be there except under emergency conditions.

In 1936, the alumni, working through an association which had been founded at Mayodan, N.C., a few years earlier, voted to make this an alumni project, setting $1,500 as the goal. This was the time of the second depression within the Great Depression as the New Deal program failed to end the severe unemployment. Hence contributions came in by pennies and dimes and dollars and not much above that.

Plans called for constructing a small chapel (32x19) which would be used only for early morning communion services and for private student devotions. At the time, it was thought that heat would be provided from the new iron-stoker just placed under the school building but this proved unfeasible. Instead an electric hot air fan was mounted in the back. The altar where Fr. Harris served so faithfully–the one carved by Fr. Wetmore–was to be placed in the Memorial Chapel and Mr. Boyd would build a new one for the main chapel. Memorial Chapel was to have been dedicated in the spring of 1937 but the actual ceremony was delayed a year because construction was intermittent–on a pay-as-you-go basis and work was not complete in 1937.

With construction languishing, the students at Christ School sought an opportunity to help in the project. Mr. Dave suggested they underwrite the floor, with tile to be used in place of wood. In this way, the project could be divided into square feet of tiling so that the cost of a square would be within the means of every student. The response of the students was instantaneous. Fr. Boynton sketched a huge thermometer which he placed in study hall, showing the goal of 500 square feet. Almost overnight the temperature soared to 300 and a few weeks later reached the top. As one of the students observed, "This was a tribute to Fr. Harris and a gift to future Christ School students." Jim Patty '41 called this spontaneous effort one of the most memorable events of his years at Christ School.

The dedication, rescheduled to Easter Sunday, 1938, went ahead as planned although the cloister had not been built, the pathway was not in place, and the infirmary burned down early that morning. But the ceremony was scheduled for 3 p.m. and the service was to be followed by a meeting of the Alumni Association. Intermittent showers slacked off at 3 p.m. and chairs were placed around the side of the Little Chapel to provide seating for the nearly 400 people present. In addition, a piano was placed on the lawn to provide music. Bishop Emmett Gribbin conducted the forty-five minute service with the choir leading the singing. After this service, the alumni met and vowed their continued commitment to the school and voted to try to establish "alumni units" in Asheville, Charlotte, Gastonia, Williamston, Winston-Salem, Charleston, and Columbia.[5] The meeting adjourned to St. Dunstan's Hall where Mrs. Dave served tea and cake. It was to be some months before the cloister was completed, the floor poured, and the path leading to the cloister finished. In later years the little chapel's functions were expanded to include baptisms (a women's auxiliary in New Hampshire donated a fount), marriages, and funeral services.

Somehow through the years confusion emerged as to the name of the two chapels. From the very beginning, the small chapel was the Fr. Harris Memorial Chapel, shortened by common usage to the Little Chapel. More recently some chaplains have incorrectly called it St. Mary's Chapel. The main chapel was dedicated in 1907 as Christ Chapel and that is the title used in Diocesan reports. More commonly, it was called Christ School Chapel or The Chapel. Somewhere along the line the name St. Joseph's Chapel emerged, though this name does not appear in the school newspaper until around 1960. Mrs. Dorothy Thomson said the chapel was referred to as St. Joseph's while she was active at the school. Fr. Boynton (Chaplain from 1933-39) said it was his understanding that the Wetmores intended to call it St. Joseph's Chapel and that this was the name he knew it by. Issues of *The Warrior* (1929-38) speak only of The

[5]In the spring of 1939, a group of 30 alumni met at Brighton Cafeteria in Asheville to hear a progress report.

Chapel and articles in the *Christ School News* for the ensuing ten or fifteen years make the same reference. The log of school services kept by the chaplains show Fr. Harris referring to it as Christ Chapel or Christ School Chapel, and not until Fr. Thompson's time does the name St. Joseph's appear.[6] After that, the name St. Mary's appears in log records about services held in the Little Chapel, perhaps as a companion to the name St. Joseph's.

Mrs. Dave was a gracious lady who served Christ School tirelessly. Although she served the school without pay, it required three people to replace her when she retired.

[6]These records include vast gaps; either they were incomplete or some log books misplaced during intervening years.

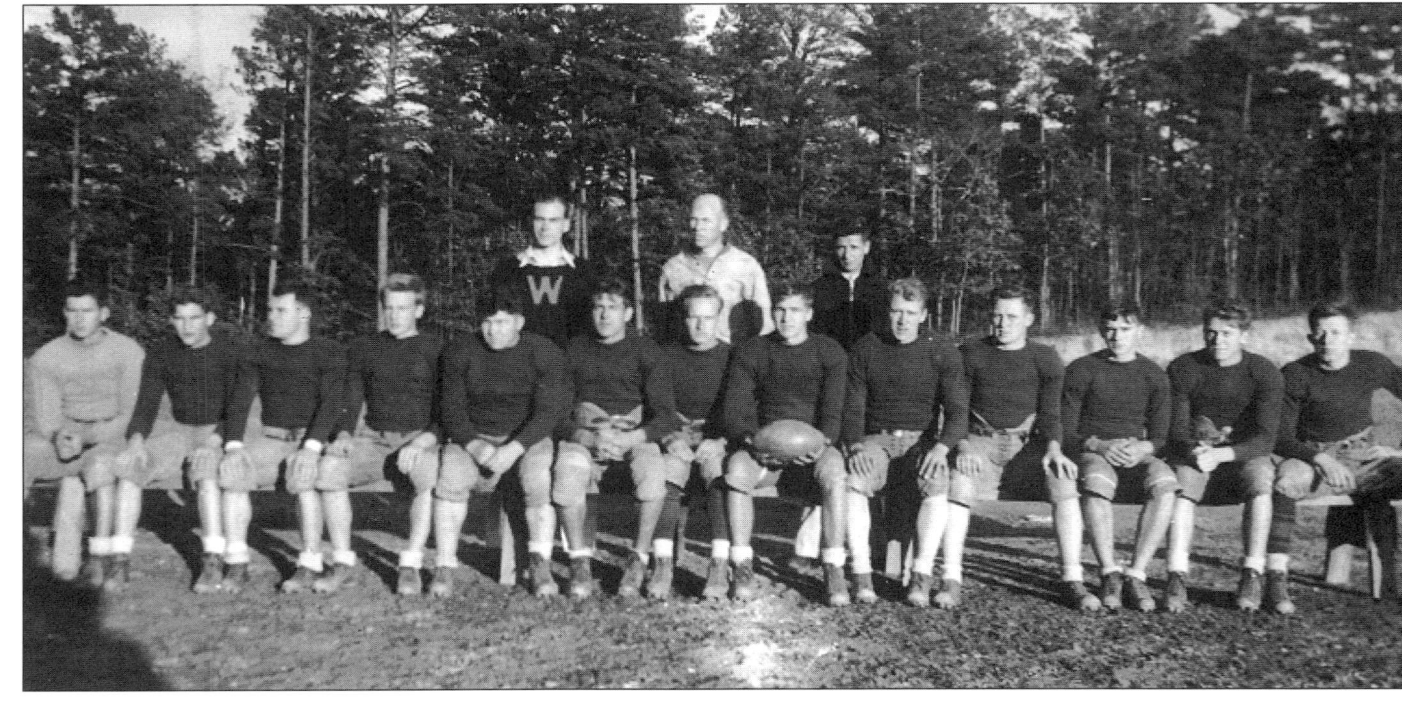

The Fall of 1933 produced Christ School's first undefeated football team. New on campus to assist Fessor was the chaplain, Fr. Boynton (W), who was a Little All-American at Williams College.

V: 1933-1939

21

An Easter Blaze

Throughout the years, Christ School maintained an excellent fire record–even though many of the buildings prior to 1940 could be classified as fire hazards since there was so little fire prevention except for the carefulness of students and faculty alike. The first major fire occurred in December 1919 when Thompson Hall (the first Old Dorm) burned down, sending some students home for early Christmas vacation and sending others into Mrs. Wetmore's cottages on Cottage Hill. The second one was that infirmary blaze on Easter morning 1938, a $10,000 loss which was covered to the extent of $4,000. The general alarm (clanging of the sawbell) was sounded by Fr. Boynton at 5:10 a.m. and by six o'clock the one-story frame structure was ashes, despite the massive efforts of a campus bucket brigade. Most attention was centered on keeping sparks from setting the Little Rectory on fire.

No one knows for certain what caused the fire which was detected by the nurse, Maude Watkins, about five in the morning. She aroused all the occupants of the infirmary while Mrs. Clara Patty spread the alarm. Two theories emerged as to the origin. One attributed it to a short circuit in a bathroom of the new wing added to the infirmary in 1932. Because someone reported an "orange glow" in the furnace room, another theory attributed the fire to ashes–either from the furnace or from an illegal cigarette. Built in 1921, the infirmary replaced St. Mary's, razed to make way for Fessor's Cottage. The 1921 infirmary was made possible by a gift from St. Bartholomew's Church in New York City. Another gift, one from Helena Spraker, a classmate of Mrs. Wetmore's, paid for the new wing. The necessary $10,000 to provide a more modern infirmary faced with sandstone was raised by Mrs. Wetmore within a few days of the fire.

In general, fire loss on the campus has been minimal. In 1936, the pump house burned down and this forced the school to lay down a pipe to hook up with the Asheville city water line. In December 1944, the Fraternity House was completely destroyed, the fire apparently starting from pipe ashes a careless smoker spilled on an upholstered sofa. In the 1960's the Frat was again partially damaged by fire. A minor scare developed in early 1970 when a student left a hot plate on in the Sacristy and smoke began to emerge from the Chapel. Fortunately the damage was minimal and most of the campus remained unaware that a tragedy had been narrowly averted. Other smaller scares–undetected–have doubtless occurred. Once such scare involved J.D. Jones '36, who stacked some leaves up on the porch of the First Cottage and then attempted to see if a magnifying glass and the sun could really ignite them. The smell of billowing smoke broke up the Sunday tea gathering at Fr. Boynton's house as those students rushed over to see what was wrong. J.D. went on to become an outstanding scholar at North Carolina State and was chairman of the alumni effort which helped to revitalize the library in 1965 when it was moved into St. Dunstan's Hall.

The school's infirmary caught fire early Easter morning and burned down. The conflagration did not stop the sunrise Easter service and the dedication that afternoon of the Fr. Harris Chapel.

V: 1933-1939

Some Giants In The Chapel

For those who misinterpret boys' griping and take it too seriously, chapel services on The Hill would never have survived and grown in majesty and beauty over the first seventy years. Given the option of going to chapel (or classes) every day or goofing off, there is little doubt what the normal boy would choose. But as Fr. Boynton taught the boys on many occasions, one learns to do by doing and in the process learns to appreciate what he is doing. Anyway, as previously observed, Fr. Boynton introduced many of the things that became traditional in Christ School spiritual life. He introduced singing and chanting into the chapel services, revamped the Candlelight service to fit the tradition of Lessons and Carols sung in English preparatory schools, and contributed a series of other innovations that involved Lent, Holy Week, and other seasons during the school year. For most of these seventy years, Christ School was blessed with priests of high church tradition who developed and improved the distinctive character of the services here. These chaplains sometimes added to or refined the richness of the services but did not subtract from the traditions that developed, except in 1967 when the service of Adoration was abandoned. Strangely enough the student commitment to the services–vigorous singing, chanting, responses–did not grow because most of the students were Episcopalians. Almost never in its history was half the Christ School student body Episcopalian. The evolution came from strong, dedicated leadership and commitment to a tradition whose mystery and beauty inspired students and guests alike. It is not surprising during those years that about the first thing an alumnus did upon returning to campus was to visit the chapel and go to evensong, early communion, or Sunday sung mass. After all, he had been a part of the ritual and had raised his voice with vigor in singing and chanting, even if not always on key. There were sags in student participation even during the best of years, just as there are sags in participation in whatever any one is doing. But when one sagged another stepped in to take his place and after some chiding, perhaps an editorial in the school paper or remarks by Mr. Dave, the chaplain and/or the faculty, the quality would return to normal. If one were to use a yardstick to compare the quality of one year's participation to another, that yardstick would be the senior class. Basically, they determined the volume. And generally the volume was loud.

Fr. Boynton's impact on the chapel continued to be felt during the ensuing years. When he arrived on campus in the fall of 1933, there was a daily mass before breakfast, evensong nightly, and a holy communion service Sunday at 11 a.m. None of these services were sung except for the hymns. "It was my privilege," Fr. Boynton said, "to introduce singing at the high mass on Sunday and a choral evensong."

Actually, he did more than introduce it. He wrote what was to be called the Boynton Mass for the Sunday eucharistic services. It was a mass he had written to be sung at his ordination to the priesthood. After his arrival here, Fr. Boynton taught the boys the full mass all the way from the Kyrie through the Gloria, as well as the Creed and the Sanctus and Benedictus, in order that they have something to sing during the high mass on Sunday. In chapel the student body was divided into four parts and Fr. Boynton was the director until Urq Chinn came aboard a couple of years later. "After Mr. Chinn came as organist and choirmaster," Fr. Boynton said, "he improved the composition so that now it is correct to say that Mr. Chinn and I composed the music."

In effect, Fr. Boynton introduced the tradition both of music and ritual which Christ School used unwaveringly until 1970. Why did Christ School adopt the use of the mass? Fr. Boynton's answer is simple and direct: "It was because I taught it to them and gave them no choice." With Fr. Boynton's leadership to continue until 1939, the service continued with only minor alterations through the ensuing years because the setting used for the service was the one the boys practiced and passed on from year to year. The ritual Fr. Boynton introduced was carried forward in the same manner.

As many alumni recall, Fr. Boynton's chapel talks incited interest and curiosity and brought the point home in memorable, often dramatic fashion. These talks seldom lasted more than ten minutes and one memorable though brief one occurred at an Easter service. The Gospel for Easter was quite long, carrying the message of Christ's resurrection, and Fr. Boynton felt the message could not be improved on. He decided that the Gospel should take the place of the sermon. When the time came for his sermon, he simply said, "In the name of the Father, the Son, and the Holy Ghost." But there was a problem–a several minute delay in the service. He had to dispatch an acolyte to the grandstand to retrieve the thrufier and the incense pot.

When Father Harris died in January 1933, he had the title of headmaster and rector. At a special meeting, the board of directors made Mr. Dave headmaster and decided upon the course of selecting a separate rector and placing the school for the first time under lay leadership. At the time of Fr. Harris's death, Mrs. Wetmore was in New York raising money for the school. Mr. Dave telegraphed Mrs. Wetmore not to return for the funeral but to seek someone to become chaplain to succeed his father.

Mrs. Wetmore, always active in whatever she did, immediately turned to a friend who introduced her to Fr. Fielding, an instructor at General Theological Seminary. The next day, Fr. Fielding walked into the room of a young man who was planning an evening lecture in aesthetic theology and, without preliminary comments, asked him, "Would you be interested in becoming a chaplain at a mountain school for boys in Western North Carolina?" The reply: "Yes, very much. I think I would like to take that position."

The next day, Fr. Boynton had lunch with Mrs. Wetmore, and it was arranged that he come to Christ School for Holy Week. During that period, he preached at Christ Chapel each evening and at the three hour service on Good Friday. At the end of the three hour service, Fr. Boynton came out of the chapel and found Mr. Dave sitting on the wall next to the steps. The conversation was brief. Mr. Dave spoke without the assurance that his students remember so well: "Oh, if you would only come and be our chaplain." Fr. Boynton's reply was even more to the point. "I will come." Thus was to begin a six year ministry which lay the foundations of our church traditions and our choir. As a close friendship developed between the Boyntons and the Harrises, Fr. Boynton was to become a key architect in significant academic and extra-curricular changes that were to assume an equally important traditional role.

Sometimes it seems that a person who follows a giant must of necessity be swallowed up by the footprints. Such is not the case when the successor does not try to become that giant but brings his own force of personality into play. Fr. Harris was such a giant but Providence was kind and Christ School found in Fr. Boynton a man who could never replace Fr. Harris but who provided a new leadership and continued and improved the traditions which made Christ School Chapel the unifying focal point on campus.

When Fr. Boynton left Christ School in 1939 to become Chaplain of St. Francis House at the University of Wisconsin, the same problem of shoe-filling emerged. His chapel talks, many of them sequence narratives, were memorable and applicable to daily life. His work in athletics and in creating a more vital extra-curricular program helped move Christ School forward to becoming a first class boarding school in every respect.

In the Spring of 1939, Fr. Boynton was deep in thought about the chaplaincy offer and put it from his mind, only to have the Bishop remind him that he could not stand in the way of God's call simply because he loved the ways and life of his present position. That discussion inspired deeper thought and yet Fr. Boynton still had not wrestled his way to a conclusion. The decision appeared to be made during a Sunday talk in Chapel after Easter. Choirmaster Urq Chinn recalls the incident well:

> Fr. Boynton gave a talk on the old hymn, "Lead Kindly Light." It says "One step enough for me." There were only about a hundred students then and he would come down and stand in-between the first two pews. That's where he preached each Sunday. (That way the kids had to behave themselves; not bad psychology.) During his talk, Fr. Boynton kept saying "One step enough for me." And he would take another step down the aisle each time he said it. After the service as the boys and visitors left Chapel, there was the usual "Nice sermon" and that sort of pleasantry. The last person to leave Chapel was Mrs. Wetmore. She paused, looked into Fr. Boynton's face, and said softly, "I hope you are happy in your new job."

Part of the credit–a large share–for the school's continuing the church traditions begun by Fr. Wetmore, transformed by Fr. Harris, and put into music by Fr. Boynton goes to Mr. Dave and Urq Chinn. When a minister comes to a church, he has the authority to determine everything–even the hymns and music. Usually, though, a minister turns the responsibility of the music over to the organist. To make certain that tradition continued, before the successor to Fr. Boynton was even chosen, Mr. Dave told Urq to "tell them how you do it (the service) here." He repeated this formula with each subsequent new chaplain. "Generally," Urq said, "the new chaplains wanted to be told of the traditions and seldom attempted to modify or rearrange anything before being here at least one year."

The first of the four men to succeed Fr. Boynton was Fr. Reid Hammond, who was here for only two years. Homesickness–that experienced by his bride of a few years for her native California–cut short his stay. Like Fr. Boynton, the new chaplain was quite young and came here shortly after being ordained a priest at St. James Church in Chicago. He was not athletic but had an excellent singing voice to carry on the choral services begun by Fr. Boynton. Because Fr. Hammond had such a beautiful voice, Mr. Chinn found himself modifying the service a little. "I told him he had to sing the introduction to 'Oh Lamb of God' and a few other things like that. His chanting was magnificent."

Besides having a splendid voice, Fr. Hammond had a gifted mind. He taught history and English and continued the "Question Box" extra-curricular activity started by Fr. Boynton as a substitute for sacred studies, a session in which boys submitted in advance written questions on life and religion and ethics. One student attending Christ School then (he chose to remain anonymous) recalled that Fr. Hammond was a demanding second form English teacher.

> He would require us to write a 3-5 page theme each week, including the weeks when we had examinations. Sometimes I had to write two during the week–one for another second former as well as myself. Writing the extra theme was not voluntary. This second former–a man at seventeen–was stronger than most of the seniors. The first two fingers on his steel-like right hand could bruise a wrist. Interestingly enough, I got A's and B's on my compositions while the other boy made C's and D's.

What moved Fr. Hammond deeply about the campus when he came was the beauty of the landscaping which "does not destroy the primitive feeling" of natural surroundings. Such effect had not simply happened; it was the work of Mr. Dave as he carried out a plan sketched for him by a well known landscape architect of the 1920's. Few things at Christ School were left to chance. Fr. Hammond continued the tradition begun by Fr. Boynton of writing "The Chaplain's Column"for the *Christ School News* each month. His first column provided insight into the background of our Prayer Book (The American Book of Common Prayer). Another custom which Mrs. Hammond and he continued was the inviting of various forms to tea at the Rectory on Sunday afternoons.

Innovation also marked Fr. Hammond's brief stint at Christ School. For the week of the first Sunday after Advent, he invited Fr. Wood B. Carper, who had just become minister at Calvary in Fletcher, to hold a mission in place of evensong each night during that week. His topic, "The Doctrine of the Incarnation," received a send-off the preceding Sunday when Bishop Gribbin discussed the incarnation in a talk at Christ School Chapel.

Fr. Hammond also provided the organizational framework for the acolytes, as described in the February 1940 issue of the *Christ School News*: "For some time there has been a rumor that an organization for the acolytes would be started. Here-to-fore there has been no initiation into the group, no service for dedication, and no regular meetings. To this end, it has been decided by the chaplain and acolytes to form an acolyte guild." The decision was also made to affiliate with an established guild rather than to form an independent chapter on campus. The result was the St. Vincent's Guild, which required that an acolyte meet certain disciplines of faithfulness in order to become a member and remain in good standing.

Members were inducted into St. Vincent's Guild at a special early morning communion service in which Mr. Dave served as sponsor. At their second meeting, the acolytes chose their first officers–Byron Clee, president; Sam Logan, vice president; and Jimmy Patty, secretary-treasurer. Fr. Rogers, a visiting priest from Lake Forest, Ill., gave a résumé of the origin of the Mass in relation to the acolyte and the part he plays.

An upbeat innovation came on Passion Sunday in 1940, when the entire Christ School student body–choir, acolytes, faculty, et al–was transferred to Calvary Church in Fletcher in the coal truck and cars provided by the faculty and Calvary parishioners. *The News* described the occasion:

> Their arrival at Calvary took on the complexion of an invasion, and the church was packed. As always, when put to the test, the choir excelled itself, and the rest of the student body demonstrated their ability in a way that they have never surpassed. Fr. Hammond, assisted by his own acolytes, was the Celebrant (at this Sung Eucharist). Fr. Carper preached a most beautiful sermon on the implications of the Baptismal promises for us as doers of the work of God.

For the next six years, the position of chaplain was filled by Fr. Gale D. Webbe, and he too made an indelible impression upon Christ School boys. For most of that time, the war was on the minds of many students. Fortunately for them, the three leadership roles (headmaster, chaplain, athletic director) which touched the daily life of each student provided manly leadership. All three (Mr. Dave, Fessor, Pop Webbe) were strong Episcopalians–vigorous, and wise in the ways of boys and in understanding human nature. These were the qualities to be found in these roles at Christ School throughout most of its first seven decades of history. The strength in each area reinforced the whole. Pop Webbe was one of those pillars. It was easy to confuse him in looks and character and action with Spencer Tracy, who epitomized the best in priesthood in an epic movie called *Boys Town*. Like Fr. Boynton, Pop was athletic (a splendid swimmer at Amherst and a tumbler) and he helped coach football here. He also had the ear of the students and offered advice and counsel easily from a bench on Yard A or while wandering through the dorms in the afternoon or night. His offbeat humor–often at the expense of himself–helped relax the tensions which built up on campus during these very restrictive war years. His invention of the term "Thud" to designate the awarding of a worklist helped to lighten the punishment, and it became a major word in the daily lexicon of most students. To help boost morale, Pop put on the Christ School adaptation of "The Sixty-Four Dollar Question," a popular radio show, and secured some horizontal and parallel bars and mats to introduce tumbling as a healthy energy outlet.

Although the North Carolina mountains have four distinct seasons, the winters are most unpredictable, springlike sometimes and like the Rockies at others. It was the snows which produced moments of great fun, especially for that large contingent that crossed the swamps around New Orleans to get here and who had never before seen snow. One such snow Fr. Webbe recalls vividly occurred in March 1945:

> That blizzard deposited 18 inches or so of snow on campus. Classes continued (We didn't have to worry about buses not running) but there were no state vehicles to clear the road to Arden and the school ran out of food after two or three days. Mr. Dave had a solution to the food supply problem, one which the students thought fun. He lined everybody up four or five abreast and had the boys march to Arden, with the truck following close behind. Shuford's Store was the destination.
>
> The snow brought in drifts which were five to eight feet deep off the edge of the football field as the wind howled much like it does across the Russian steppes. Student work forces shoveled snow in order to dig a trench to the dairy barn so that the boys could carry 10 gallon milk cans to the dining hall. One morning Mr. Dave divided the school into sides. Forts were constructed on the football field and World War III began with the whiz on snowballs and the storming of those forts. Perhaps The Man's greatest display of anger came when a Frat member, using a pick to search for a nearby frozen waterline at the Fraternity, struck oil, so to speak, by putting the pick through the pipeline. Water pressure on campus, low even at the best of times, such as the middle of the night, collapsed, leaving a tiny trickle for bathing and shaving.

In his work at the chapel, Fr. Webbe liked doing things and doing them right. This characteristic rubbed off on the acolytes and there was much competition to be the best server or best serving crew without arousing animosity among the competitors. "In this way, Fr. Webbe was carrying on the traditions of his predecessors," Urq Chinn said. "Gale was a perfectionist, like Fr. Boynton and Fr. Hammond, and the boys were quick to do things in an orderly, prescribed manner while serving at the altar. You didn't just flop around; you practiced, as many times as necessary to make it professional."

Fr. Webbe continued the traditions in the chapel which came before him, such as Candlelight Service, daily communion, and Lenten services, and so forth. In several ways he made his own mark. For one thing, he involved the faculty in serving at the early communion on Sunday morning, including Mr. Dave. He revived a discarded practice of the past by having seniors read the lessons at some evensong services. (Who can ever forget Jim Washburn '45, reading the lesson one night, a dog wandering down the aisle at one point, and then the burst of laughter as he read "and Saul tied his ass to a tree and walked for a mile"). "And, if I'm not mistaken," Mr. Chinn said, "it was Fr. Webbe who started the chanting of the Gospel and the Epistle."

That the Chapel was the heartbeat of all aspects of Christ School life is seen in a letter of October 29, 1945, in which Fr. Webbe responded to a recent graduate who was in the military service. The boy had inquired as to how things were going at the chapel:

> We had a nice High Mass with procession and the works today–Feast of Christ the King–and Adoration tonight. It (High Mass) went well in spite of the big dance last night when the Fraternity netted over $100 and everybody had a good time. Corporate Communion is coming up November 1 (All Saints' Day), so the school year is well under way.

Stability was restored to the chapel in 1950 with the naming of Fr. Webster as Chaplain. He had spent one year as assistant chaplain in 1944 and now returned to serve for 13 years, second only to Fr. Harris in tenure. Like his predecessors, Fr. Webster was a man strong in faith, devout, upright, and manly. To him, as those who came before him, The Chapel was the center of life at Christ School, and they were of the Anglican tradition–believing in and upholding the traditions which brought it strength.

These were a series of remarkable men, who seldom missed an early morning communion (seven days a week), even on near zero winter days. The significance of "praying for the state of Christ School and the world" was an occasion not to be missed, even at the expense of health or personal comfort.

Fr. Webster's years here were productive ones. He introduced the Anglican Missal into the Sung Eucharist. While he was here, student interest in the early morning communion services grew dramatically, with anywhere from 1,500 to 2,600 people receiving communion each year at these pre-dawn services. Incredibly, attendance ran high even on those days when the acolyte had to break the ice in the water pitcher.

One of the programs which Fr. Webster introduced was the student-organized and student-run compline services which were held immediately after study hall let out–that thirty minute period when students generally ran to the Frat or the Grandstand to grab a smoke or to the cottages to take a shower or write a letter. The services, instigated by Rodney Kirk, who was later to be a priest at St. John's Cathedral in New York City, quickly became popular and by the second year, there were two compline services held in chapel each weekday evening, one beginning at 8:45 p.m. for the first and second formers and the other at 9:15 p.m. for the upper four forms. The chapel register shows that the first such service in the second year–called meditations and held during Lent–was celebrated by 36 students in Fr. Harris Chapel at 9:25 p.m. on Thursday, February 19, 1953, with senior Leland Jamieson as officiant. Altogether 537 students attended the 32 student-led meditations. These compline services ran for about ten years, with total attendance each year in the 400 to 550 range. An exception came in 1957, when the compline services were discontinued March 8 because of a flu epidemic which put 60 boys into bed at one time and brought on early lights out. Although ten meditations were eliminated during this epidemic, attendance still topped the 300 mark for the remaining services.

The Chapel was without doubt the heart of Christ School. There was the daily 6:30 a.m. mass, evensong or benediction before supper and high mass on Sundays and on all the great feast days. The Rev. Walter Hooper, who taught here for a couple of years and now administers the C.S. Lewis estate and papers, recalls his feelings about the Chapel.

> If you took a consensus of what the boys liked or disliked about the school, I doubt if you would have found one who did not love the Chapel. The book which Pop (Webster) used for Mass was the *English Missal*, a combination *Book of Common Prayer* (1928) and various other prayers. It was in the Chapel of Christ School that I, for the first time, witnessed the Sung Mass splendidly and unashamedly observed . . . .
>
> As long as I am able to remember anything, I will remember the ringing of the Angelus in the evening. If you were outside, you could see boys standing here and there in complete silence as this devotion was paid to God.
>
> It was considered a great privilege to serve at High Mass and no boy took the privilege lightly. I still regard the High Masses at Christ School the most beautiful and spiritually rewarding of my life. The recent descent into liturgical language as

boring as saw-dust only helps to remind me how fortunate we were at Christ School.

As the incense rose to the ceiling as Fr. Webster elevated the Host, one of the servers rang the chapel bell, and it still gives me a shiver of awe and pleasure to recall that everyone within hearing distance of Christ School knew that the Body of Christ occupied the premier place on The Hill.

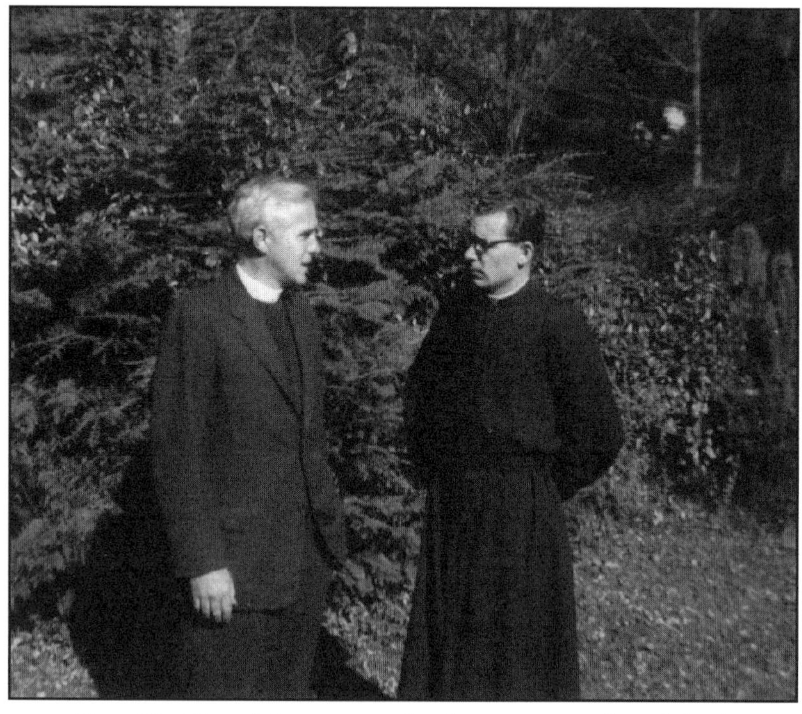

Two of the Chapel giants got together for a reunion at Christ School. They are Fr. Gale D. Webbe (left) and Fr. Ralph K Webster.

V: 1933-1939

23

The New Hand Is Firm

In physics class, Mr. Dave taught one principal over and over: That matter can neither be created nor destroyed. He hammered this principal into practice most visibly as he patiently went about his goal of rebuilding the school's physical plant into a more permanent, durable one. He set about removing–as conditions permitted–the many temporary structures that dotted the campus and replaced them with buildings of sandstone exterior. Nothing of the old was destroyed in the process as whatever was usable in the old found its way into the substructure of new dorms and faculty homes. Mr. Dave pursued a cost effective approach long before that term became current. In every aspect of the school's development, Mr. Dave felt obligated to see that the parents got their money's worth. Recycling solid old material was one part of the process. Supervising the construction himself and making use of Mr. Boyd and local labor was another way of keeping costs down. Using the raw materials available on campus (stone from the quarries and lumber harvested on the place) made building less costly. Following a pay-as-you-go approach kept borrowing down to short term situations and prevented the waste of income going to long-range interest payments. And more important, he provided a living workshop for the students–permitting them (like Tom Sawyer) through worklist or assignment or voluntarily to be a part of the process. No building was torn down or built in which the students, under his direction, were not participants. In some ways the troublemakers had more fun than the others because they were able to work closely with Mr. Dave in circumstances he so clearly relished. The Rev. Scott Root recalled this very aspect in an interview a few years ago:

> I have a vivid memory of the tearing down I did. I think I did more demolition work than most boys at Christ School. I never got old enough to have a claim but I caught plenty of worklists. I remember tearing down the old school building darn near

> single-handed, because Mr. Dave and I were a team and I was always on the worklist. Through constant practice I learned how to pull nails and pull down two-by-fours. After that I learned how to build things and it was a good feeling to know that I'd learned much of this stuff at Christ School–how boards fit together and hold a building up.

What Fr. Root has immodestly forgotten over the intervening years was that he had lots of brother on the demolition team–a group that Mr. Dave often fondly referred to as his fraternity, the Alpha Sigma Sigma. Small wonder that Christ School alumni return to the campus filled with pride and eager to point out to all who will listen the part they played in the building of the campus and athletic field. By now it does not matter whether their contribution of time was voluntary or involuntary. What is important were the lessons of hard work and faithfulness to the task that they carried with them into their own lives. In this day when the term "cost effectiveness" is used to justify most anything, Mr. Dave might appear to be an anachronism. Included in the formula as he applied it were patience and student involvement. A man frequently impatient with himself, Mr. Dave did not seek short-cuts or attempt to burden the school with big debts but kept his objectives in mind until the time for carrying out each one of them was right. Many today might consider his use of time–so much spent with the boys and so little in public relations–to be inefficient. But Mr. Dave considered the time he spent with the boys the most important time of all. In this way he showed them the values which he felt were necessary to life and important to them–hard work, faithfulness, doing the best one can, and working together. In a sense, Mr. Dave was much like Sam Walton, the man who converted Wal-Mart from a few stores into a billion dollar sales empire. Walton attributed his success to staying out of the office and being among the employees. "A manager who spends more than twenty percent of his time in the office," Walton said, "is messing things up for everybody." To Mr. Dave, the office was where the students were.

Part of Mr. Dave's feeling for the boys came from his own experience in going off to Kent. Both Dorothy Thomson and Bob Harris recalled how homesick he was the first year. On one occasion, Mrs. Thomson, who was two years younger than her brother, went to visit him from St. Mary's on-the-Poughkeepsie to help quell an attack of homesickness that had landed him in the infirmary. After graduating from North Carolina State, Mr. Dave entered the Air Force and served in France. (His brother Don, also in the Air Force, was shot down in 1918 and landed in Holland where he was interned for the remainder of the war.) After returning home, Mr. Dave went to work in Akron, Ohio, as a salesman but he wanted to come home. He was homesick. "Fr. Harris reluctantly let him come back," Mrs. Thomson said, "for he had no idea that Dave might be interested in teaching." Thus Mr. Dave returned to the campus and did some maintenance work at Christ School and worked as a salesman in Asheville.[7] As Bob Harris put it, "Dave liked to run things." He was not a trained teacher (which may have been to his advantage) and his degree was in horticulture. But Christ School was an outdoor place, and that plus the farming appealed to him. When Mr. Dave returned to help out around the place he resumed a project Coach Nichols had started in 1916–digging out the area which was to become the main athletic field. To do this, Mr. Dave organized the worklist/claim process even before he was established at Christ School. With Mr. Dave still hanging around, Fr. Harris put him on the faculty to teach science and he quickly became his father's strong arm. About 1927-28, Fr. Harris, like an overworked clock, began to run down and Mr. Dave gradually took over the duties of headmaster, leaving Fr. Harris free to concentrate on his duties as chaplain. In 1932, Fr. Martin was added to the faculty as a math teacher but mostly to help understudy Fr. Harris in conducting services, teaching Bible to all the students, and training the acolytes. When Fr. Harris died in New Orleans in January 1933, his successor–a man who at one time was just hanging around–was well prepared for his new role.

In June 1936, Mr. Dave presented to the board the idea of building a new dormitory (St. Edmund's) next to the 30 Dorm with the two being connected by a covered passageway. Conditions seemed ripe for such a proposal. The trustees had approved the sale of property in Rosscraggon that had been donated to the school by Miss Marion Meade. This sale would net the school $6,000 which the board earmarked for the new dorm. In addition, water would presumably no longer be a problem because the school was connected to the city lines shortly after the pump house burned down. Thus there would be a sufficient water supply to provide for an expanding enrollment. In his proposal, the headmaster also pointed out that this increase of twenty to twenty-five students could be absorbed with little added expense.

Mr. Dave's plans for building a new, permanent campus on top of the old was not limited to this one dormitory. At the July 1937 board meeting he called for construction of a new school building. To support the need, he read to the board a letter from J. J. Highsmith, superintendent of schools in North Carolina, in which Mr. Highsmith called attention to the "unsatisfactory condition of the administration building." More to the point, a new building was necessary, Highsmith explained, if the school was to retain its accreditation. The proposal got the swift backing of the trustees and an immediate pledge of $8,000 to get it underway. Six thousand was to come from the liquidation of some notes while Mrs.

[7]In some ways, Mr. Dave's return to Christ School may have been intensified by his desire to relieve his father of some of the burden which was wearing away his life.

Wetmore had raised an additional two thousand dollars.

An unexpected tragedy occurred on Easter morning (1938) which slowed down plans for the school building. The infirmary burned to the ground. While making the rounds to awaken students for the Easter sunrise service, Fr. Boynton saw a bright orange glow in the furnace area of the infirmary. Students were quickly aroused by the clanging of the sawbell and a bucket brigade was formed but it was too late to save the infirmary. Fortunately Mrs. Wetmore, who had an apartment there, was unharmed but her false teeth, later found in the rubble, were a temporary casualty of the fire. Smoke hovered over the campus like incense but did not prevent a beautiful sunrise service in which Fr. Boynton's message underscored how frequently "good emerges from tragedy." The need for an infirmary was immediate, but for the moment the students were moved out of the Second Cottage, which became the dispensary. Mrs. Wetmore responded quickly to the emergency and within forty-eight hours she had raised through telephone calls the $10,000 necessary to construct a new, bigger, better infirmary. Many other individuals–alumni, parents, and friends–also contributed additionally for medical supplies and equipment. The foundation of the infirmary came from the huge blocks of cement that had been a part of the dam at the Old Mill Pond.

The dam at the Mill Pond was central to the life at Christ School for nearly a quarter of a century. The Mill Pond (often referred to as Wetmore Pond) backed up the water from a rock dam built across Gap Creek to the north of the Rock House and ran east and west. Fifteen feet from the dam the water dropped to a depth of twenty to twenty-five feet and it backed up 300 feet north of the dam. Almost every winter the pond froze over to a depth of three to eight inches from which ice was cut and stored for use by the Wetmores, the Harrises, the school, and other people in the community. Refrigerators as we know them had not come into use then, though there were ice-boxes. Both school and community used the lake for swimming, fishing, and ice-skating. In 1916, the great flood which swept through Western North Carolina partially destroyed the dam but it was rebuilt. The dam was also the site of a dynamo which generated power for the Wetmore House, the Rectory, and a couple of other buildings on campus. The dynamo operated from dawn until around nine at night. The light produced was frequently of such poor quality that Fr. Harris installed four gas light reflectors to light up the study hall at night. Candles and oil lamps augmented the flickering power grid. By 1925, the need for the dam as a source of power came to an end as Carolina Power and Light extended its lines to the campus and the need for grist and saw mills declined. For a time, Mr Dave experimented with generating power from a dynamo operated on campus by hook-up to a Fordson tractor but the process was too noisy and cumbersome and was quickly discontinued. The foundation stone of the infirmary, which came from the old dam, was carried over from Burney Mountain by slaves in the early days of Struan. Over the years much silt washed into the pond and all attempts to remove the silt proved futile. When the lake dried out, it left many acres of very rich soil, which became a source of supply for corn and potatoes for the school during World War II.

Shortly after Fr. Boynton arrived, he instigated the building of a small pond on the Christ School road. For the years between the discontinuing of the Mill Pond to the building of Boynton Pond, Christ School boys continued to swim in the fall and spring but had to trek long distances to Grove Lake or Cane Creek beyond Meadows Store. Although Boynton Pond had to be cleaned of silt every year, this was no trouble because Mr. Dave always found ways of increasing the worklist in March in time to drain and clean the pond for swimming. More than sixty volunteers appeared in the spring of 1942 after they were caught with food in their rooms the Monday following Easter Sunday. Not only did this group spend two days in the muck, but all of their Easter candies and cakes were sent to the dining hall to provide dessert for the student body for several meals. For a few years the pond was full of sizeable goldfish. The population growth started when Elizabeth (the cook) emptied her aquarium into the pond before leaving for summer vacation. Others followed suit and for a time people within walking distance would come over to the pond to feed the goldfish.

Although providing pleasure for many and being an economic necessity for many years, the Mill Pond was not without tragedy. Two drownings occurred there, one in 1913 and a second in 1924. According to Fessor, both were accidents but the second one was inexcusable. The first drowning involved a young boy from Flat Rock who, immediately after arriving on campus and putting his luggage down, went straight to the pond. He climbed to the top of the boathouse and dived in where the water was about twenty feet deep. Exactly what happened afterwards is beyond memory, but apparently he took in too much water and drowned.

The second incident happened a couple of weeks before graduation and the victim, Roy Wingate, was a senior from Asheville. A stained glass window in the Chapel pays tribute to his memory. That drowning occurred on a Saturday afternoon. A number of boys had gone down to the pond to wade and fool around in the water. There wasn't too much swimming because the Mill Pond had filled up with silt two or three feet deep on the bottom. One of the boys (his nickname was Greasy Spoon), a lanky youth of 6'3", waded out pretty far into the mud and slime. The rest of the group had left the pond to play in a field nearby. Suddenly they heard cries of distress as Greasy's feet stuck in the mud and he began to panic. The nearest person to the screaming youth was Roy Wingate and two friends who had just returned from a hike to Little Baldy and they were traveling a path that ran alongside the pond. From a distance, the group in the field could see Wingate wading toward Greasy. When Roy reached the panic-stricken boy, Greasy suddenly sprang on Roy like a monkey would jump on some place of safety. The force of that springing action sent Roy sprawling and he sank deep into the mud, possibly too stunned to move. While others on shore were trying to throw a rope to Greasy and finally succeeded in pulling him out, Roy was apparently overlooked in the excitement. Then several boys began to dive in search of him but his body was not to be found until sometime later when Mr. Dave dived and brought Roy up in his arms. This was Mr. Dave's third year at Christ School and, according to his brother Robert Harris, this had to be one of his saddest moments. Roy Wingate was perhaps the most popular boy in school. As a commemoration to him, recalled by Dr. John Dougherty '24, the fifth and sixth formers sat under the big white pine next to the Christ School Chapel as Dorothy Harris read to them heroic poems from Byron, Shelly, Keats, and Wordsworth. "When I think of the real meaning of Christ School, I think of her. I think of her generous, kind, graceful attendance to us in this moment of deep sorrow."

With the infirmary having been destroyed by fire on Easter morning, with work continuing on the 38 Dorm, and with the state pressing the school to construct a new administration building, the board meeting that June 6 grappled with serious financial problems. The trustees discussed liquidating some of Christ School's invested funds for building purposes. Before reaching a decision, they decided to refer the matter to the finance committee and the headmaster for their consideration before reconvening the annual meeting a week later.[8] The finance committee called for the creation of a building fund of $20,000. The finance committee would be empowered to manage the fund and to authorize expenditures for building and improving school facilities. The plan was simple. The board would turn over $20,000 of invested funds to the committee. The school would borrow $5,000 on these funds at 3 or 3½ percent and keep adding to the building fund from time to time to maintain the $20,000 balance. The board expressed some dissatisfaction with the bank's management of these funds (the interest return was low yield) and this transfer would provide more flexible management through the finance committee. The board approved the plan and transferred the $20,000 in various funds and set up a building committee consisting of the finance committee and the headmaster. The building committee was granted authority to use the $20,000 as security to borrow up to $10,000 to construct new buildings and improve present facilities. The fund was to be maintained at $20,000 and the finance committee was authorized to sell, buy, invest, or reinvest.

[8]The finance committee was made up of J.G. Merrimon (chairman), Reginald Howland, Harvey Heywood, and the headmaster.

In effect, this paved the way for Mr. Dave to build on a pay-as-you-go basis. At this same meeting, Mrs. Wetmore, who was in failing health, resigned as secretary of the board to be replaced in that position by Mr. Heywood. She remained on the board, though. Morris Plan Bank was selected as the depository for the building fund.

At their August 1938 meeting, the trustees heard news both good and bad. Mrs Wetmore said that she had collected $5,500 which was transferred to the building fund. The headmaster reported a financial loss for the year of a relatively negligible $1,382.75 ($11.43 per pupil). He said a $50 raise in tuition (room and board) to $400 would balance the books. At the time, the school was receiving an average of $270 from each pupil, a shortfall in income of about thirty percent. The enrollment was 121. "We are prepared to take 130 boys," Mr. Dave said, "which is now the physical limit of our buildings and equipment."

Though badly needed, construction of the new school building had not begun when the board held a special meeting on May 3, 1940 (about the same time that Nazi Germany was overwhelming France). Mr. Dave again outlined the dire need for a new school building. He described the present one as "inadequate, a fire trap, one which would safely accommodate only eighty pupils." Plans for the proposed new building, already approved by the North Carolina Department of Education and the Southern Secondary School Association, would accommodate 150 boys, permitting some expansion of the student body. In case of expansion, the task would be to reconcile this number with other facilities–gymnasium, dormitories, dining hall, and chapel.

In July the board held its regular meeting, reiterating its desire that work on the school building should begin as soon as practicable and electing William M. Redwood to the board to replace the late Reginald Howland. At this meeting Mrs. Wetmore announced her intention to resign from the board, but she was dissuaded because of some changes such a resignation would make in the school's legal status.[9] What she did say was that the school was now on a firm foundation, which made it unnecessary in the future for her to make appeals for contributions to running expenses. Mr. Dave's financial report for the year showed an operating deficit of $4,911.45 without including revenue from the farm and other income sources. These additions brought the deficit for the year down to $8.08. The board expressed its continued confidence in the headmaster by raising his salary to $250 per month, beginning September 1. Ever mindful of the severe burden Fr. Harris

[9]"I am glad to report that owing to the efficient management of the Headmaster, it will not be necessary that appeals should be made for contributions to running expenses.

"Christ School will (like all educational institutions) need buildings, improved equipment, and endowed scholarships . . . .We have friends who would wish to continue giving to these objects and I hope to keep in close touch with them.

"It is a joy that Christ School has never had one cent of debt, but the cause of our greatest thankfulness is that through all the years the aim of the school has been to make known to all who come here the Living Christ, ever present, to love, to serve, to imitate Him, through the power and beauty of the Church He has given–that Christ may be all and in all.'"

carried as Rector/Headmaster, the board urged Mr. Dave to delegate duties as he saw fit.

It was about this time that Mr. Dave was confronted with what is currently called "career advancement." The board was apparently unaware of this opportunity and this did not figure into his modest salary increase. About 1940, according to his sister, Mr. Dave received an offer to become headmaster of Kent School. The temptation to take it could have been overwhelming. He had attended Kent (as had his brothers), was a prefect and football player, and was especially beloved by Fr. Frederick Sill, the founding headmaster. For many years the two men wrote each other, with Mr. Dave frequently seeking advice on some concerns. "I had no conversations with Dave on this matter," said Mrs. Thomson, "but I don't think he hesitated very long in turning it down. Christ School was his and Kent was somebody else's. Fr. Sill loved Mr. Dave and would have done anything to get him back there any time he could."[10]

Betty Grable was standard fare in 1939,even in a Christ School Dorm decorated in spartan simplicity.

[10]Mrs. Dave (the former Elizabeth Merrimon of Asheville) brought a practical balance into Mr. Dave's life and many credit her with "taming the temper of his youth." She also kept it straight that Christ School was a separate entity. From time to time, she could be heard gently admonishing him with the words, "Remember, Dave, you are only an employee."

24

Urq Builds A Choir

Before Urquhart Chinn's arrival, many people contributed to the development of the Christ School Chapel choir which served the entire mission community. The first choir, according to Fessor, was started by Susannah Wetmore, who was a very accomplished musician. Vestments were worn for the first time at the sunrise Easter communion introduced by Fr. Harris in 1908. They processed in vestments made for them by the Girls Friendly Society and other women's groups from materials donated by friends. Cassocks were obtained from time to time from churches, especially those in the North. The choir would not possess robes continuously until around 1939, when a friend of the school, Glenn Marston, donated vestments in memory of his wife. In addition, he provided cabinets for the sacristy. In 1948, Mr. Marston donated a set of bells which Urq played often for some years.

The make-up of the choir in those early years was quite mixed–ranging from children to adults and including families from the community as well as boarding students. After Miss Wetmore went off to college, different women took over the direction of the choir. When Fr. Harris arrived, Mother Harris became the director at different intervals. Since she did not play the organ, frequently a faculty member, nurse, or student filled the role of organist.[11] One student, Clyde Clark of Canaan, N.H., a gifted musician who could play almost any instrument, provided the accompaniment for two years. A student favorite during the period from 1918-20 was Miss Myrtle Peacock, who taught, played the organ, and directed the choir. (While Miss. Peacock was on the staff, there were two other members of the faculty who had intriguing names–David Owl and Joe Crow.) The last organist before Mr. Chinn arrived was Mrs. Sula Pearce, who was also the nurse and matron of the dining hall. Her son June was a key figure in a last minute blocked punt victory over Asheville School which enabled Christ School to go undefeated in 1933. For three years Fr. Boynton directed the school's musical efforts and spent a great

[11]Mother Harris was not a talented musician but she managed though long practice sessions to develop the kind of vigorous hymn singing Christ School students became noted for.

deal of time teaching the boys the new mass, which he introduced for the Sunday morning service, and the chanting, which was an integral part of evening worship.

Christ School has always had a choir, but not in the sense that boys, alumni, parents, and friends remember it in the years 1936-70. Until Fr. Boynton came in 1933, the service involved no singing or chanting except for the hymns. There was no Candlelight Service until 1936. What Fr. Boynton did was to entice Urquhart Chinn, a graduate of the Boston Conservatory of Music and a man who played both in churches and movie theatres, to come to Christ School and organize a leading choir which would sing anthems and the setting for the sung eucharist, a mass which Fr. Boynton wrote to celebrate his ordination. As Fr. Boynton described it, Fr. Harris was "high church without music." His voice was not strong enough to endure the strain of chanting. What Fr. Boynton claims as his greatest contribution to the school was his "bringing Urq Chinn to the campus."

December 1936 was notable on campus for two major musical events. The choir sang in public for the first time at the Candlelight Service and Mr. Chinn presented his first recital at Christ School five days earlier on Sunday afternoon, December 13. His half hour of Christmas music attracted a large group of faculty, students, and friends. His program consisted of *March of the Magi* and *Noel* by DuBois; *Reverie* by Dickinson; *Gesu Bambino* by Yon; *Hallelujah Chorus* by Handel; *Silent Night*, arranged by Harker; and *Toccata* by Boellman.

The Candlelight Service told the story of Christ through the six readings, and the choir and students sang the same story in metrical form. Neil Hurst sang two solo parts: The *First Noel* with the school as chorus and as one of the kings in *We Three Kings.* Joining him as the other two kings were Richard Goodlake and Joseph Duncan. The climax of the service came with the choir humming *Silent Night* while the rest of the students processed down the Chapel stairs carrying their lighted candles out into the darkness of the world. Other selections sung by the choir and/or the school were *Deck the Halls with Boughs of Holly*, (processional), *O Come, O Come, Emmanuel*; *O Little Town of Bethlehem*; *Lo How a Rose E'er Blooming*; *O Come All Ye Faithful*, and *Break Forth O Beautous Light.*

When Mr. Chinn reached Christ School in September 1936, the seeds which he would bring to fruition were already beginning to sprout. For one thing, Mr. Gray McAlister, a math teacher with degrees from Hampden-Sydney and Duke, organized a Glee Club in 1934 with great encouragement from Fr. Boynton. It stirred up great interest among the students and twenty-four boys joined, with the aim of presenting two concerts on campus and perhaps going on a trip. The Glee Club sang simple, traditional music and sang a couple of carols at the Candlelight Service of December 1934. The Glee Club also helped the Drama Club produce a minstrel show in December 1935, singing *Steal Away* and *Road to Mandalay* while the four endmen (John Collins, John Sammons, Tommy Suiter, and William Dorsey) drew the laughs. The Glee Club took the lead in learning the mass Fr. Boynton brought to Christ School but it did not sing as a separate group in chapel. In April 1936, the Glee Club went public, appearing on radio station WWNC in Asheville following a try-out. Eleven boys sang Stephen Foster's *Old Folks at Home* and a musical setting of Longfellow's poem *Star of the Summer Night* with Tommy Suiter's mother playing accompaniment. What served as the choir for this period in which Fr. Boynton was introducing the setting for the sung eucharist and other services was the student body. He would divide the congregation into four parts and teach them the mass. In the process, he convinced Mr. Dave of the need to have a professional choirmaster and organist to develop a first rate choir.

What Mr. Chinn found on hand when he arrived were ten boys from the Glee Club and an organ with fewer stops than there were on the foot pedals of the one he played in Boston. His first impulse was to return to Boston, but he couldn't because his car slid off the Christ School road on a rainy night and was mired axle deep in mud. He reached school at 11 p.m. and saw nothing of the campus except the old infirmary, with its big old hospital bed, a bureau and a chair, a crucifix over the bed, and a chain hanging down from the ceiling with an uncovered light bulb dangling at the end. "This was my introduction to Christ School." From that point on, everything got better over breakfast at the Boynton's and after a couple of days to settle in at the Old Dorm before the students came. He was in the two room apartment below the stairwell. In a few months he would move into the 30 Dorm, then to the apartment in the Lower 38, and finally settle in Boyd Dorm in 1950.

The high church service was no problem for it was very similar to the one Mr. Chinn played for in Boston. "Everything there was sung or chanted but incense was used only on special occasions." Those first years, the sung eucharist involved using only the Boynton Mass. By 1948, after Mr. Chinn had written a mass, the school sang the Boynton Mass from September to Advent, the Chinn Mass during Lent, and alternated the two the rest of the school year.

One of the major hurdles facing Mr. Chinn that first year was Fr. Boynton's expectation that the choir would be singing the next day. "Every week Fr. Boynton would come up to me and say, 'Well, when are you going to get the choir going?'" Mr. Chinn said. "I kept wondering if I was ever going to get a choir going at all. We had ten boys from the Glee Club and we sang in unison. I kept putting off the process of learning parts. But we practiced regularly in the infirmary and were ready to lead and to sing anthems at the Candlelight Service in December." The beauty of the process was that Mr. Chinn had the support of everyone–Mr. Dave, Fr. Boynton, the faculty, the choir members, and the student body. All were hungry for success.

How important the choir was in the scheme of things was apparent after the Easter service of 1937. The service went so beautifully that Mr. Dave declared Monday to be a holiday. (This may have been the origin of what was an uninterrupted Easter Monday holiday from 1937-70.) Fortunately for the choir, Mr. Dave had an interest in music which was matched by what Mr. Chinn described as a "wonderful tenor voice." Whenever the choir (or other groups) had a picnic, Mr. Dave would sing *Old McDonald Had a Farm* and the boys would come in with the chorus. Another favorite, which Mr. Dave sometimes accompanied with a guitar, was *I Got a Gal in Cumberland Gap*. Students who sat next to Mr. Dave in chapel remember that he sang the hymns–down through the sixth and seventh verses–without opening the hymnbook. While Mr. Dave never gave a scholarship for athletics, legend has it that he would provide one for a good soprano.

The choir grew rapidly over the ensuing years from its initial successes, limited only by space, until by the mid-1950s there were thrity or more members. Every year Mr. Chinn tried out the new students, taking them one-by-one to chapel during evening study hall to hear them sing *Silent Night*, something everyone would know. "It starts slow and you have to hit high notes," Mr. Chinn said. "For the sopranos, I'd pitch it up a little, and for the basses I'd pitch it down a little bit."

Choir rehearsals were held initially in the infirmary and then were moved to the loft of the 38 Dorm, a space built specifically as a place for the choir to practice. Mr. Chinn's practice sessions were both fun and serious, and the boys quickly learned when he was joking and when he meant for them to get down to business. The most enjoyable moments came when he wanted to loosen up the group, and he would play barroom music with which he used to accompany silent movies. When he was serious, and you weren't, it was a good idea to avoid his shoes, which were pointed like the prow of a ship. Though no blood clots were ever reported, a good crack on the shins made many youthful singers sit up and take notice. Mr. Chinn recalled one such incident involving David Harris, Jr., who, at the time, was too young to attend Christ School but was a member of the choir.

> Maybe I shouldn't say this, but I remember David at rehearsal one day messing around some. Unfortunately for him, he was sitting right next to the piano. I moved my foot quickly

sideways and kicked him on his shin. He didn't show up for the next rehearsal, his feelings hurt more than his shin. I think he stayed out one week; then he came back and was one of the leaders of the soprano section for the next two years.

Those pointed shoes, by the way, were not designed as instruments of correction. Rather they enabled an organist to maintain better control over the pedals. "Actually," Mr. Chinn said, "the kicking wasn't that bad. It became a kind of game."

Until the 1950s the choir was limited in size to about twenty members who sat in the first four pews of the chapel next to the organ pipes and the console. When the organ was renovated in 1949, the console was moved to a position directly opposite the pipes and another pew was added for choir members. As the school grew to 150 students, additional pews, given in memory of Mr. Reginald Howland, were placed on the landing leading to the altar and this arrangement (coupled with a few chairs) accommodated thirty members. Thanks to the Howland family and the Marstons, the choir was properly robed and provided with sufficient funds to create a sizeable inventory of music, enabling them after World War II to represent the school on many trips. Actually, the first trip, as Mr.Chinn recalls it, was to Calvary Church in Fletcher before the choir owned any vestments. "Since we didn't have any of our own, the boys put on the vestments worn by the choir members at Calvary."

After World War II, the chapel service attracted numerous parents, visitors, and alumni–both at evensong but especially at the Sunday sung eucharist. It was soon necessary at Easter, Christmas, and other times, to place chairs down the aisle to accommodate everybody, even when the enrollment was only about 130 students. "It was not long before we had to tell the boys not to invite their girls to the Candlelight Service," Mr. Chinn said. As time passed, the Chapel was decorated by the students in evergreen and the only lighting was provided by racks of candles sitting in the windows and hanging overhead. The creche, which someone donated to the school, was quite expensive and stood in the corner out from the organ pipes.[12] Originally a small electric light bulb provided a rather bright glare for the manager. In 1948, Fr. Rossmaessler made a little square lantern and used pieces of tissue paper for the windows. Inside was a light bulb. He hung it on the arm of one of the shepherds and this provided a warm glow over the Baby Jesus. One tradition, the choir's humming of *Silent Night*, was an improvisation rather than the result of design. After the candles were lit, the choir sang *Silent Night* while the congregation marched silently out into the darkness. "When the choir completed the three verses," Mr. Chinn said, "the Chapel was only half

[12]One of the oldest decorations in the Chapel, the creche with its plaster of Paris figures, was given to the school in memory of Eleanor Heckscler, who died at the age of two. In the 1980's, it was allowed to get wet in the basement of the chapel and it disintegrated.

empty and it was now too dark for the choir members to read the words in the hymnbook. Searching for a solution, I whispered to them, 'Hum!' This humming was so effective, we carried it on." There was one thing about the Candlelight Service which Mr. Chinn refused to let anyone touch. "Because of the beauty–even the awe and majesty–of the service, I thwarted any efforts to introduce anyone other than the chaplains to read the scriptural lessons. Their well-trained voices brought greater solemnity to the service."

Fr. Charles F. Boynton brought many gifts to Christ School during the period 1933-39, but many feel his greatest was the inspirational lift he gave to the campus, including developing a service which became the school's most memorable tradition.

VI: 1940-1945

Keeping The School Afloat

The wartime years (1940-45) presented special problems and tested the headmaster's leadership qualities in many ways heretofore untried. He always met the challenge–with amazing success. With the war came wartime controls–rationing of food and fuel, which not only affected a boy's stomach but greatly curtailed his mobility. It was a period in which morale became the critical factor as there was little opportunity for one to leave campus or even to be visited by parents or friends. Gas rationing greatly limited travel as did Japanese seizure of the rubber plantations in the Dutch East Indies. Those throngs of alumni and parents who were attending Thanksgiving dinner and the Candlelight and Easter services and graduation suddenly dwindled into a handful. Choir trips were dramatically curtailed and dances were sharply reduced in number from what the boys considered too few to almost none. In many ways many of the boys felt shut-off from the world (and they were) and they were restless about a war in which they were going to be involved and their energies sometimes turned toward outlets which were previously considered unsavory by most.

The war years tested Mr. Dave's managerial skill. Rationing, shortages, inflation were the big enemies. Keeping the school afloat financially on a shoestring budget was a major problem. Despite the obstacles, Mr. Dave kept the school in the black for most of those years, with cash carryovers ranging from $1,905 to $7,054 on income that ranged from $52,860 to slightly over $70,000. To make balancing the books even more difficult, he was providing $6,000 a year or more in scholarship aid, the equivalent of ten to fifteen full scholarship in a student body whose enrollment averaged around 130, with the exception of 142 in 1942 and an average of 119 in 1943. Inflation was a continuous problem. The average cost of maintaining a student in 1940 was $305. This increased to $512 six years later. During the same period, tuition (room and board) rose from $350 to $500. But even here, parents of students already in school could continue to pay the lower tuition figure if they so desired.

Feeding a school full of boys requires ingenuity in the best of times. When the war began about eighteen percent of the school's budget went into the dining hall, compared to about sixteen percent which went into faculty salaries. As is obvious, room and board was a hefty part of faculty remuneration. To deal with growing food shortages and rising farm prices, Mr. Dave put the school into the farming business. By producing more meat, dairy products, poultry, eggs, and food crops, he reduced the cost of feeding the students to a per pupil average of twelve cents a meal. The one year's exception was 1942, when this average abruptly shot up to twenty cents per meal. Dairy production skyrocketed under better management of a professional herdsman. Other improvements included better breeding of the Holstein herd, increasing production of cattle, pigs, and chickens, and bringing more land under cultivation. Mr. Dave's 1943 farm report to the board was rather typical of this period. The cost per meal per student had dropped back to twelve cents at a time when the cost of maintaining each student rose twenty percent. What warded off serious belt-tightening in the dining hall was a farm operation which provided all the school's flour, potatoes, chickens, and eggs for a six month period beginning in December 1942. Based on the December commodity price index in 1942, the farm provided the dining hall some $10,853 in produce, or about sixty percent of the cost of operating the dining hall. The list of produce was impressive: 16,200 gallons of fresh milk, 4,800 pounds of beef, 4,500 pounds of pork, 5,000 pounds of veal, 1,030 pounds of poultry (hens and fryers), 265 bushels of wheat for flour, 250 pounds of Irish potatoes, and 420 pounds of butter. The increased dairy operation, which was to continue into the 1960s, meant an endless supply of cold pitchers of milk three times a day.

Although the students were not on campus for the summer planting and growing season, they became a part of the process at harvest time in the fall. Harcourt Waters '43, who was to have a fine career on the Tulane University tennis team, captured the general tenor of this farm labor in the November 15, 1942, issue of the *Christ School News*, of which he was the chief editor.

> Due to the shortage of labor, Christ School is now offering a course in agriculture with special emphasis on harvesting. It proved itself very popular, especially with members of the Alpha Sigma Sigma (worklist). Also there were a surprising number of boys who "volunteered" for the course. So far most of the work has been done on field trips, which were made to the corn fields, the potato field, and the hay field. Although a few of the boys were old hands at harvesting, most of them were "city slickers" (or "country squires") who didn't know the difference between a

corn knife and a pitchfork. But under the guidance of Charley and Laz they soon acquired the knack of handling these tools and in a short while felt right at home in a corner hay field. In fact, working in a cornfield actually made Bob Berkeley homesick. He said the cornstalks reminded him so much of the weeds in his victory garden back home in Detroit.

In the spring of 1943, Mr. Dave outlined for the students his intention of expanding the farm program even further the next school year. In the planning was the growing of more vegetable crops to serve in the dining hall that fall. On the upper field behind the old sawmill (an area rich from silt that had built up for years in the Wetmore Pond), he was going to plant four acres of potatoes. In this same field would be smaller plantings of carrots, beets, cabbage, and onions–all crops that could be kept in storage.

Down on the lower farm, Laz Allen would be planting ten acres of silo corn to feed the growing dairy and beef herd, ten acres of feed corn (for the pigs, chickens) thirty acres of soy beans, ten acres of oats, two acres of cane, one acre of sunflowers, and ten acres of lespedeza. When talking about the farm, Mr. Dave's enthusiasm sometimes produced a rhetoric that exceeded reality. He enjoyed the farm operation if for no other reason than it meant more farm equipment–tractors and planters and other machinery which he dearly loved. In addition, he planned to add 200 chickens to the 350 the school already had. Not all of the above plantings came about that summer but there were many acres of corn and other silage crops for the boys to cut and store in the silo.

By 1943, a critical shortage of farm labor had developed everywhere because the draft was taking every man available, even into the forty age bracket. Such a farming program would require labor, a problem which was solved when a few students volunteered to remain at Christ School during the summer. They worked six or eight hours a day, lived in the dorm, and, according to Hugh Brown, '46, the major excitement was downing an Orange Crush at Mr. Shuford's service station in Arden. One monumental failure was the four acre sweet potato crop. After the slips were planted, the area was struck by a long, hot, humid drought. Those sweet potatoes begged for water and the farm-hands trooped to the creek and lugged countless buckets of water, sloshing each sweet potato plant with a can full. Since sweet potatoes were a big item on the menu during the war, the student body probably applauded that crop failure. But, unfortunately, Julius, the cook, rose to the occasion and grew his biggest sweet potato crop ever at his farm in Lake Lure. He profited by generously selling those sweet potatoes to Mr. Dave. Those boys who spent a wonderful summer here also remember the pay checks which kept down too much nightlife. The younger boys in the group were paid $3 a week while the older ones got $5.[1]

Throughout the early years, both Fr. Harris and Mr. Dave planted gardens at various places about the campus, but in the 1930's the garden was located in an area now roughly occupied by the Susan Wetmore School Building. The Alden brothers also used the garden and beautified the area with prize-winning dahlias and other flowers which they planted about the campus. During the war, victory gardens began to sprout up in new locations since the school building obliterated the previous site. Mr. Dave planted one behind the infirmary and another one over at Wetmore Hill. Fessor and Mr. Peoples, a wartime Latin teacher, put their vegetables in a plot near the dairy. Fr. Webbe raised his crops behind the Little Rectory. In addition to gardening, Fr. Webbe also purchased some chickens for eggs and eating. Those faculty who lived on campus during the summer (and not many did before the 1940's) enjoyed some nice perks. Grain was stored in the old gymnasium; faculty could have it ground into flour to make bread. The cows kept giving during the summer, and, with the boys home on vacation, this meant plenty of milk, cream, and butter. Home-made ice cream and steak were a summer's dividend.

Whatever farm chores the boys were engaged in came early in the fall, with the seniors sometimes returning a week early to help put the campus in order, to haul coal from Arden, and to help both school and neighbors with their harvesting. While the older boys would miss some class time helping gather hay and cutting corn for storing in silos, the smaller ones would in the afternoon harvest the potato crop, storing the potatoes in the dark room under the basement, which also housed apples, cabbage, and other root crops. Hungry boys were not above slipping into the basement storage bin to grab a potato to eat raw or take into the woods to cook. Over a period of time thousands of yellow jackets swarmed around the same spot and boys working around the kitchen were likely to be attacked. Perhaps the most disagreeable farm job belonged to those who stood inside and packed the silage as it was shot into the silo. Even a long bath would not quell the itching for days to come. Among the neighbors whom the students assisted were Mr. Baldwin (whose son Tommy attended Christ School), Mr. Holt (whose father had been on the Christ School board), Mr. Sigman, and Mr. Anderson, whose daughter was to teach French here for several years. There was a great deal of wartime sharing; the school allowed neighbors to use its trucks along with the student labor. Mr. Sigman, who always insisted on paying the students the prevailing wage for their help, also fed them a farm meal–fried chicken, mashed potatoes (which were real), beans, corn dumplings, hot rolls, and ice cold milk. With a reward like that, who complained about war.

[1]Besides Hugh Brown, the other workers were Joe McCullough, Stewart (Ooee) Walker, J.C. McDuffie, Buck Brittle, Fulton Norvell, and David McCullough.

VI: 1940-1945

26

Keeping Up Morale

Keeping up morale. That was the number one concern of everyone at Christ School during the war years. The excitement, the uncertainty, the urgency all had a way of distracting students from their primary purpose–getting a good education. Keeping up morale was a thankless task and one saw more lines creep into Mr. Dave's face during this period than at any other time.

Helping to create this instability was the constant turnover of faculty members and the loss of several excellent teachers to the draft. Zach Alden, Lee Bethurum, and Charlie Hurst were the first to go. All three were bright teachers and knowing in the ways of Christ School. During the three-year stretch from 1942-45, a dozen new names appeared on the faculty mail boxes. Half of them were sixty-five or older, doing their part for the country by leaving retirement for the classroom. Not all were wise in what it was like to live in a boys school and some found their life here hard and of short duration. Certainly meanness–not of the heart but from an inability to control that part of adolescence which must probe and shove until something hurts–sent several teachers packing. For that we all bear shame.

The credentials of the teachers then were impeccable: Frank Read (Hobart), Dr. Willis Parker (Harvard), Josef Nelson (a man who knew fourteen ancient and modern languages and could sight read nine of them), James A. Peoples (Vanderbilt), Dr. Stephen Huntley (Ph.D., Toulouse), Fr. Ralph Webster (Hobart, General Theological Seminary), Jim Darsie (Hiram), Clyde Joyce (Memphis State), E. Huling Woodworth (Amherst, retired Chase National bank executive), Sam Hill (Georgia), and Jim Heinold (Penn State). Academics did not suffer from a lack of good minds. And the prefects found the Coffee Room sessions to be full of intellectual zing.[2] Of these teachers, a few were to remain here to establish a name. Frank Read would leave in 1950 to go to the Harvard School in Hollywood where he was seen attending the horse races with

[2]Mr. Dave never had faculty meetings. Whatever he wanted made known came out of coffee after lunch, when the teachers would gather in the 38 Dorm (later St. Thomas Hall) for demitasse.

Lana Turner in arm. Fr. Ralph Webster, who spent a year here before going to Puerto Rico to start a mission boarding school, returned to Christ School to be chaplain from 1950-63 and then moved on to be headmaster of an Episcopal church school in Baton Rouge, La. Jim Darsie taught math in Classroom 3 for nearly thirty years. And Jim Hein old taught here during two stints, leaving a soccer legacy in a sport he organized here.

In January 1943, Mr. Dave made a mistake. He inadvertently exacerbated the morale problem. Enrollment in September began with a capacity 131. By the end of the year the number of students dropped perilously close to the hundred mark, with an average of 119 on campus for both semesters. This serious drop in enrollment tortured the budget and placed the well-being of the school in jeopardy. There were several reasons for this precipitate decline. The draft took several of the older students; some seniors dropped out along the way to enter college; several boys were sent home for misconduct; and a couple ran away. By Christmas, Mr. Dave closed the Fifth and Sixth cottages, sending the remaining occupants to other dormitories. Four seniors moved into the two basement rooms located in the 38 Dorm.

To fill these cottages and to generate more revenue, Mr. Dave agreed to house a group of twenty naval cadets who were to be trained at the Old Airport, since the Navy had been unable to find suitable housing elsewhere in the area. These cadets ate their meals in the dining hall with the rest of the students but at separate tables. They did their own crumbing. Mr. Dave was in charge of inspecting their quarters. The cadets drove back and forth to the airport several times a day in two station wagons to receive flying and ground instructions.

Their presence created untold morale problems on campus. What Mr. Dave was unaware of at the time, or lightly dismissed, was that these were cadets who had been washed out of one or two other programs, mainly because of disciplinary reasons. This training at the Old Airport was their last chance to get a commission. Failure this time meant a hitch in the navy as third class seamen.

What these cadets brought with them were their gripes, bitterness, and bile which quickly infected a senior class already restive as a result of the changes and uncertainty brought into their lives by the war. The senior class became deeply divided, some listening to the voices of the cadets and other heeding their own senior leadership which underwent drastic changes during the year. Of the four seniors named prefects in May, only one (Allen Johnson) remained in authority at the end of the year. One prefect did not return in the fall but chose to enter college; another, the replacement for the one who didn't return, was drafted into the army after Christmas; and two others resigned (one of them not returning to school in January). In February, Mr. Dave attempted to pull the senior class together by creating a senior council (all sixth formers) which would meet each Wednesday night to deal with school affairs. This effort proved futile when the seniors elected as one of their leaders a student whose record was pock-marked with second chances and who was strongly influenced by the cadets. Students like lots of praise, whether they deserve it or squirm in disbelief at hearing what they don't deserve. Mr. Dave was not a leader who was given much to public praise. You knew when you were doing your part: it might show in the corner of his eyes, in a memorable moment when he joked around with you on the worklist, or when he took time in class to discuss his dreams for Christ School or world politics. When the 1943 school year came to an end, with its division and brooding belonging to yesterday, Mr. Dave made his feelings clear when he awarded the Headmaster's Cup to Allen Johnson. "He is the best prefect Christ School has ever had." Certainly no one present would deny that Allen held steadfast in a year of daily crises.[3]

In an editorial entitled "A Year to Remember," *The Christ School News* in April 1943 tried to provide some perspective on what had happened. It called 1943 a year of "unusual changes" and suggested that only the future could tell whether it was a success or not. The article cited some of the major changes:

1. Students working in shifts on the fall harvest.
2. Four new masters (replacing several drafted).
3. Three boys were drafted; another left to join the Marines.
4. Some seniors dropped out to enter college.
5. Government cancelled interscholastic athletic competition after Christmas.
6. Student government shake-ups: prefect turnover.
7. Quartering of naval cadets on campus.
8. Senior Council formed.

These were changes which enhanced the natural restlessness created by the war. None of these were to have lasting impact on the school, since most would disappear as war turned to peace. The editorial listed several other changes, two of which would later become part of the fabric of school life. For one thing, room study was granted to honor roll students. In years past, such privilege was granted to seniors (sometime on a selective basis, sometimes as a group) but it was taken back when abused. This reward for academic achievement was to continue in the future and some time in the 1960's was extended automatically to all seniors, ostensibly to help them prepare for college by assuming responsibility for meeting their academic preparation. The faculty was not unanimous on this extension, and all agreed that failing grades must be given to nudge any of the wayward back

[3]Strangely enough, under normal circumstances Allen would not have been at Christ School in 1942-43. His twin brother graduated in June 1942 and went into the navy. Allen heeded advice to continue in school for another year to strengthen his work in math.

into reality. Another change involved discontinuing Chapel services on Monday night. With transportation uncertain at best, this provided a few more minutes for boys to get back to assembly on time. In 1950 this practice became permanent to allow the Chaplain to have a family night at home. Two other adjustments did not become permanently attached. One was the change in the daily schedule. The previous year breakfast was served (sit-down for all) at 6:45 a.m. and classes began at eight. Because Congress had enacted double daylight savings to provide more light at night, breakfast was moved to 7:45 a.m. and classes began at nine. There was a slight change in the supervised study hall and extra-curricular periods that followed lunch: attendance at both became mandatory. Then what proved to be a one year change involved Christmas vacation, a decision in which Mr. Dave gave both parents and students an opportunity to consider. Christmas vacation was extended to a month and Spring vacation was reduced to a week-end. This decision saved the use of hard-to-get-coal to heat the campus and it cut down on the expense and crowdedness of train travel in the spring at a time when military personnel were sent by train. Early in 1941, Mr. Dave sought permission of all the parents in a letter asking their consent to move commencement back a week. His daughter would be graduating from Chatham Hall and he wished to be there for the occasion. This letter went out early in the fall to allow parents to arrange their travel plans and to point out that the days lost would be made up during the winter.

The Grandstand, attached to the Old Gym, was where juniors and seniors would go to smoke their pipes. This 1944 scene was typical.

VI: 1940-1945

27

Physical Fitness

One thing which came to the campus in 1942-43 whether the students liked it or not (and few really did until later) was a new vigor in regard to physical fitness. In September the United States had been in World War II for nine months and victory was nowhere in sight. Mr. Dave and Fessor (thinking of our interest when we didn't know what our interest was) decided that Christ School boys were going to be thoroughly prepared for the rigors of military life. It seemed unlikely in 1942 that anyone would escape the armed forces but even those who were not physically qualified to serve could be made more physically fit. The result of his summertime conniving was the introduction to all students of an obstacle course and steeplechase equal to that found at Parris Island. Later on some basic military drill was added for upperclassmen. Such drill would prove beneficial to many graduates when they found themselves in basic training with recruits who turned left at the command "right." Also Mr. Dave reinstituted calisthenics about this time, with students assembling on the terrace in front of the First Cottage and doing, among other things, that killer exercise known as the Russian Dance. As a sidelight, early morning communion attendance began to spiral during this period to a point where it was reported that fifty-three students squeezed into the Little Chapel at one service. Attendance at early morning communion was the only excuse for missing the predawn exercise. Fessor, who routinely went to early morning service three or four days a week, reportedly stopped attending communion for a time because of the "bad company."

That obstacle course, designed in a military training manual but modified by Mr. Dave and Fessor to fit the Christ School terrain, circled the athletic field and boggled the mind. About twenty-five obstacles like those seen at similar courses on military bases stretched over a quarter of a mile and were run by brats and seniors alike. No one knew when the war would end and everyone would learn how important it was to be in condition. Included in the grand design were a board walk, a ladder, a solid wall for scaling, a maze, a remnant of the claim bank to scale in the southeast corner, numerous hurdles of varying sizes, and a small draining culvert running under the road which you had to crawl through. (What excitement was generated when a boy of hefty size became lodged in the culvert.)

Students ran the obstacle course every day before going to afternoon athletic or recreational activities. Once a week the boys ran the course against time and a record was established by Stewart (Ooee) Walker of Charleston, who did it in one minute and fifty seconds. His nearest rivals – Allen Johnson and Harcourt Waters– required eight more seconds. The average time of the student body in the spring was two minutes and nineteen seconds. Some forty-eight boys ran the course in below average time. In general, speed in running was not as important as speed in getting over the obstacles. An article in the *Christ School News* put the whole matter in a humorous vein: "The scaling wall and the higher hurdles present difficulties for the smaller boys. However, Doc Cree has found a way of overcoming the difficult obstacles. He just goes around them." Before the end of the year, the 530 yard course had been strengthened with five or six more obstacles including a monkey swing, parallel bars and an inverted "V" ten feet high (you ran up the boards on one side and climbed down the logs on the other.) Two weeks before graduation, Walker again set the record for the extended course, running it in 2:19. Following him were David Kimberly, Bill Towne, Lon West, and Allen Johnson.

Thursdays became a monster shape-up day. When Fessor blew the whistle, all students turned out on the athletic field for the only extra-curricular activity scheduled that seventh period: a field day. The students were divided into groups of smaller and larger boys. First came calisthenics. Then came special activities for each group with plenty of competitive relays. At first, the period ended each Thursday with a timed run over the obstacle course. Later in the year, the Thursday run over the obstacle course was replaced by running the steeplechase course which extended about three miles across school property. It led off from the south edge of the ball field down to and across Wetmore Hill and then wound around, ending up at the back of the headmaster's house. Many obstacles dotted the course including a hollow log to crawl through, another log ten feet above the ground which you crossed over like a raccoon or walked on, and a tree you had to climb to reach a wire walkway across the creek as well as a rope swing. Bob Berkeley was the first to fall into the creek and Hank Lathrop had the honor of being the first unable to let go of the rope while swinging across the creek. In time, everyone become commando proficient.

In addition to the regular running of the obstacle course and the steeplechase, students had to pass a physical fitness standard. That program included a six-mile hike, a mile run, chins, push-ups, hundred yard dash, clearing hurdles, and many other agility feats. Boxing matches were staged in the Old Gym almost every Saturday night, providing exciting entertainment for the onlookers and an opportunity for perfomers to display their stamina and strength and, sometimes, ability to keep out of range.

And then there was the case of Joe McCullough. He graduated in 1942 and returned to the campus in February 1943 after completing a semester at The Citadel, where he played freshman football. He was waiting a call to the Air Force and it turned out to be a nine months wait. Some of his attention was directed toward Betsy Harris, who had graduated from Chatham Hall and was working in the office and Jigger Shop at Christ School. Joe's presence was an unfair advantage to about half of the Classes of 1940 and 1941 who had or were writing Betsy. The problem for Mr. Dave was to find something for Joe to do. His energy was turned into other directions. In February 1943, compulsory military drill was introduced into the physical fitness program and Joe was named to direct it with several seniors chosen as lieutenants. Rudiments of military discipline and simple formations were taught on the football field every day, with three forms drilling on alternate days. Each instruction period lasted about an hour. The February issue of the *Christ School News* seemed to take a good natured approach to this training:

> Attention! Forward March! These were a few of the commands given by General Joe McCullough to the newly formed Christ School Commandos in their first drill session. Before the first instruction, Fessor gave a brief talk on the importance of military training and discipline. Then Fessor showed the class some of the elementary movements used by the "leather pushers." After practicing these maneuvers for a while, the regiment marched around the ball field several times. At long last, with all ceremony, the Commandos were dismissed by Lt. Harcourt Waters. After the drill Buck Private Bob Berkeley declared that his legs got so mixed up he felt like a corkscrew, and Yardbird George McAden decided to transfer to the Navy.

Even in April, as the *News* looked back to eight weeks of such training, it was noted that the Commandos had not yet become a precision drill team. "It seems that a few boys liked Alex Harris and Pee Dab Kendrick still don't know their left foot from their right hand."

Bishop M. George Henry confirms students at a service in the Chapel on Easter evening.

The 1944-45 Faculty, first row: (left to right) Jim Darsie, Fessor, Mr. Dave, and Frank Read. Second row: Edward Kennedy, Jim Heinold, Dr. Stephen Huntley, Fr. Webbe, E. Huling Woodworth, and Urq Chinn.

VI: 1940-1945

28

Doing Their Part

It was no minor miracle that Mr. Dave kept Christ School afloat during World War II. He was confronted by declining enrollment, a growing restlessness on the parts of students whose minds were more on foxholes than studies, and the finding of qualified teachers to replace those who were being drafted into the armed forces. As head of the Buncombe County draft board, Mr. Dave showed favor to no one, and in the process several of Christ School's best teachers were shunted off to war. As younger men were being drafted into the service, the school found itself with older replacements, many coming out of retirement as a sense of duty to help schools in need. All were experienced and knowledgeable (sometimes too knowledgeable) but some were in their 70s and 80s and not fully aware of the eccentricities and strains of a boys boarding school. Despite the constant turnover, the school's academic achievement remained high.

What the war did was challenge Mr. Dave every moment in his search for teachers. "The war days were the worst," said Urq Chinn, "because Mr. Dave never knew whom he was going to get." While looking, Mr. Dave taught everything from science to math to Latin and other teachers found themselves equally flexible. One of the more interesting and scholarly was Dr. Nelson, who was hovering around eighty and could speak about a dozen languages. He came from Puerto Rico and was reading the Koran in Arabic when he arrived on campus. He taught French and Spanish. With his mind a dozen floors above that of the boys, they were frequently able to lead him astray. For instance when the boys entered the French class, they would protest that it was Spanish or Latin and sidetrack him for that day. Another boy used to climb and swing on the hot water pipe every morning and Dr. Nelson, who had a difficult time remembering their names, would call out the name of a boy and give him a worklist. For about three months, the wrong boys kept reporting to the worklist every afternoon.

Another of the older teachers, every inch a scholar, was Dr. Parker, a graduate of Eureka College. (Besides Ronald Reagan, what other Eureka graduates come quickly to mind?) He taught both history and biology–his field was history–and his lectures sometimes belonged in the classroom at the University of Chicago. He lived in Asheville with his wife and undertook this assignment as "duty to his country in wartime."

For some years, Christ School had volatile Latin teachers. The wartime presence of Mr. Peoples was no exception. He thundered Latin as though talking through a megaphone and had many years earlier been headmaster at one of Christ School's major athletic rivals in the area–Bingham Military Academy. Whenever students wanted to shift the topic from Latin (a self-defense mechanism), they merely had to utter two words and Mt. Vesuvius exploded. One of those words was "*Time*" (a magazine which drew instant wrath) and "Lincoln" (whose tenure in office was as acceptable to Mr. Peoples as *Birth of a Nation* is to the NAACP). Although in his late seventies, Mr. Peoples spoke and walked with a vigor that shamed people decades younger. It was as a prefect that I got to know Mr. Peoples and to be made aware that Mr. Dave did have a foible or two. One day, near the end of February, Mr. Dave came up to me and handed me a crumpled piece of paper, saying "Give it to Mr. Peoples." Innocently I carried out the task, learning in the process that it was Mr. Peoples's pay check that The Man had been carrying in his pocket for a month. I sustained the pent-up wrath.

When I returned to Christ School to teach, I experienced that same situation first hand. The first year I taught, I did not get paid until well into November (a salary that was $200 a month). After the first month, I said to myself, "Well, I guess we just get room and board." We had never talked salary and I didn't think any more about it. Another month passed. Finally in mid-November, Mr. Dave came up and put his hand in his pocket and pulled out two crumpled checks. It was not long after this that Mrs. Dave started putting checks, sealed in envelopes, in the faculty mailboxes.

Several more of the characters included the Hungry Indian (by whom boys in the 30 Dorm were fascinated), Rejoice (Mr. Joyce was his Christian name), E. Huling Woodworth (a retired New Yorker who tried his hand at sociology and economics), and Sam Hill ("What the Sam Hill is wrong with you!"). Mr. Hill, whose expensive wardrobe would have put Brooks Brothers to shame, arrived on the campus from Georgia in an open air Model-T, which he couldn't drive. His assignment was to teach Latin. He lived in the north apartment in the 30 Dorm but didn't return after Christmas, writing that he "loved the school but that the dorm was too cold." With coal in short supply and whatever heat was available usually dissipating in the 38 Dorm before it reached the 30 Dorm his apartment was frigid. But he was a nice man whom the boys liked very much.

One Monday, a group of six football players wanted to go to Hendersonville to see Waynesville make up a postponed game. The

Mountaineers were to be the next Greenie foe. The problem was how to get there at a time when gas was still rationed and transportation was almost nil. One of the boys found out that Sam Hill wanted to go to Asheville (he had not been there since school started in mid-September). The boy immediately offered to drive him to Asheville with a few friends coming along. The six of us piled into the Model-T, surrounding and cheering Sam Hill in the middle. We had a great time at the game and Sam Hill had a fine time walking around in what he thought was Asheville.

Another teacher adding color to the campus was Doc Mobley, who arrived in 1941 with a trunk like the one Pew carried in *Treasure Island*, requiring a boy on each corner to carry it upstairs to his room in the Old Dorm. The first few weeks, Mobley couldn't adjust to the fact that Saturday was a regular school day and each Friday night he roared off campus in his car to return early Monday morning for classes. In the spring of 1984, I saw a man standing alone in the Christ School library, just staring at the portrait of Mr. Dave. I stood quietly behind him. He stared at the face for three or four minutes. Then he turned around and saw me. He didn't recognize me but he said, the corners of his eyes moist, "That was a great man." At this time, Mobley was superintendent of schools in Walterboro, S.C.

This is where Christ School football players took their first steps in learning to block.

Candlelight Service

CHRIST SCHOOL CHAPEL

DECEMBER 13, 1944, 8:00 P. M.

Order of Service

Processional—"Glory be to God"—Choir

Prayer

First Reading

Hymn 66—"O Come, O Come, Immanuel"—School

Prayer

Carol—"There was a Rosebud"—Choir

Second Reading

Hymn 551—"The First Noel"—School

Prayer

Carol—"While by my Sheep"—Choir

Third Reading

Hymn 78—"O Little Town of Bethlehem"—School

Prayer

Carol—"Sleep, Holy Babe"—Choir

Fourth Reading

Hymn 554—"We Three Kings"—School

Prayer

Carol—"Slumber Song"—Choir

Fifth Reading

Hymn 72—"O Come All Ye Faithful"—School

Prayer

Chorale—"Break Forth"—Choir

Sixth Reading

Carol—"Silent Night, Holy Night"—Choir

Closing Prayer and Benediction

The Choir

SOPRANOS—Baber, Campbell, Crocker, Farr, Haywood, Holton, Kennedy, Lathrop, J., Legg, Moore, B., Newton, Norris, Osborne, Paschal, Peyton, Pickelsimer, Russell, Staton, Vaughan.

ALTOS—Belk, Crisp, Kimberly, J., Montgomery, W., Rockwell, Smith, R.

TENORS—Fayssoux, Meekins, Seitz, Shannon.

BASSES—Brown, H., Hutson, Mitchell, Norvell.

Candlelight Service Program 1944

VI: 1940-1945

Entertainment

Despite wartime restrictions that drastically curtailed trips to town on Monday, life at school was far from dull because the students became more actively involved in whatever opportunities presented themselves. Anything which some group did became the property of everyone, whether you were a participant or simply enjoyed talking about it. More often than not, the real excitement lay not so much in the event but in the preparation and anticipation that preceded it and the bull sessions that followed. The Prince Albert cloud of smoke at the Frat House or the Grandstand did not inhibit post-mortems.

Most of the students were caught up in the extracurricular activities. After a year's lapse (following Mr. Zach's being drafted into the army,) Fr. Ralph Webster brought the Drama Club back to life and it had a new stage in the study hall to work on, a new lighting system, and the strong encouragement of Miss Betsy Harris, who was working at the school then in several capacities–including general cheerleader. In December, the Drama Club presented two one-act plays, with Fred Pearce starring as "Gas" in *Gassed*, and John McCrary playing the lead in *Dress Rehersal.* Frank Bryson was the enraged director who was driven to madness by the ineptness of his cast. Among those bumblers who claimed that they were "just being themselves" were Henry Grady, Milt Borman, Jack Davis, and Henry Mitchell. The Broadway production came in April when a cast of eleven appeared in a three-act melodrama, *Eleven Against the Sea.* Things became rather harried for Fr. Webster when the number two lead ran away two days before opening night, but the part was learned quickly by another actor.

Given the wartime circumstances, relationships between Christ School and the Fassifern School for Girls in Hendersonville became cozy. In 1943-44, the two schools exchanged dances and parties on at least six occasions. Much work and planning went into each by student and faculty alike, and much energy was put into making them eventful evenings. In early October, the boys arrived at Fassifern in the school truck which had been used to haul coal earlier that afternoon. A broom made the truck ship-shape. If anyone felt embarrassed about this mode of transportation as he competed with rivals from Hendersonville and Blue Ridge School for a girl's attention, he didn't show it. Mr. Dave drove the truck to Fassifern and if Mr. Dave thought it was O.K., then there was unanimous agreement. After the dance, Mr. Dave took the seniors by a drug store for an additional treat.

A few weeks later Christ School seniors and juniors invited Fassifern over for a party held in the Rock House beyond Wetmore Hill, a house unoccupied for many years. It was swept and cleaned under the direction of Betsy Harris and the boys then white-washed the walls and scrubbed the floors. Decorations consisted of jack-o-laterns and shocks of corn. Since there was no electricity, the two connecting rooms were lit by candlelight and the glow from two fireplaces. A string band provided music and senior Bill Kirk (from the mountains of Tennessee) called a mean square dance. That was not all. Between dances, the boys and girls played several games and dunked for apples. Outside a bonfire was built and couples gathered around it to sing and tell jokes and stories.

These back-and-forth festivities continued throughout the year. In December, Fassifern had the juniors and seniors back for a party which included ping-pong, bingo, bridge, and dancing. Special entertainment was provided by a Fassifern faculty member who played the guitar and sang Negro spirituals and popular songs, with everyone joining in. The big surprise–the climax of the evening–came when a group of Christ School boys were entered in a beauty contest. When it was over, Saunders Alpaugh was crowned "Miss Fassifern."

In some ways, the entertainment exchange between the two schools developed into a friendly, competitive game of one-up-manship. In February (before Lent), the Fassifern girls attended a Valentine's Day dance in St. Dunstan's Hall. The walls were decorated with cupids and hearts artistically drawn and decorated by Pete Bennett and Jim Washburn. A make-believe bar was set up on the stage and Noble Doak Smithson and Dick Senn were the bartenders. Before intermission, a victrola provided popular dance music. After intermission, Bill Kirk called several square dances and, by popular demand, Dewitt Burkhead gave his famous rendition of "My Heart Tells Me" accompanied by a girl on each arm.

This did not end the social whirl. In April, Fassifern held a carnival and among the entertainment was the then popular game "Truth or Consequences." Thanks to incorrect answers, Dorn Gresley got to wiggle like a hula dancer (grass skirt and all) and Pete Bennett brought tears of laughter with his imitation of an infant. The school's final dance, the night before the final banquet, brought in a bevy of Southern belles from Fassifern and elsewhere with the dining hall taking on the appearance of a Southern garden–native greenery, azalea blossoms, and Spanish moss. Punch glasses provided a dignified touch. As other schools in the area learned, albeit somewhat slowly, Christ School boys knew how to throw a dance and make the girls feel warmly welcomed.

In one way or another, all the teachers joined in the efforts to keep morale high. The big three bachelors (Mr. Chinn, Mr. Read, and Mr. Alden, better known as the Session de Smut) carried on the Sunday tea tradition started by Fr. Boynton. In addition, they would invite small groups in for occasional Saturday or Sunday night suppers. Since getting to town was a problem, sharing rides with faculty members was an important event. Few who rode with Miss Mac could forget the experience as the gravel flew and one hoped the brakes would hold. In the kitchen, Julius and Elizabeth would provide a few extra nibbles for the wounded, favored, or plain hungry during the afternoon, and Elizabeth would cook fish on a Saturday night for those whose luck at the pond favored them. A leftover piece of cake or biscuit and jam awoke the taste buds heretofore inactive.

One of the most active in devising schemes for involving the students was Fr. Webbe, the chaplain during most of those years. For one thing, he was a man's man who looked like Spencer Tracy, and his athletic prowess covered football, swimming, tumbling, and archery. (He also had a rib-hunting elbow in faculty-student basketball games.) He often hunted deer with a bow-and-arrow, but the results of those trips have faded beyond recall. Besides coaching football, introducing tumbling to the campus, and bringing a variety of evening services into chapel including a revival of "song fests' every few weeks (an occasion when the students selected their favorite hymns to sing), he introduced a program which brought much mirth and merriment on Saturday night. It was "Take It or Leave It," based on a popular radio show of Phil Baker, with sixty-four cents the top prize instead of $64. If a contestant answered seven consecutive questions (much like you find on "Trivial Pursuit"), he won the top prize. If he missed an answer along the way, the money went into the jackpot. He could stop at any point and keep his winnings, and the student audience often screamed "you'll be sorry" when he continued playing. The first show, involving twelve students whose names Betsy Harris drew from a hat, occurred in February 1943. It became a tradition for three years. "The problem in keeping it going," Fr. Webbe said later, "was trying to think up enough dumb questions." There were three sixty-four cents winners on that first program. The first was Gilbert (Whizzer) White, the fastest halfback on campus; he collected sixty-four cents when he correctly guessed the won-lost record of the 1942 Christ School football team on which he played. John Hammond (to cries of "you'll be sorry") struck it rich by being able to give the name of the "slightly bald-headed man" who had attended every Christ School ball game. (The word "slightly" was intended to confuse and it took Hammond about a minute to guess the answer.) Lewis Berkeley won the top prize by identifying baseball nick-names. Called wrong for a correct answer was baseball wizard George McAden, who was a celebrity on campus for inventing baseball parlor games. He developed the "Little World Series" which became popular in the Second Cottage. Instead of using a baseball, the players used a table tennis ball and a paddle. Any ball knocked out of the cottage or through a window was a home run. In the latter case the running came when Fessor heard the glass shatter. In time heated rivalry sprang up between the Second Cottage Jailbirds and the First Cottage Railbirds.

The Rev. Norvin Duncan '07 (Front Left) never missed the Priest Fellowship meetings at Christ School.

Seven months later, many in the Class of 1941 would be marching off to war.

VI: 1940-1945

30

Wartime Athletics

Although Christ School's athletics were curtailed during the war, sports were important to morale and campus heroes emerged, though there were no super stars. In addition, some new ways to channel student energy were developed as a result of the wartime limitations imposed upon travel. Tumbling became popular, tennis underwent a strong revival, track was reintroduced. Boxing matches and basketball games were introduced as occasional happenings.

In the winter, the old gymnasium never remained idle, despite its natural air-conditioning. Besides teaching five periods, Fessor found the time to coach the varsity and junior varsity basketball teams (with assistance at the jayvee level) in the evenings and to run the large intramural basketball program (senior and junior divisions) in the afternoons. The Intramural League was the school's basketball farm system from which grew future basketball greats. Seniors who were cut from the Greenie varsity their senior years to make room for rising talent moved to a place of leadership in the competitive senior intramural league. Few seniors ever complained of such transfer, for it was a natural process of what was necessary to keep Christ School competitive against surrounding schools which had such large numbers to draw from.

At a small school which wanted to be competitive, the concentration in sports was necessarily limited to several main ones to prevent the dilution of all. In its evolution, Christ School started with baseball, added football fifteen years later, and brought in basketball another eight years after that. These remained the big three sports with alumni and students alike, and track and soccer were later to become quite popular when the student body increased from 125 to 160 in number.

In 1934 two students, Robert Morgan and Frank Zimmerman, organized tennis as a varsity sport at Christ School but, like most new ones, it took time to grow. Zimmerman's play brought American tennis great Bill Tilden to the campus on several occasions to observe him. Morgan, who was to pilot the famous *Memphis Belle* during World War II, later presented a trophy to the school which was given annually to the best tennis player. Though Mr. Dave had a strong interest in tennis (his daughter Betsy was top-ranked in the South) and coached it during the 1940's, he did not take advantage of his position to make it the centerpiece of Christ School athletics. During the war years, one of the events students looked forward to was the Intramural Tennis Tournament held during the final days of school. It was open to everyone, varsity tennis players included. The competition was fierce, upsets were frequent, many matches were played before breakfast, and at least on one occasion the singles finals was taking place on the number one court outside St. Dunstan's Hall while the final banquet was in progress. However, the match ended in time for the winner to be acclaimed. How much tennis was improving became apparent in the spring of 1945 when the varsity schedule was resumed. High school tennis programs were still restricted by the war, but Mr. Dave arranged a series of matches with the Naval Hospital, the Asheville Army Redistribution Center, and the Lake Lure Rest Center, where Air Force personnel was sent at regular intervals after combat for rest and relaxation. These teams were loaded with college players who had entered the military. Leading Christ School that year was Sidney Main, who rarely lost. One of his defeats came at the hands of a service man who had played number one on the Dartmouth College tennis team.

The seeds were sown during this period for the renewal of track and the beginning of soccer. Both were to be the handiwork of Jim Heinold who ran track while attending the University of Cincinnati and Penn State. Soccer had its roots in the intramural program of potpourri offered at Wetmore Hill for those students generally less athletically inclined or for some boys who simply grew weary of a long, hard scheduled season. Soccer would become a varsity sport several years after the war ended and after much promotion of the idea on the part of the students, especially those active on the *Christ School News.* The campus press became outspoken in calling for a new winter activity which otherwise was limited to basketball. Ultimately, the decision to make soccer a varsity sport meant that two major sports were attracting students from the same pool and the result was a decline in interest in, and later demise of, intramural basketball.

Track, which had been organized by Fr. Boynton (a four letter athlete at Williams College) in the late 1930's, provided limited interscholastic competition and much intramural practice. Many of the participants also played baseball, practicing for track for about thirty minutes after baseball practice ended and participating in a meet if it did not interfere with a baseball game. When Fr. Boynton moved to Wisconsin in 1939, track went into a hiatus. In the spring of 1945, track reemerged but in an intramural form. For the first week or so, Coach Heinold had the boys working to complete the 100 yard cinder track which Mr. Dave had started for Fr. Boynton. The track became a quarter mile around the football field with a 100 yard straightaway along the west side. In addition, the boys dug the pit necessary for field events and filled it with sawdust. Track was to become a letter sport several years later.

Since all Christ School students were not varsity athletes (no athletic scholarships were ever given and most of the students probably would not have gone out for sports in big public high schools), other activities utilizing some of the faculty had to be devised, especially in the fall and winter. Some interesting generic names emerged–Pop's Playboys, Read's Rangers, and Huntley's Hikers. As a general rule, Pop's Playboys ran the obstacle course four days a week and then went to Wetmore Hill to play touch football, softball, capture the flag, bringing home the bacon, soccer, and snowballing (when the weather cooperated.)[4] Often Fr. Webbe was aided by Frank Read who might split a group off for a three to seven mile hike. Huntley's Hikers were a small core group of grizzly veterans who only hiked–either for pleasure or as an act of defiance of authority which required participation in athletics. Sometimes their reward was blisters and cold feet, but principal prevailed and no one got hurt.

Perhaps the most exciting new athletic venture undertaken during this time was Fr. Webbe's introduction of gymnastics, that is work on the parallel bars, the horizontal bar (set up outside the gym), and the mats. Fr. Webbe was a gymnast and swimmer at Amherst College and taught the basics of gymnastics. In the spring thirty to thirty-five students participated in this activity and at the end of May, the school was treated to a tumbling exhibition. No letters were awarded and there was no interscholastic competition, but the program was popular and obviously an excellent way to teach stamina, agility, self-reliance, self-discipline, and courage. Unfortunately small schools face a dilemma–not necessarily bad–of being able to provide certain sports occasionally, depending upon the talent or interest to be found in the faculty at a particular moment. In this case, Fr. Webbe was that talent. When he left in 1947, there was no faculty enthusiast and technician to build a following. In the competition, the tumblers did work in three areas. On the horizontal bar, they did such things as cutaways, kip-ups and shoulder stands, side-kip over the bar and dismount, and lay-outs from the bar. They did handstands and different rolls and dismounts on the parallel bar, and a variety of mat stunts. In the first year of this gymnastic tournament, the champions were Lon West, Bruce Burch, and Scotty Root, who later performed on the plebe gym team at Annapolis. Some other boys later judged to be outstanding gymnasts were Alex Harris, Frank Bryson, Mariner Potts, Charles Kimberly, and Robert Cooper.

[4]Thursday was a free afternoon for all students except those engaged in varsity sports. You could sleep, walk to the store, hike Burney Mountain, or study.

Varsity sports cannot be overlooked as a morale factor, for these were the events which brought all the students together to cheer and yell and feel for Christ School as a whole. With varsity sports limited to a few activities, schedule conflicts did not exist and no varsity sports were competing with each other for support on a given day. Though attendance at games was voluntary, absences were the exception. Constant reminders from Fessor or Mr. Dave and the faculty about the Christ School tradition and pressure among the students themselves created a strong feeling that whatever happened at Christ School happened to everybody. (There were no varsity sports in 1942-43 except for football.) Despite wartime limitations and disruptions, the teams were competitive, though the record against Asheville School was not good in football and basketball. One shining note, though, were the football teams which, during the four war years, turned in the best consecutive winning record in Christ School's history through 1970. The combined mark for that period in football was 21-7-2, for a percentage of .733. The 1942 football team was perhaps the best in the school's history, at least as far as depth was concerned. Fessor was able to use two different teams at a time when no such thing as platoon football existed. A game which Fessor remembered as the best one ever played in Western North Carolina (college or high school) saw a Hubert Edney kick-off return of ninety yards trigger the Greenies to a sensational 21-14 upset over the number one Waynesville Mountaineers. Another victory which gripped his memory was a 6-0 upset in 1944 of the visiting Canton Bears. Christ School had a backfield which averaged under 135 pounds and a line that hit the 145 pound mark, with the biggest lineman weighing 165 pounds. Canton outweighed the Greenies nearly fifty pounds per man. The highlight was a Christ School goal line stand in which Canton began the drive on the Greenie two yard line. Four plays later the Bears stalled a foot away from a score.

Baseball had its moments in the sun during the war, particularly with successes over Asheville School. In 1944, Phil Boatwright (the football team's 123 pound end and punter) struck out eighteen Blues in pitching the Greenies to a 9-6 victory. It was a game in which hammering Hank Lathrop went five-for-five. A year later that left hander with the cute stuff, Weedie Ferguson, drove in the winning run at the top of the ninth to edge the Blues 7-6.

Two other contributions to morale in those years should not go unnoticed. As a part of its effort, the *Christ School News* organized in 1942 a ping pong tournament to establish a ladder for the rest of the year. Seeded at the top after the tournament were Harcourt Waters (he later played tennis at Tulane) and Ham Bartley. The other was a boxing and wrestling program introduced by Coach Heinold in the fall of 1944. The group began the day with fifteen minutes of calisthenics and then alternated between roadwork and learning the skills of boxing and wrestling. To keep interest high, some ju-jitsu was worked into the program.

What you see is what it was. The Old Gym had no insulation or heat. Manager of this 1947 baseball team (far right) was the Old Dorm's electronics genius, Douglas Jarnigan.

Above: Processions in-and-out of Christ School Chapel were standard fare for Urq's choir. Mr. Chinn was recruited by Fr. Boynton, who was later Bishop of Puerto Rico and Suffragan Bishop of New York.

Below: Students playing tennis on the court across from St Dunstan's Hall.

VII: 1945-1950

Two Big Events

Two events happening outside of Christ School during the war years awakened the students to the harsh reality of the other world. One came on a Sunday afternoon when most of them were in a rather relaxed posture as Christmas vacation was fast approaching. Some were listening to the Skins and Giants battle it out on the professional football field. Others were playing ping-pong, reading, writing, sleeping, or lazily assembled at the Grandstand or the Frat. Still another bunch had started walking toward Burney and the Old Airport, looking for something to do. A jarring note occurred when a bulletin interrupted the football game in mid-play to announce that the Japanese had bombed Pearl Harbor. This dramatic news moved quickly around campus, and for most it was unreal.

By now the student body contained many boys whose fathers were already in military units at home and abroad and their lives were most abruptly changed. Small groups huddled quickly in cottages and dorms to try to decide what was going to happen. The angelus rang shortly thereafter and Mr. Dave told the solemn assembly that a long war would follow. "Before it is over," he said, "most of you will have seen action and many of you will not return. One thing will hold steadfast: Christ School will always welcome you home."

The other event came in April, 1945, with the dramatic bulletin that President Franklin Delano Roosevelt had died of a heart attack at Warm Springs, Ga. Though occasional pictures of the President during the preceding year had shown a man weary, worn, and sick, the nature and extent of his illness had been withheld from the public for a year and was not seriously searched for by the press–ostensibly under the umbrella of national security. Taking advantage of the wartime emergency, FDR had sought an unprecedented fourth term six months earlier and had just returned from the Yalta Conference only a few weeks before. As his body was moved by train from Georgia to the nation's Capitol, thousands of people with heads bowed and eyes moist lined the railroad track to pay homage as the train moved somberly northward. The uneasiness that followed FDR's death was as alive among the students as their parents. The war with Japan was not over and an invasion of the Japanese mainland might cost a million American lives. And . . . who was this Harry Truman?

The first yearbook, The Warrior, was published 1928. Little Betsy Harris stands with the Staff.

No Asheville School football game could be played without a bonfire rally.

VII: 1945-1950

Loose Ends

The war was over (Hiroshima did that with one blow) but not the loose ends. A certain restlessness still remained–both in the nation and at school. Although the number of new students admitted each year remained proportionally about the same, there was an increase in the number who were just passing through or not passing their work. Some families remained dislocated because of their jobs and military service and the school found itself with a few more students who were stopping off for a year or two while their families resettled. The restlessness showed itself in an increasing number of runaways, usually right after Christmas or the first few days of the school year. Two or three would suddenly depart in the middle of the night. Most of them were boys who could not or did not meet the required academic standards and most of the runaways were not received back into the student body. Otherwise, yearly reports showed little of a break-down as far as general discipline was concerned. In November 1946, a couple of boys were shipped for illegal smoking. In 1947, one was sent home for thievery. In 1949-50 three boys were expelled as a group the first month. It apparently had a salutary effect. Mr. Dave noted that this action "cleared the air the rest of the year, with an improvement following both in attitude and scholarship." This was a restless period in which the percentage of failures had increased until that precipitous action in the fall of 1949. Pointing out that the number of failures declined sharply for the rest of the year, Mr. Dave said the percentage was still too high. He resisted any notion that the way to deal with this problem was to reduce academic standards. "There seems to be no way at present to lower the rate other than by reducing our standards. A move of that kind does not seem wise." Still the poor quality of work of a sizeable number of students apparently contributed to unrest among the faculty and five masters–including several with long and deep ties to the school–left in 1950. This broke up a continuity and stability that had begun some years earlier, a stability Mr. Dave had praised as the strength of the school during this period of wartime and de-acceleration. In his report to the board in July 1950, Mr. Dave was optimistic about the future and the new staff which he had assembled–one of whom was to serve as chaplain for thirteen years (second only to Fr. Harris in tenure) and another was to teach at Christ School for nearly thirty years (second only to Fessor and Mr. Dave).

This period of time saw Mr. Dave begin to put together the pattern and routine which was to be the Christ School trademark until his death in December 1969. That routine was followed, though it was not rigid in the sense of being unchanged. Mr. Dave shifted schedules and tactics from time to time to accommodate circumstances, but on each occasion he demanded that the routine in place be followed. The routine was not up for vote. How important he felt regularity to be was expressed in the Headmaster's Letter which appeared in the October 1946 *Christ School News:*

> No better place can be found than school for the planting of the best of habits, and it is important that those habits formed be of the best as all habits are hard to break.

Small wonder that orientation periods were brief, for Mr. Dave believed that every student knew the basic difference between right and wrong, between working and loafing, between cooperation and selfishness, and that the best correction was to learn immediately by doing. Things done correctly were so noted; those done wrongly brought forth a worklist or correction that produced better results the next time.

The five years after the war were a period of readjustment for teachers and students alike. The student body would become a little older, for the military draft was no longer dipping down into high school. A renewed interest in extracurricular activities would surface and a greater release of social energy would unfold in the form of dance exchanges with Fassifern and St. Genevieve's and the introduction by the Fraternity of the Smoker. One change in America's ways which the war encouraged was marriage at a younger age. As a result, Mr. Dave found it more and more difficult to find bachelor teachers, the kind who lived in the dorm and dedicated their lives to their charges since they did not have conflicting family responsibilities. Thus, until Jim Darsie came to Christ School in mid-1944, there were only three faculty homes on campus–the Little Rectory occupied by the chaplain, the headmaster's house, and the cottage built for Fessor around 1925 with the promise of a home in the future.[1] Other married faculty lived in apartments in the three dormitories (30, 38 and Old). And some of these apartments were not satisfactory for

[1]Fessor was scheduled to get his new house in the fall of 1960. At this point, I did Fessor (a man whom I never ceased to admire) an unwitting disservice. In January 1960 I met the sister of a student; by May we were engaged and in August we were married. Somewhat startled that an old line bachelor was getting married, Mr. Dave switched plans and provided that the new house would be for the McCulloughs. It was years later before I knew of this intrusion on Fessor's dreams. If he was aware of the change in plans, he never said a word. God bless him.

faculty with children, especially more than one. Until Mr. Dave began to dot the campus with new homes, faculty housing was a source of agitation for some members of the staff.

The designer of many of the faculty homes on campus was Mrs. Dave. The house which was built in 1960 for the newly married McCulloughs was one in Iowa, whose picture Mrs. Dave had seen in a U.S. Gypsum magazine. The school wanted a house with a more modernistic look without altering the basic lines which dominate the campus. This house, with its marine siding, provided a nice off-set sloping roof and a large sandstone fireplace which gave it traditional links to the other buildings on campus.

According to David Harris, Jr., Mrs. Dave used a different approach on the house built for the Darsies, the first faculty home to be constructed on campus since the Little Rectory when Mr. and Mrs. Dave were married. "She designed the Darsie house by cutting different rooms out of magazines and piecing them together. The house was constructed out of material salvaged from the old school building. The rafters over the living room are probably ancient 2 x 14's which are godawful pieces of heavy timber. The Boyds built the foundation and then walls and went in later to roof it. They had to eyeball the roof."

All of Mr. Boyd's sons liked to work with rock, picking up the skills he had learned while serving as a teenage apprentice on the construction of the Vanderbilt Mansion. Mr. Boyd was skilled in all the building crafts. He left Christ School during World War I to go to Norfolk, Va., to build houses for the workers involved in shipbuilding. On the first day, he was put to work on a house. The next day, he was made supervisor of construction. Some time before he came to Christ School, Mr. Boyd moved his family to Arizona to work in a gold mining camp. In time the call of the mountains became too strong, and he returned to help Fr. Harris as carpenter, landscaper, worklist boss, and shop teacher.

Of his several sons (who worked for the schools in streaks), Glenn was the most skillful in wood but he preferred working in stone. His chief characteristic in stonework was infinite patience required to shape the stone so that he didn't end up with a mass of big ends in one part of the building and stone with only small ones in another. The arrangement required imaginative balance, like making a mosaic. Christ School students were seldom if ever involved in quarrying the stone though they did help haul it. Bob Harris recalled the limited use of dynamite in getting stone for the Chapel in a quarry running southeast of the dairy barn.

> We (Dave, Alex, and I) used to go watch them get the rock out. To do so, they would do what was an ingenious process called driving steel. One man with a hammer would drive a steel bar

> held by another into the stone. The holder would twist the bar and the driver would strike again. The sledge hammer didn't have a stiff handle but a wiggly one called a hip handle. I kept waiting for the driver to hit the other guy's hand but he never did. Finally they would break the rock into big wedges. From time to time, they would pour black powder into a hole, put mud over that, tie a fuse in, light it, and run for the trees. The explosion would expose a big chunk on the surface.

By the time Mr. Boyd was here, the use of dynamite was mostly a thing of the past. The quarrying process involved simple brute strength with bars and wedges as the chief tools. The mica sheist itself was fairly soft so the men took out great slabs and then used the wedges to break the rock across the grain. This would reduce the size to hefty chunks with the men, standing around on benches, cutting the face on the sandstone with chisels and hammers. Most of the shaping of the pieces was done at the quarry site rather than at the building. After the rocks were hauled to the construction site, they were placed on a scaffold where Glenn (sometimes Ralph and Virgil) would pick out the fittings with an imaginative glance. "There is more mortar in the walls than meets the eye," said David Harris Jr., "It's well-mortared but all behind the stone. It is built like a drywall but the stone is bedded and backed up."

Though most of the major construction work was done during the summers, some boys remained on campus to help build the 38 Dorm and Infirmary, carrying the stone and doing other things. The money for both of these buildings was raised through the efforts of Mrs. Wetmore and her *Galax Leaf* publication. Those women from the North who gave so generously to the school both of money for buildings and clothes for the mission during this period of financial struggle were referred to by Mr. Dave as the "Old Clothes Episcopalians."

It was in the construction of the Susan Wetmore Administration Building, which was begun in 1939 but was not completed until 1941 because of financial delays, that Mr. Boyd demonstrated the exacting nature of his skills to their fullest extent. At one point, when the weather closed in, he went into the old wooden shop and hand-sawed the whole roof out–all those cripples and short rafters. In the spring, the workers hauled the roof up and it fit together to perfection.

In walking around the campus, a trained eye can see improvement in the stone work as years progressed. David Harris Jr., provides this commentary:

> I think the stonework in the school building is much too clean (smooth). I prefer the rougher stone such as in the Chapel and St.

Dunstan's Hall (old dining hall). The Boyds cut the school building stone finer, chiseling every stone. The stone in St. Dunstan's was just hammered, with the edges remaining ragged. There is very little face on it. You can see a vast difference by looking at The Chapel, the Memorial Chapel and the cloister. The Chapel was built from stone almost as it came out of the ground. They are rough with only a few of them faced up. In the cloister, you will see a lot of cut stone in the archway. The stone was refined more in more recent buildings. The stone in all the buildings varies in size, with the largest being determined by how much each individual rock mason had the strength to handle.

David Harris Jr., who was headmaster from 1967-71, came to Christ School in 1953 because of the construction of the new gymnasium, a memorial to all Christ School boys who died in wars for their country. He explains the circumstances:

> I came up on July 4 (he worked for Jones Construction in Charlotte) and borrowed an instrument to lay the building out. (He was working in Chapel Hill at the time and had a two months old child.) Mr. Dave asked me to come help with the building because he did not want to undertake engineering responsibility for putting up the steel undergirding. Later that summer, Jones Construction wanted to send me to Norfolk so I took Mr. Dave up on his offer. I told him no one should be on campus who didn't teach and he gave me a class in physics. When Jim Heinold resigned that summer, I ended up with three additional sessions of math.

The building of Memorial Gymnasium marked Mr. Boyd's last appearance on campus. Serving as supervisor emeritus, he was at the site every morning observing what was going on. By now his hair was totally white and his glasses a half inch thick. He remained small and wiry, a man who kept to himself but showed a fiery temper when willfully crossed by the students. "I remember one occasion," Mr. Harris said, "when Mr. Boyd jumped off the Old Gym roof (he did not take time to climb down the ladder) and chased Geezil across the farm, a hatchet in his right hand. Geezil was late to a lot of things that night, sneaking back after Mr. Boyd had gone home. Geezil's punishment was Mr. Dave's hearty laughter, complete with the knowledge that Mr. Boyd could take care of himself."

It took nearly five years to raise the funds necessary to construct the Memorial Chapel named after Fr. Harris. The nation was gripped by depression and Christ School had no wealthy alumni. Contributions ranged from fifty cents to as much as ten dollars and ultimately $3,000 was raised by students, alumni and some boys who attended but did not graduate from Christ School. In later years, Fessor, who instigated this project, said his greatest regret was that Memorial Chapel had not been built before Fr. Harris died, because he had early communion services every day of the year. "The big chapel was very difficult to heat and ordinarily there would be no heat in there, and sometimes the water used for communion had turned to ice. I know that many, many, many times he had services when it was so cold that a fellow would just kneel and shiver."

In athletics during the immediate post-war period (1945-50), the big news at Christ School was the introduction of soccer into the winter sports program and the reintroduction of track as a letter sport. Both were badly needed to expand the opportunity of Christ School boys to develop as varsity athletes. Heretofore, varsity possibilities in the winter were limited to just basketball, but the appearance of soccer in the winter of 1947-48 ended that monopoly.

Soccer was a winning sport from the time it was begun under Coach Jim Heinold, but it did not become a letter sport until a few years later. In a sense, soccer was not new to the school for students as far back as the 1900's kicked a soccer ball around for recreation. During the war years, the Playboys played intramural soccer on Wetmore Hill but it was a run-and-shoot brand without instruction. What Coach Heinhold did was bridle the energy and give it direction. Some students felt that the development of soccer was retarded by Coach Fayssoux out of concern for the basketball program, even though the varsity cage squad was limited to about a dozen players. However, a large intramural basketball program which Fessor directed was a feeder system for future cage teams. That first year forty-two boys turned out for soccer, even though no letters were to be awarded, no matches had been scheduled, no playing field existed, and it was a winter sport–frostbite and all. But no one complained about the weather when the opportunity to play existed. Helping (or possibly aggravating) the development of soccer was the *Christ School News*, whose staff campaigned vigorously in the press–first for the formation of soccer and then for making it a letter sport. The reason offered for soccer not being a varsity-letter sport those first two years was that it was difficult to arrange a complete schedule because not many schools in the area had teams. Before he left Christ School several years later, Coach Heinold was scheduling matches with Darlington and McCallie.

How much soccer affected the basketball program with two varsity squads drawing from the same limited pool of students remains to be explored. During the five or six years before soccer was organized, the varsity basketball team won about forty-five percent of its games against the best competition in the area. During the first four soccer years, the percentage of victories remained about the same. During the decade of the 1940's, Christ School basketball had few winning seasons. There was nothing to compare to the cage record from 1927 to 1933, when the Greenies were undefeated in all their home games. There is little doubt, though, that the emergence of soccer did greatly reduce the number of boys playing intramural basketball and thereby cut into the feeder system. Soccer, then, began the demise of intramural basketball which was completed in the mid-1960's when wrestling was introduced as a winter sport. Some of the lower formers who were trained in intramural basketball became a part of an eighth and ninth grade soccer squad organized later. There is strong evidence to support the claim that when soccer was shifted to the fall in 1980, this did greatly reduce the talent available to either football or soccer, with each sport attracting some who would have been an asset to the other. In recent years, both Christ School football and soccer–as the records show–have been damaged by this inevitable conflict for athletes.

The appearance of soccer was announced to alumni and parents in School Notes of the November/December 1947 issue of the *Christ School News:*

> Included in winter sports this year is soccer, a new sport at school. Although Coach Heinold says it is a complex game, some boys feel it is a form of "legalized murder." However it is not as bad as it sounds and it's lots of fun.

Whenever a new activity began at Christ School during the first seventy years, it automatically involved the students in some physical labor. Soccer was no exception. The first two weeks found the forty-two students leveling Wetmore pasture, filling in holes, using the tennis court roller to pack down the playing surface, and then lining the field and erecting goal posts for two fields, one for the senior division and the other for the juniors. As a by-product, the Brat football team had a new field on which to play its games.

Soccer was not to be a sport in which players made a half-hearted commitment and simply kicked the ball around all day for the fun of it. Since none of the candidates were experienced in soccer, Coach Heinold set out to teach them through constant drill the techniques of heading, passing, and ball handling. As he told the first group, a message he was to repeat in subsequent years, "The objective is to enable you to keep complete control of the ball at all times." What this meant was practice . . . practice . . . practice. What Coach Heinold formed that first year were two senior division teams which he coached and two junior ones under Bill Chalker. To provide scrimmage conditions for future play, he divided the two senior teams into offensive and defensive formations to learn the patterns for the five-match schedule.

This system of practice . . . practice . . . practice worked. In five years, Heinold's booters compiled a 26-7-3 mark without a losing season. After dropping their first two matches–to Asheville School and Canton–the Greenies closed with three straight wins. They were undefeated for two seasons (playing 19 matches without a loss before falling to Marion 7-4) and were Blue Ridge Conference champions for four straight years–a league which included Christ School, Asheville School, Ben Lippen, and Canton. The first ever soccer win was a 4-2 victory over Ben Lippen, with Ray Midyette and Kenneth Rockwell scoring two goals each. That first Christ School line-up may not have been the best squad in those early years, but it was a memorable group which uncomplainingly withstood the rigors of a cold winter on Wetmore Hill. The starting eleven were:

> Goalie Tad Johnson, LF Richie Meech, RF Dorsey Crocker, LH Williard Colby, CH Bill Kennedy, RH Raymond Sharp, LW Joe Troitino, LI Bobby Moore,[2] CF Kenneth Rockwell, RI Ray Midyette, RW Bob Giles.

When Coach Heinold departed in 1953, he left forty returnees and most of the starters from a fifty-nine-man squad. Something was lost in the transition and the team dropped to a 3 to 5 mark, and though some good squads were to be developed in ensuing years, none reached the magic of those who had to "kick the cowpies off" before passing the ball.

Some boys who knew nothing about soccer when they arrived became fine players during those formative years. Forwards Pete Cothran and Tommy Mebane set a school record for a season with seventeen goals each in eight games, a mark which had not been broken even in later years when the schedule was expanded to fifteen or twenty matches a year. The February 1954 *News* applauded three graduates who learned under Coach Heinold for their important roles on the University of North Carolina team, the best in the Atlantic Coast Conference. Charlie Damerson (FB) and Cothran (F) lettered at Carolina that year and Tommy Kirkland (F) played in several matches. A couple of other graduates–Ross Smyth and Tom Burns–played key roles in organizing the first intercollegiate soccer team at Davidson College.

An unforgettable moment for the Class of 1949 came on Monday night, April 25, when the Christ School faculty, aided by some of the staff from Fassifern School for Girls, put on a one-time showing of *Arsenic and Old Lace* in the study hall. In addition three students (George Wheeler, Jack Hudson, and Jimmy Guy) played minor roles while a lot of others worked backstage.

[2]In subsequent years, Bobby Moore has seen much Christ School soccer, officiating games at Wetmore Field and elsewhere.

Drawing acclaim for her role was Mrs. Lucy Root, school secretary who ran the Jigger Shop, kept the students on a close financial leash, and had a three minute sand dial in her office to speed up outgoing student phone calls at a time when that was the only telephone available for student use. *The News* reporter said:

> Mrs. Root played the part of Abby Brewster. There were moments when Mrs. Root seemed to become Abby Brewster in heart and soul, and, at those moments, no one would recognize Mrs. Root.

English teacher Frank Read drew praise for "drawing laughs" in his role of Teddy Brewster; Fr. Ed for putting his soul into the part of Jonathan Brewster, and Spanish teacher Bill Chalker for making Dr. Einstein, a German of low repute, come alive. The most praise was reserved for English/French master Zach Alden:

> It is to Mr. Zach that full credit is due for the success of the play. In playing the role of Mortimer Bewster, he was excellent in a part calling for a great deal of speaking as well as acting. Mr. Zach also directed the production and designed and built the set.

Other Christ School faculty members in the glittering cast were Mr. Chinn, Mr. Darsie, Mr. Thompson, and Fessor.

One of the early gifts to Christ School was the nativity scene located in front of the organ pipes and across from the console

No matter how rigid the schedule and how limited the means, circumstances, and transportation, Christ School students were never without recreation and entertainment–whether provided by the school or by their own devices. Much of this has been described in the earlier years. Even in the immediate post-war years when griping became a universal yardstick, Christ School students were not in a monastic order. Their Monday trips to Asheville were limited to once or twice a month and an off-campus Sunday dinner to once a month. Thursday and Monday afternoons were free to walk to the Old Airport, Arden, and Fletcher–unless a worklist interrupted that exercise of choice. There were a variety of extra-curricular activities available, much beautiful country within hiking distance, and 600-700 acres of farmland on which to build caves, huts, trap beaver and rabbits, and roam to one's heart's content. There was the Frat and Grandstand for smokers and story-tellers, the gymnasium for basketball or tumbling, the lawns and athletic field for sunbathing, the library for reading, a ping-pong table or two, and the faculty homes to visit on weekends to play games, cards, talk, or listen to radio, records, or (later) television.

In addition, there were things that happened each year which were peculiar to that particular time and circumstance–memorable occasions that united the students. In sports, the Asheville School games were always a unifying force and seldom did less than one hundred percent of the student body turn out for the big one. Attendance at all sporting events was high, in part, perhaps, because usually only one varsity event was scheduled on any given day. Fewer games were scheduled and more time was given to learning how to play. Other normal special events which were highlights to all were such things as the Candlelight and Easter Services, a play or two put on by the Drama Club, special religious services that resulted in half-day of school, and the dedication of a building or a stained glass window or new acolyte robes.

Scattered about the campus in the 1950's were several wrought iron benches. Much of Fr. Webster's one-on-one counseling took place on them.

CHRIST SCHOOL
SUCCESSUS FIDELITATE

St. Dunstan's Hall as it appeared to students during the period 1940's-1970's. Built in 1916, it served as a dining hall and a place to hold dances.

VII: 1945-1950

The Choir Hits The Road

The choir became much more than just the leading group in the Chapel services at Christ School. After World War II, it became the roving ambassador, taking overnight trips to sing at the Cathedral in Atlanta, St. Paul's in Winston-Salem, and churches in other cities like Greensboro, Pinehurst, Columbia, Charleston, and Knoxville. People judged the school in part by the choir–not merely its singing (which was of excellent quality) but by the appearance and behavior of the boys themselves. Those, too, received high marks.

No trip was ever without its humorous moments, no matter how well planned and prepared for. Many are etched forever in the mind of Urq Chinn. We'll let him relate some of them:

> We used to sing regularly at St. Mary's in Asheville at the Candlemas service. One afternoon we arrived there with little time to prepare. The choir sang from the balcony in the back and I tried to place the kids so that they sounded all right back there. We only had time to go through one anthem before the service started. The choir was singing beautifully until we came to the anthem we had practiced. During this one there was a pause when the basses were supposed to come in like a fugue and the other parts would join in later. I raised my hand for the basses to start and I didn't get a thing. Nobody sang. I don't know what happened, but I just threw the piece of music down and we started the next anthem, just as though that were the end of the previous one.

An organ malfunction created a different problem one year when the choir was in Marion.

> The choir was singing in a large Protestant church instead of the smaller Episcopal one I was used to because of an expected

> large crowd. The other church had a bigger organ and more space. I was playing and the choir was singing the "Hallelujah Chorus" and we reached the part where I needed to add a few more stops for emphasis. All the stops were right in front of my fingers on the top row of keys, so I pushed my hand up, and bang, I knocked down every stop on the organ. Their was total silence and the kids looked at me and I looked at them and then I looked at the organ. This all happened in seconds. I took my hand and slid it across the stops and we went on singing. Afterwards I found out what had happened. There was a little bar of wood which, if you hit it, cancelled all the stops on the organ. That was what I had hit by mistake. Apparently most of the people didn't even notice the near disaster.

In a trip to Charlotte, Urq recalled the embarrassment which can happen to a soloist. "We were doing an anthem and one of the boys had a solo part in the middle. We were singing a cappella and the boy was standing next to me as I directed the choir. In the middle of his part, he dropped his music and it fluttered toward the floor, hitting me in the chest on the way down." Fortunately for all concerned, Urq's choirs practiced beyond perfection and the soloist had memorized the anthem.

Almost every choir trip, whether it was a short trip or an overnight, provided the members an opportunity to socialize with young ladies in the various churches. These meetings frequently sparked letter-writing romances. Always there were refreshments afterwards and parties and dances and on overnights the members usually stayed in the homes of members of the congregations. Usually these trips were organized by parents of boys then in school and many alumni were present. Often Mr. and Mrs. Dave would show up unexpectedly in Winston-Salem or Greensboro for the Sunday morning service in which the choir would present a concert. Often the choir was accompanied by a Sunday acolyte crew, especially on those occasions when the school sang its solemn evensong service at an out-of-town church. While misconduct was generally not a problem, there were occasional misadventures. Mr. Chinn recalled one such event in Charleston.

> We were singing at St. Phillips, I believe, and the boys were staying at homes all over town. There had been, I suspect, some gallivanting around. A bunch of the choir and other young people from the church were feeling a bit hilarious on the third floor of a home in the downtown area. Somehow, one of those things that remains a mystery in the telling, a vase worth $600 separated into 600 pieces as it ended up on the floor. I didn't think we'd ever live through that, but we did. Nobody had to pay for it. The hostess

(obviously being nice) said the vase was up on the third floor because she didn't like it. "It's one of those Chinese dynasty things, you know." Thank goodness, things like that were rare occurrences.

With lots of seventh and eighth graders at school, Urq always had a sound soprano section. In addition, often a boy's voice changed late so that he might still be able to sing soprano (falsetto) while turning in outstanding weekly performances as the starting guard or tackle on the varsity football team. Given the right encouragement, Urq said, such late sopranos would rise to the occasion, even in the most embarrassing circumstances.

The choir was singing at Fassifern School for Girls in Hendersonville (probably in the spring of 1939) and I asked Joe McCullough to sing the solo part in the middle of "Beautiful Savior." By then Joe, who roughhoused with seniors while he was a brat, was a big, muscular fifteen or sixteen and a starter on the football team. To sing a soprano solo before this group of girls while you were standing in the soprano section required unusual courage. It was a question of whether the lure of girls would outweigh the embarrassment of singing a soprano part. So I asked Joe if he would sing the part. Happily he found a solution to his dilemma. "I'll sing if you will let me stand by the basses." I did, he did, and never has a bass reached such a high-pitched performance.

End Magnus Halldorson (42) lateraled to fullback Gordon Fitz-Simons, who ran for a touchdown in a 27 to 20 victory over Asheville School.

Urq Chinn practices with the sopranos in the 38 Dorm choir loft.

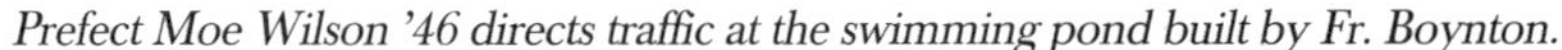

Prefect Moe Wilson '46 directs traffic at the swimming pond built by Fr. Boynton.

VIII: 1950-1970

Rebuilding The Campus

World War II and its controls over production and distribution forced Mr. Dave to delay for several years his plans to continue upgrading the physical facilities of the campus. During those years he concentrated on maintaining the old in good repair and improving the appearance of the campus by carrying out the landscape scheme drawn up for him in the 1920's by Col. Malcolm Ross. This involved planting trees and evergreens and other shrubs and improving and extending pathways and terracing on the West side of the campus.

With the war in Europe (but not Asia) ended, Mr. Dave reported to the board in July 1945 that the present buildings on campus were in good repair but cited the need for two new ones:

1. A dormitory to replace Thompson Hall (rebuilt after the fire of 1919) at a cost not to exceed $25,000.
2. A permanent gymnasium to replace the one which Fr. Harris authorized as temporary in 1922.

"I am having plans drawn up by Mr. Earl Stillwell . . . and upon their completion will attempt to raise money for their construction," Mr. Dave said.

Events were to show that raising money was to be a problem perhaps more difficult than imagined and that the school could not possibly fund two such endeavors at the same time. Ultimately, the gym gave way to the dormitory. At the 1946 board meeting, Mr. Dave repeated the need for both buildings and said that over $5,000 had come in as contributions toward a new gymnasium. Both structures would be of sandstone to blend in with the other major buildings. He also reported that the Alex Harris Memorial (Alumni Room) had been completed and that a room had been added to Fessor's cottage. In comments about the Old Dorm, Mr. Dave underscored that it was inadequate in every way, including being a fire hazard. He planned to ask Stillwell to sketch a dorm which would house seventy boys and three masters and replace the first three cottages.

The next year, Mr. Dave was pressuring the board with new arguments. He urged the expansion of the school from 130 to 150 students, saying that twenty more could be added with little additional overhead cost to the school. Pointing out that the physical plant prevented such "economic expansion" and that the Old Dorm was expensive to keep in repair, he urged the replacement of the Old Dorm.

"When the time comes," Mr. Dave said, "I suggest building a dorm to house 100 boys and sufficient masters . . . . making it possible to eliminate the Old Dorm and all six cottages." These buildings–all frame–were getting older and Mr. Dave argued that "getting these fellows all under one roof would result in a real saving in operating expenses." The effort to raise money for the gym, which was in an unorganized state, had by this time secured $13,500 and the need was set at about $100,000.

In July 1949, the board gave the green light to the construction of a new dorm but not the mammoth 100-boy dorm that the headmaster had, probably facetiously, suggested the year before. Instead the new Dorm (to be named after Mr. Boyd) would house thirty-some boys and would dislodge only one cottage–the second one. Before the board approved this construction (the cost estimate presented by Mr. Dave was $35,000) Mr. Dave had presented an alternative plan of more modest proportions. He emphasized that presently thirty-two boys were housed in this trap and he suggested building a temporary one story wooden structure to house eighteen boys and one master, while the remaining fourteen boys would continue to live in the lower floor of the Old Dorm. This would relieve some of the congestion and not expose second floor students to the danger of conflagration. Instead the board went along with what had been the headmaster's initial proposal in 1945. And Mr. Dave proved to be quite accurate in his estimate of $35,000. An audit showed the actual cost of the dorm to be $34,922.29.

The plans for the Boyd Dorm were among those Mr. Dave drew up on the back of envelopes. Oral changes were implemented by Mr. Boyd as construction went along. This was to be Mr. Boyd's last major construction effort at Christ School and, at the time, he had no knowledge that this building would become his legacy. Once construction began in the fall of 1949, Mr. Dave found it necessary to enlarge the dorm to house forty-eight students to make-up for the loss of the second cottage plus the addition in the fall of eight students more than the 130 capacity. By February 1, 1950, the boys who were living in the Old Dorm and on the back porches of several cottages moved into Boyd Dorm. Since the first floor of the Old Dorm was faced with sandstone, Mr. Dave had hoped to salvage it for some use–as a place for the school publications to work or as a recreation center with bathrooms for visitors. During the second semester of 1950, both the school paper and yearbook staffs had quarters in the Old Dorm but the next year the building was torn down, mostly by boys on the worklist. Mr. Dave informed the board that this (Boyd) dorm and another one about the same size "will solve our housing problem for many years to come." In Mr. Dave's mind, the processing of rebuilding a campus of permanent durability was continuing.

Perhaps the only major dream Mr. Dave had which did not ultimately materialize was the construction in the late 1940's of a new gymnasium. It was badly needed. The old one was unheated, the roof leaked badly, it had no showers or locker facilities, and it did not provide space for more than one activity in wet or cold weather. After the board meeting in July 1945, Mr. Dave wrote some alumni of the need for a new gymnasium and this was the beginning of an unofficial campaign to raise money, the amount needed estimated to be about $40,000 but raised to around $100,000 a couple of years later. Enthusiasm showed itself among students and alumni alike and the official announcement brought in over $4000 the first year, including $1,090 raised by the efforts of the *Christ School News.* In October 1946 some twenty-five captains were named to spearhead the effort in various areas but by June 1948 only $13,520 had been raised. Though more money had been contributed by 1952, the goal was still more than seventy-five percent short of the total needed. However, Mr. Dave still intended to go ahead with the plan drawn up without charge by architect Earl Stillwell of Hendersonville, N.C., but the dream came to an end when President Truman decided to remove Korean wartime price controls on steel. Suddenly, the cost of the steel supports would amount to more money than the sum allocated for the entire structure. With the help of Moreland Hogan, Sr., whose New Orleans construction firm built the first main airport in Atlanta, the school was able in 1953 to build a gymnasium of brick exterior for under $100,000.

The original building was to have been a dream. It was to have been located in the area where the old shop and laundry stood (near the present dining hall) and the exterior would be hollow tile veneered with the sandstone in keeping with the rest of the campus. It fit into Mr. Dave's feeling that the layout of the facilities should be one in which the headmaster could easily see and keep control over the daily life of the school. That's why his goal was always to keep the number of students down to a total in which the headmaster knew each boy. The gym was to be three stories in the back (south side) and two stories on the north. The main floor would house the varsity basketball court, with two cross-courts for intramural play. Elevated folding bleachers would run the length of the north side with storage rooms beneath. A low roof extension on the east would provide space for an office, training room, and a trophy-assembly room for athletic squads. A fifty by fifty foot extension on the southwest side would provide an area for tumbling, parallel bars, wrestling, boxing, and so forth. The hollow tile would be glazed on the inside to provide a smooth finish. Steel trusses would support the metal roof and windows would be of metal frame. The downstairs area, built into the natural contour, would contain an oil burning furnace providing steam heat and a laundry and workshop. A concrete porch would run along the backside (south) and it would have a fireplace for cookouts by athletic and other groups. The basement would also have showers and dressing rooms for school and visitors alike, eliminating those cold runs from the Old Gym to the Old Dorm. It was to be called Memorial Gymnasium in honor of all Christ School boys killed in any war, with their names to go on a bronze plaque placed in a prominent area. The construction of this gym would have provided plenty of athletic facilities for a student body extended upward to 150 or 165, leaving the problem of expansion limited to the chapel and the dining hall as far as the physical plant was concerned. The problem in the chapel was solved when the choir was moved to new pews on the landing leading to the altar rail. By placing twenty-five to thirty choir members there, there was plenty of room in the rest of the Chapel–five to a pew–for students, faculty, and visitors alike except on occasions such as Candlelight Service, Easter, and graduation, when extra chairs were placed down the aisle. The dining hall was not crowded to its limit because the staff was much smaller, food was sent home from the dining hall for faculty wives and their children, and generally non-faculty staff did not eat their meals in the dining hall.

The gymnasium built in 1953 met two crucial requirements: it came in under $100,000 and the roof didn't leak. It was superior to what had been temporary for thirty years but not as grand as the one Mr. Dave had planned. Actually Memorial Gymnasium was a great step forward. Heat was provided by a coal furnace. No longer would visiting coaches wear ear muffs. No longer would games be postponed because of rain or melting snow. It had storage facilities, showers, locker rooms, an office, a training room, some tumbling equipment and a small room for weight-lifting and wrestling practice. There was one main basketball court and two cross-courts for intramural purposes. It was big enough to permit indoor tennis practice and a volleyball net provided recreation for inclement weather. For two seasons prior to the building of Memorial Gymnasium, the basketball team played all of its games on the road. The first of those two seasons saw the Greenies win two of seventeen games. The second season was a winless 0-12. The only other Christ School basketball team to lose all of its games was the one which played the first season in the Old Gym in 1922-23. Their record was 0-13.

The need for a new gym reached the desperation stage in 1951. At the

July board meeting, Mr. Dave informed the trustees that the Old Gym was no longer usable; it was unsafe for practice. "The roof trusses are sagging and could snap at any minute," especially when the students were cheering and "beating on the grandstand."

Raising money and trying to arrange financing took time so that work on the new gym did not begin until June 30, 1952. As agreed to by the board, the school was to borrow $40,000 with the four or five year note to be paid off from money raised from the alumni and quarterly interest from the Mary C. Kistler Trust. Any further amounts necessary to meet payments on the loan were to come from the Lawrence S. Holt Trust and/or other unrestricted funds.

Before construction began, Mr. Dave was forced to scale down plans for the gymnasium. Steel, copper, and other items were in scarce supply because of the Korean War and required a government allocation permit. This involved such long delay and the prices of such items inflated so rapidly, that Mr. Dave had to dispense with the architectural plans of Earl Stillwell. For help, he turned to Moreland Hogan, a New Orleans contractor whose son was attending Christ School. Thanks to the efforts of Mr. Hogan, the school acquired the plans Metairie High School in New Orleans used for their gymnasium and secured the necessary steel and other metals, including Raymond Arches, which enabled the school to reduce costs by building the inside walls of concrete block with brick veneer on the outside. Mr. Hogan was also present to help see that the trusses went up properly. Also on the job–in a kind of emeritus role–was Mr. Boyd. This was the last building at Christ School which he would be associated with.

As in the case of other buildings on campus, the boys were able to do their share of the work. The application of the floor (hardwood maple) involved several processes. Student crews hauled by wheelbarrow tons of crushed limestone that was used as the foundation. Then a mixture of asphalt and sand heated on metal was poured over the limestone. The next application was the pouring in three stages of concrete, with the boys again manning the wheelbarrows. The maple floor on top then provided a playing surface that was quiet and more resilient than found on most basketball courts. The students also did the cleaning up, grading, and landscaping that completed the construction process.

When the gymnasium was dedicated on Alumni Day (May 17, 1954), the final cost was placed at nearly $95,000. Instead of having to borrow an estimated $40,000, Mr. Dave had to borrow only $24,000 on a personal note from the bank. When work began, some $26,168 had been contributed by alumni and friends. At the alumni meeting that day, another $2,697 was pledged at the instigation of Richard Hutson '43. Other money ($45,000) came from the sale of a few acres of land (about $11,500), gifts, interest from unrestricted funds, and additional contributions. In addition some alumni and friends contributed materially: Col. Robert Morgan of Morgan Manufacturing contributed the hardwood floor; Donald Jenkins '23 provided a reduction on the aluminum sash; Hayes and Lunsford of Asheville gave a discount on the electrical equipment; and Dillon Cobb '32 raised funds to purchase an electrical scoreboard. Mr. Dave expected to eliminate the remaining debt within the next twelve months. His faith that things would work out had been vindicated.

Christ School was to win the first game it played in Memorial Gymnasium in December 1953, with a 45-41 victory over Flat Rock. The victory came after forward Gene Presley put the Greenies ahead with a jump shot at 41-39. He was a high scorer along with John McDonald. Both scored ten points. Others playing in the sweet opening victory were Reed Finlay, Boone Dougherty, Hugh Murray, and Bill Underwood. Things turned worse later in the season and the Greenies ended up 5-12 for the year, with a three year mark of 7-39.

Mr. Dave loved athletics, especially football, but he was often appalled by the injuries and he did not want sports to disrupt the routine. He was constantly vigilant against overscheduling and had a strong ally in Dick Fayssoux. Even while struggling to find funds to build Memorial Gymnasium, Mr. Dave kept in focus a more important aspect of school. His view appeared in the October 1951 issue of the *News* in an annual column he wrote entitled "Headmaster's Report":

> There is no reason to believe that improvement of the school property is worthwhile unless we can see a corresponding improvement in our student body. This improvement is not going to become apparent until every boy considers his classroom work the most important aspect of school life. Top grades are not too important but top effort is essential . . . .

Interestingly enough it was not the physical plant which attracted students to Christ school, through the campus grew more beautiful as the sandstone buildings appeared and the landscaping continued. What did attract was the character of Mr. Dave, the role of the Chapel, the beauty of the setting, the strength of the faculty, and the demonstrable academic results. The new gymnasium was nice; it provided better facilities for playing basketball and a more flexible program. But in athletics, like academics, it was not the physical facilities that set the tone or taught sportsmanship or developed manliness and character; it was the coaches. If this were not true, no Abe Lincoln would ever enter the White House.

VIII: 1950-1970

Able, Stable, Faithful

It required several patient years following the dislocations of World War II for Christ School to begin a new surge of academic programs which was to highlight the next two decades. Before this transition was completed, the largest turnover in the faculty in the school's history occurred at the end of 1950 with five of the eleven masters being replaced that fall. Of the five coming in, one was a Christ School boy just graduating from college and another was the new chaplain who had spent a year here during the war, being ordained in Christ School Chapel in October 1943. The Rev. Ralph Webster spent a year on campus then learning how to run a self-help school which would be a model for one he was to establish in Puerto Rico.

Many factors were involved in the faculty turn-over, not least of which was the concern over a decline in the quality of students being admitted. Any such decline was swiftly corrected during the next several years as Christ School was to enter an academically competitive era in which its students were to receive many handsome scholarships and a growing number began to move away from enrolling in a few select southern schools to entering colleges and universities in the Northeast–both big and little Ivy included.[1]

The decades of the fifties and sixties were to be ones of remarkable faculty stability, even though three of the five hired in the fall of 1950 departed within three years. Five of the six faculty remaining from the spring of 1950 (Mr. Dave, Jim Darsie, Urq Chinn, Fessor, and Capt. Reid) and one of the new teachers (David McCullough) were on board for the entire twenty years. Fr. Webster was to be chaplain for thirteen years, second only to Fr. Harris in time served in that capacity. During those twenty years, these seven men gave a combined total of 133 years to Christ School. Two alumni were lost in the five who departed in June 1950. They were Frank Read, who went to the Harvard School in Hollywood to teach in a rather glamorous setting, and Zach Alden, '24,

[1]The faculty member most active in getting Christ School boys to consider a wider range of colleges was Sandy Hand, who taught American history and coached soccer.

who taught and then became headmaster at Chamberlain-Hunt Academy in Mississippi. To Chamberlain-Hunt, Mr. Alden brought many of the values traditional to Christ School, values which he had learned under Fr. Harris and Mr. Dave and which he supported strongly both in his academic and leadership roles.

That seven men in a staff which ranged in size from eleven to fourteen teachers served so long together underscored how strongly each believed in the system of education that was the Christ School way of life. It imposed heavy sacrifice and limitations upon the time of each. Boarding school was a twenty-four hour-a-day life and the teacher's time-off came only when the students enjoyed time-off at Christmas and in the spring. Off-campus social life was quite limited and most faculty were busily engaged in all phases of Christ School life–the church, extra-curriculars, athletics, and the work system. Dedication was the strong incentive for salaries remained quite low. For those who might argue that raising salaries is the only way to produce academic quality would have to overlook two decades that were rich in scholarship and academic achievement. To demonstrate that money was not the primary reason for teaching at Christ School, a beginning bachelor teacher (five classes, two sports, an extra-curricular or two) was paid $200 a month on a nine months basis. In 1970, that same teacher, thanks to an increase of $1,200, would be paid $6,600. By that same year, the salary of the headmaster was raised to $8,400. Obviously when Mr. Dave turned down the opportunity in the 1940's to become headmaster of Kent School, he was rejecting an opportunity to follow a path of advancement which would have provided a much larger stipend.

One problem about hiring teachers which vexed Mr. Dave no end was the difficulty in getting single teachers. He held to, almost with religious veneration, the idea that "a certain number of single men is absolutely essential" to school life. After World War II ended, it became more difficult to attract single men. For one thing, there was a dramatic increase in early marriages during the post-war period and this meant children at a much earlier age. Part of the problem, then, was economic. This meant the school had to build more homes on a budget which was nearly bare, for total charges (room, board, tuition) in 1951 was only $750 per student. When Mr. Dave retired as headmaster in 1967, the total charge per student that year was only $1,600. Until the end of the war, there were only four faculty homes on campus–the Rectory (Mr. Dave's house), the Little Rectory (the chaplain's house), Mr. Darsie's house (just north of the infirmary), and Fessor's cottage. Rooms were expanded in the dormitories to provide for married couples and an apartment was added beneath the back side of the infirmary. But the moment a faculty member got married or a couple began to have children, the need for houses became urgent. By using the school's resources carefully and wisely (lumber from school trees, salvage from buildings previously torn down, and so forth), Mr. Dave succeeded in building about ten faculty homes that ranged in cost from $12,000 in the early 1950's to $19,000 in the 1960's for the McCullough and Hess houses. Fr. Webster's house contained much of the salvage which came from both the old school building and the Old Dorm. Included in the McCullough house were walls of three-quarter inch cherry in the living room, dining room, and halls–preserved from the last cutting of cherry trees on the school's property in the 1940's.[2] This house-building effort reflected the extent to which the board of directors approved of Mr. Dave's leadership and guidance of the school, for in many instances they approved the construction long after the work on such quarters had already begun.

Frequently Mr. Dave evaluated the year through his comments about the faculty in his annual July report to the board of directors. From 1946-50, Christ School had three chaplains, and the frequent shift in one of the main centers of responsibility was always disruptive to the students and the tone of the school in general. Mr. Dave appreciated the importance of having stable leadership in the chapel and in 1951 commented to the board, "Fr. Webster has improved the religious atmosphere of the school immeasurably." In June 1955, while informing the board there would be no change in faculty for the coming year, he added:

> This is a particularly strong group which works well together and it is hoped that the present situation can be maintained for some time to come.

What he regretted most was the retirement of Miss Harriet McCoy, who had been a nurse here for ten years but was retiring because of declining health. If not loved by those students who wanted to goof off in the infirmary, Miss Mac was loved, admired, and respected for her ability to detect the genuinely sick and to provide a diagnosis of serious illness even before the doctors were able to call the shot. Her background as an army nurse provided an in-depth ability to see through sham and pretense, and she knew how to boss a Monday crew of not-so-angelic hosts so that the infirmary floor matched Fessor's gym for polished brilliance.

In 1958, Mr. Dave had this to say about the staff which had just completed the year. "All of our instructors are capable and efficient and all have done a first class job."

Five years later, Mr. Dave reminded the board about the difficulty of maintaining a competent staff. "Good teachers with the proper background are very scarce, and when you find one he is practically always married and has children or will have within a few months." Everything

[2]A moment of crisis occurred some years later when a new occupant decided to add a decorator's touch and paint the cherry walls white. Fortunately, the action was not carried out.

else equal, a good single man took precedence over a good married one. A year later Mr. Dave was offering high praise for a new Latin teacher. "He (Tom Curtis) is almost as good a Latin teacher as our Capt. Reid, and no higher compliment could be paid any young man."

In 1964, the school hired a female teacher for the first time since day students were dropped in 1924. She was Miss Tops Anderson, who gave up her job at Ashley Hall in Charleston to come to the Cane Creek area to help care for her ailing mother. It was at Mr. Anderson's farm that many of the older students helped harvest crops during the war years. "Miss Anderson is going to come in by day to handle the work," Mr. Dave told the board. "She is a well-qualified and experienced teacher and should have no difficulty with either her job (teaching French and Spanish) or the discipline." For whatever reasons, no students attempted to challenge Mr. Dave's estimation of her ability to control a class.

In 1967, Mr. Dave again reminded the board that the problem of finding qualified faculty members was becoming more critical each year. That year, three vacancies had to be filled, including one precipitated by the withdrawal in late spring of the chaplain who had replaced Fr. Webster in 1963.

Those two decades were the years of golden harvest. No beauty surpasses–at least to a farmer–the endless sight of a field of wheat just before harvest time, rustling in the wind, glimmering in the sunset, every grain ready to burst forth. Christ School, during this period, was much like this. The harvest years ran together with such harmony that it grew difficult to separate one year from the next. Christ School grew in reputation, not only in academics but even more so in character as the self-help system and chapel-centered schedule created a oneness of purpose which demonstrated that faithfulness is success.

Track became a major sport in the late 1950's.
George Holt (left) hands the baton to Charles Webb in a meet at Asheville School.

A Mighty Symbol

On an occasion or two, Mr. Dave suggested that the board of directors should give some consideration to enlarging the chapel, but he did not exert great pressure in this direction. Instead he found ways to make the problem manageable. By increasing the number of pews to thirty (fifteen on each side), 150 people (five to a pew) could be accommodated in the main section of the chapel. When the choir was moved up to the chancel, this provided seating for twenty-five to thirty choir members, taking them out of the front pew on the main floor. This meant that 180 people could be accommodated. Chairs down the aisle (to a maximum of twenty to thirty) provided for overflows on Christmas, Easter, graduation, confirmation, and some Sundays during the year.

Obviously the wear-and-tear on the Chapel increased significantly as the student body moved from 120 students to 160 and beyond. This entailed more maintenance and a continual watchful eye to make certain that the substructure remained sound. But these concerns were manageable. As long as the Chapel was the center of school life–not just symbolically but from the standpoint of lively participation–few voices dared suggest a new one. Whether such voices rise anew to clamor for a new or altered chapel may depend on future numbers.

What became a major problem during this period was enrollment. The problem was two-fold: an overabundance, rather than a lack of applications, and how big Christ School should be. In the latter case, Mr. Dave often voiced the view that the school must be small enough to enable the headmaster to know and influence the life of each student. In 1938, he suggested the maximum limit should be 130. With the building of Boyd Dorm, Mr. Dave talked of an enrollment of 150. When the cottages were replaced by Harris Dorm, he indicated that the manageable limit had been reached–around 160 students.

Forgetting the pressure from mushrooming applications, Mr. Dave saw at various stages several physical limitations which had to be overcome if the school were to grow from 130 students to a still personally manageable 160. The dormitory space became available with the construction of Harris Dorm. The academic space became available with the addition of the science wing and conversion of the old labs into classrooms. Athletic space became available with the construction of Memorial Gymnasium. What remained was the problem of coping with increased numbers in the chapel.

Doing something to the chapel was a matter which Mr. Dave was reluctant to tackle. He knew it was Christ School Chapel which alumni first returned to, wanting to recapture the thrill of singing and participation that made evensong and Sunday sung eucharist not just a service but an event. Lusty singing was the rule rather than the exception. And the high service in a simple chapel setting was an unforgettable experience on a daily basis. Besides Mr. Dave had memories of his father who gave every day of his life to early morning communion services in Christ School Chapel, often alone when frigid weather outside embraced the unheated interior. There was also another problem. Christ School, which incorporated and became independent of the Diocese in the 1940's, did not own the immediate grounds on which it stood. If it chose to do so, the board could have built another chapel elsewhere on the campus and closed the original one. To do so would have sparked angry cries of heresy from Christ School past. Even to alter the chapel in a way that detracted from its eye-catching approach as visitors made their first turn on campus, the huge ivy vines overlaying one side of the entrance, would have produced great anguish. During this period, before the Alumni Association was organized to be a fund-raising tool, small groups of graduates often discussed how the chapel could be enlarged without really changing it. Various ideas came forth but no movement. There were no voices for re-building or radical revision–inside or out.

VIII: 1950-1970

By Word Of Mouth

From its very inception, Christ School was in a situation in which the demand for enrollment far exceeded the space and finances available to care for such numbers. While Christ School was founded as a college preparatory boarding school, the larger part of its student body were day students, mountain children who had no access to public school education. In the 1920's, when Valley Springs High School was built in South Buncombe County, Fr. Harris discontinued the day school operation, with the last walk-ins graduating in the Class of 1924. From this point on, for a few years, Christ School had to struggle to increase the number of boarding students and to provide the facilities for such an increase. It crept from sixty to eighty to one hundred, expanding to 125 students when the 38 Dormitory was completed. When day students were on campus, the size of the student body ranged from twenty the opening year to a maximum of 260. One must keep in mind, though, that many day students attended part time during the year, dropping out to work or for sundry reasons, and many attended a few years and then dropped out to marry or go to work.

It was not too long after World War II that Christ School's reputation and enrollment began to grow in geometrical proportions. During the first several years of 1950, Christ School admitted around 137 students each September. When reporting on the admissions picture to the board at its annual July meeting, Mr. Dave noted each year that all except five or six places had been filled by June 30. He wrote in the Headmaster's Report of June 30, 1953:

> "There has been an amazing demand for places in our student body for the next session. . . . There are already sufficient applications on hand to complete our enrollment and many for next year. . . ."

At the July meeting in 1954, Mr. Dave informed the Board that 150 boys had been accepted, "ten more than can satisfactorily be accommodated." As a result of the growing admissions pressure, he asked the board to authorize the future construction of a new dormitory to house the students who were then living in the five remaining cottages. It was to be a dorm similar to Boyd. For Christ School, the upswing in applications pre-dated the Brown v. Topeka decision of 1954 which called for desegregation of the public school system across the nation. At that board meeting, Mr. Dave discussed the effects of this Supreme Court decision.

> Three factors are now contributing to a rush to private schools: adverse criticism of the public school system in general, growing parent awareness of the (current) educational system, and recent Supreme Court rulings on segregation.
>
> We're turning away students in droves. Now seems to be the time to expand to 150, which is the limit for our type of operation. Now is the time to make that decision.

In 1955, Mr. Dave pointed out that the number of applications was "overwhelming," and he informed the Board the school had been full since March and had only a few places remaining for the 1956-57 school year. With the need for a new dormitory in mind, he added, "It seems that we are in a boom period, and it looks as though we had better get in shape to handle the situation." A year later the school was accepting only one of every four applicants and nearly forty applicants were already in hand for the expected forty vacancies two years down the road.

The crush of demand and the ensuing paper work taxed the Christ School admissions department, which consisted of one man, Mr. Dave, who also doubled as headmaster, maintenance man, teacher, business manager, counselor, and so on. The downside of increased popularity was the pressure it exerted upon the school to overcrowd. In order to get a better handle on admissions, to put it on a more business-like basis, Mr. Dave announced in 1957 the beginning of a series of entrance and placement tests, with only those passing the examinations being given consideration for admission. The aim was to insure that the school admitted a better prepared group, one "capable of first class schoolwork." In strengthening the admissions process, Mr. Dave was responding both to the parents and the demands of the colleges. "In as much as all parents send their children to us to prepare them for college, it is only right that we accept only those capable of that type of education."

By 1958, a subtle change had been occurring in the enrollment profile. There was heavy demand for the ninth grade and the tenth. Almost no students were admitted into the fifth form. But there were signs that the lower two forms were in trouble, at least from an economic standpoint. "Our seventh grade is invariably too small and in most years the eighth is in the same condition. Both are expensive to teach, but necessary in planning for the future." There is little doubt that the seventh grade would have been hard for Mr. Dave to give up. He loved the choir and the seventh graders were the main soprano section. Besides he enjoyed their naive youthfulness as they roamed the school grounds barefoot and in short pants, running, shouting, and finding time to build model airplanes and shoot marbles and play mumbletypeg. Besides, half of the choirmaster's pay came from his role of teaching English and American history to the seventh graders.

The screening process, which included conferences with parents and students and strong recommendations as to character, paid off. In comments to the board in July 1959, Mr. Dave observed that the process had resulted in "a better scholastic record" and has "practically eliminated the student who drops out at the end of the school year." By this time Harris Dorm had been built and dedicated and the school had extended its admissions to 162.

For the next few years, the reports to the board simply echoed the remarks of the previous year: the school is full (beyond capacity) and several hundred applicants have been turned away. One year, more than 135 boys applied for about fifteen ninth grade vacancies. In 1961, Mr. Dave wrote: "The school is a little more than full with 166 enrolled and the only problem is where to put them."

The pressure for admissions created such a plethora of tedious and burdensome paperwork that Mr. Dave gave up his duties of teaching after forty-one years in the classroom. In informing the board of his decision to leave the classroom in July 1962, Mr. Dave apologized for the necessity of having to hire a teacher to replace him. "Prior to this time," he said, "I have carried out a full teaching load and managed the administration in my spare time."

In 1963, the headmaster again expressed deep concern about the future of the seventh and eighth grades. He cited two reasons for the decline of applications to the Lower School: an increase in the cost of education and the rapid growth of parochial and day schools. (It might be noted that the total cost of attending Christ School was raised to $1,500 in 1963, well under the room, board, and tuition charges of other excellent preparatory schools and below the charge of many day schools.) "It would be much easier to operate on a four year basis," Mr. Dave said, "but I would hate to see us reduced to that number of classes as the eighth grade, in particular, is of great importance." The importance of the eighth grade lay not so much in the number of sopranos it provided for the choir, but rather because it was an important year in teaching the boys to adjust to the school's academic demands, the self-help system, and to learn its way of life. In his report a year later, Mr. Dave's pessimism about the future of the lower two forms was underscored. He expressed the belief that the lower school would "eliminate itself" in the next few years and that "we should be prepared to adjust our staff and our curriculum accordingly."

With Mr. Dave's retirement came another surge in admissions when 185 students were accepted for the 1968-69 school year. In a report to the board of directors on April 8, 1968, the new headmaster, David P. Harris Jr., said that applications for the next year "overwhelm me and I stay behind on acceptances and rejections."[3] That the fall of 1968 would see a dramatic increase in the number of boys admitted was foreshadowed in the new headmaster's additional commentary:

> (All) old boys have been invited back. I find it difficult to drop any of them even while it is obvious that the boy will have a difficult time.

Although the school had been accepting eight or ten students beyond comfortable capacity for several years, the overcrowding was always relieved somewhat by the dropping out or dismissal of five or six students each year. This appeared to be the expectation and it seemed a less disruptive process than adding a handful of students at mid-year who would be behind in their schoolwork and totally unfamiliar with the self-help way of life.

But that overload, even when it involved only eight or ten students, created new problems. For one thing, it made discipline a little more difficult to maintain, going beyond the 160-65 figure Mr. Dave felt to be the maximum if he was to remain a close, personal influence upon each boy. It was during these same years that drinking and smoking began to grow to be a more serious problem, especially during the last several years of the 1960's. To alleviate some of the conditions which seemed to provide students a greater opportunity and access to drinking, Mr. Dave began to curtail the admission of students from the immediate area, reaching out more to students from other states. The increase in numbers–particularly the quantum jump to 185–threatened the very fabric of the self-help system. It meant that the basic jobs on campus were fragmented into smaller bits, requiring less time and becoming less meaningful to the boy involved. The same disintegration was beginning in the inspection process. Suddenly thirty-five or more seniors were doing the supervision which had been effectively handled by twenty to twenty-five. A decline in the quality of inspections and work became more apparent, and with it an undermining of the pride and self-respect previously engendered by the work system. It was a problem which the board was becoming aware of in the early 1970's.

[3]Beginning in the fall of 1967, the Board of Directors began to meet on a quarterly basis rather than annually.

VIII: 1950-1970

No PR Allowed

Mr. Dave was unpretentious. He didn't believe in blarney. He didn't try to fool anyone. That's one of the reasons parents–even the more sophisticated ones who might not at first relish the idea of shaking hands in the office with a man whose khaki trousers were soiled from his work moments before on a busted water or sewer line–left that office knowing this was the place for their son. Mr. Dave never heard of PR. He believed in what the school was, what he was doing, and the way in which he did it. Hence, there was no pretense. What you saw and heard was it.

For example, visitors–distinguished or otherwise–were not treated to special meals. In fact, there was no such thing as distinguished visitors for everyone was considered distinguished and treated so. When the Priest Fellowship of the Diocese met here once or twice a year for many years, they would find the day's menu (drawn up by Mr. Dave that morning on an envelope) unchanged: thick split pea soup, navy beans soaked to the fill in rich juice, corn bread, molasses, and a never-ending pitcher of fresh milk providing nourishment for the rest of the day. If a board member appeared, he was afforded the same gracious, democratic treatment.

There was no such thing as a special clean-up day to impress anyone. The regular Monday clean-up period and the twice-a-day regular job periods left the housekeeping in good order. Whatever blemishes there were, were there for all to see. Even the school catalogue was not intended to flatter. It was small, contained few pictures, provided the basic facts, and stated simply and clearly and unashamedly the philosophy, purpose, and program. Basically, the only changes occurring in the catalogue were the names of new faculty, vacation dates, changes in courses, and any increases in tuition. The unchanging catalogue not only made economic sense but, more importantly, symbolized the steadfastness of the school to the ideals and principals and values to which it adhered. Cosmetic changes might occur, but the basic Christ School way was ingrained in those catalogues.

The Drama Club came back strong in the late 1950's. The crew of "Mr. Roberts" gets into action.

Dances continued to be popular as this foursome conversed during intermission.

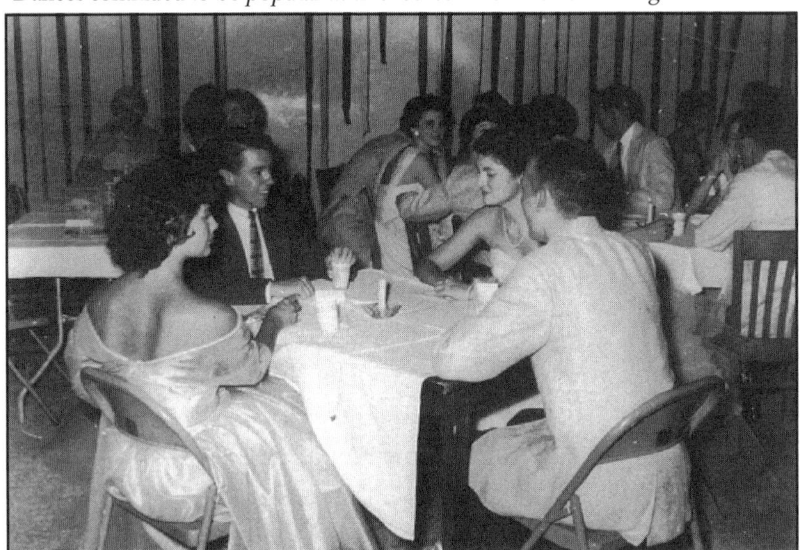

39

CS News: A Strong Voice

From its beginning in 1929 until 1970, the school newspaper had a strong editorial voice. Shortly thereafter, the editorial section disappeared from that publication. For the most part, the editorials were student oriented, dealing with problems that affected life on campus, but occasionally topics broadened to fit the national or world situation.

The editorials were timely, thoughtful, sometimes provocative, giving insight into some problems of the moment. There were editorials of exhortation, in which students were urged to take advantage of trips to concerts in Asheville, to support the drive to raise funds to combat polio, and alumni and friends were asked to contribute $30,000 to wipe out the remaining debt on Memorial Gymnasium, a structure dedicated to all Christ School boys killed while serving their country.

There were editorials of praise, such as thanking the dance committee for an especially festive occasion, or to the unsung student heroes about campus who did their jobs thoroughly without attention, and praise for nurses like Miss Harriet McCoy and Mrs. Virginia Klose for their dedicated care to the health of the school community.

The editors focused attention on areas where the students sagged in dilgence and reminded them of what it was to be a Christ School boy. There was criticism of student misuse of the newly installed telephone in the basement of the school building ("The Battle of the Booth"), of a slump in chapel performance ("A Case of Laryngitis"), some misconduct when the Angelus was ringing ("A Moment for Silence"), student abuse of the laundry ("Rough Spots Ironed Out"), and the need to own up to misconduct ("The Measure of a Man").

Healthy opinions were expressed on a wide-range of topics from national affairs to changes in the school routine. The paper editorially discussed the issue in the 1950's of extending the right to vote to eighteen year olds and concluded they were too immature. The editors brushed aside the argument that being able to fight (eighteen year olds were drafted then) was a sign of maturity. It concluded with the judgment that no one should have the right to vote without taking a course in American history. In June 1954, the paper applauded summer reading as a step forward. It required students to read three books (from an assigned list) and then to write an essay of several pages on each.

Sometimes the editorials stepped on toes–in unexpected places. Editor Hagood Ellison found himself in that uncomfortable spot in 1968. For the first time ever, a group of Christ School students began to whistle, make cat-calls, and jeer the opponents–during play and especially at the foul line. It was un-Christ School conduct. Ellison denounced such conduct editorially. Much to his surprise and embarrassment, Fessor, who no longer coached football or basketball and who silenced with strong voice student or parent alike who might be out of line at a Christ School game, sternly rebuked him for "criticizing Christ School."

When the October issue of *The Warrior* came out in 1934, reporter J.D. Jones wrote an editorial of welcome. While enlightening newcomers as to the purpose of the school ("the building of character") and the improvement of facilities, he managed to inject a bit of wry humor: "For the edification of a few, it might be noted that the bathhouse contains showers. Last year some were hard to impress with the fact."

Editorials–even graduation ones–did not fall into the modern psychological mold of "I'm O.K., You're O.K." The June 1949 edition under the aegis of Rutherford Smith distinguished between Christ School types in an article entitled "Sermon on the Hill:"

> Now you who entered here last fall have fallen into one of two categories. Namely, one that could be headed Christ School Boys in which you have tried to cooperate and to do your share of the work. The other group can be headed by a single title, that of "Bums" in which you have tried your best to get by with as little effort as possible. Think carefully. How many of us with a clear conscience can say "Christ School Boy?"

Year-opening editorials often called upon the senior class to exercise strong and united support of the school program. Such was the case in 1941, when *News* President Robey Bradham spoke in the November issue for a class that would a few months later find itself entering World War II:

> Members of the Senior Class can be of service to the school in many and varied ways. School discipline can be maintained better by prefects and masters with the aid of the Senior Class. A sincere desire by the Seniors to improve their inspecting would lead to a cleaner and more attractive school. An ambition

> to aid in seeing that study halls were better kept would prove of inestimable value.

Editors did not hesitate to explore the philosophy of living. In November 1942, one of them wrote about the dangers of sacrificing personhood and character to curry popularity:

> Popularity is coming down the track of your life, and, if you are not careful, it will wreck your character and destroy your principles. Do not be afraid to stand alone for the right. Never sacrifice your principles for the sake of popularity.

For the most part the Class of 1945 was graduating into what was expected to be a long, costly war against Japan. The war in Europe had ended the previous spring but the invasion of the Japanese mainland lay ahead and resistance was expected to be fanatical. Hence the editorial pointed out that some members of the class would fall in battle to help preserve institutions of worth like Christ School.

> We have received the spiritual, mental, and physical training necessary to cope with the pressing problems of today and of the future.
>
> We are not leaving Christ School but we are actually taking it with us. Whatever we do reflects on our beloved school . . . . This should give us added incentive (to do our best) because Christ School, the institution, stands for much more than just any one individual.

Ward Hamilton considered in an editorial October 10, 1958, an announcement by Mr. Dave that the seniors would be banished from all study halls–day and night. No more supervision, they would be free to study when, where, and to what extent they pleased. The writer did not know whether the new freedom from supervised study hall would be a "boon or a bane."[4] But he added:

> This is not to be considered a general holiday for deliverance from study . . . . Being able to allot your time among your duties is a basic skill in learning to accept responsibility.

Later that year, a pair of editorials–one by Mac Smyth and the other by Bill Wells–pointed to several things that both reflected and generated better morale on campus. Smyth, the editor of the *News*, wrote in a "Pat on the Back:"

> For the first time in many years the Christ School fraternity is again an organization–not just a smoking club but a recreation

[4]See Exeter Word List.

place for all Fifth and Sixth Formers. This year the Headmaster has allowed upper formers to hold parties on Saturday nights at the fraternity house . . . and the boys should be commended for not trying to take advantage of their new privilege.

In the same issue, Wells, who was to become a Morehead Scholar, praised the new team organized at Christ School which improved morale about campus generally– "a new, self-organized cheerleading group." What was their contribution?

These energetic sixth formers have been among the deciding factors in our splendid record. Thanks should go to all the cheerleaders under the direction of Tony Leonard. They are John Griswold, Bill Wasson, Sam Robinson, Overton Erwin, Steve Bitter, Chris Parsons, John Hankal, and Pat Riley.

All graduating classes make their contribution to and mark on Christ School, good or bad. The *Christ School News* of June 6, 1965, concluded that the Class of 1965 had left a "good legacy." It took root with four first formers in 1960 and graduated twenty-five who had a deep sense of unity and purpose.

That unity began to manifest itself three years ago. Together the class published two editions of *Green Leaves* (a fourth form literary magazine), sold tickets for the student body to hear a talk by Charlie (Choo-Choo) Justice with the proceeds going to provide for a needy family to whom a group of the class paid a personal visit, and ended that year with a hamburger cookout and square dance at the Frat House.

This year that unity has manifested itself all year and has been best expressed in its contributions to the new dining hall– not in the form of several hundred dollars as a class gift for shrubbery, but in the free time labor expended in digging and grading the grounds around St. Thomas Dining Hall.

It is a class that constantly kept rising to the top. It carved its own well deserved niche.

The editorial page played a vital role. Through it the *News* kept alumni, parents, and friends alive to the concerns and conscience of Christ School at a given moment. Editorials served as a reminder that though times may change, basic problems don't. They showed that the school had fewer problems in the long-run because it gave sunlight to those that existed and provided solutions as needed.

VIII: 1950-1970

Academics: A Full Harvest

Academic excellence taught in an environment of Christian nurture was Christ School's mission from the opening day in 1901. The school made its first academic expansion in the fall of 1902 when Celestine McCullough was hired as a history teacher. She was also to be matron of the boarding girls who were to be placed on the third floor of the Old Red School House when the plastering was completed. Though the plastering was finished, girl boarders were not taken in.

In 1910, the board of directors advised Mrs. Wetmore that the school should "stop the practice of automatically accepting pupils from towns or cities solely on the recommendation of the clergy." It was apparent that sometimes the clergy let their heart outrun the mind. The next year, Fr. Harris, who returned as rector and headmaster, was named chairman of a committee to set scholarship policy.

Towards the end of Christ School's second decade, Fr. Harris saw the need to move the school into a boarding only situation, for public education was being rapidly extended into Buncombe and Henderson counties. In 1922, he called upon the board to begin discussion of the role of the church schools in the face of this expansion. The answer came in 1924 when Fr. Harris dropped the school's day program–a decision which created some resentment in the neighborhood.

During the 1920's and 1930's (years of the great Farm Depression), not all Christ School graduates enrolled in colleges, but there were more avenues open then to a young man who had a good high school education. Those who did attend college distinguished themselves, and the colleges and universities most attended were the University of North Carolina, Annapolis, Virginia, Pennsylvania, Auburn, Cornell, New York University, Harvard, North Carolina State, Duke, Tulane, Kenyon, Georgia Tech, Maryland, Clemson, George Washington, Wake Forest, Sewanee, Lenoir Rhyne, Mars Hill, and Asheville-Biltmore College.

During the post WWII years, academic development accelerated, with those not attending college becoming rare exceptions. With Mr. Dave successful in keeping costs low, the school drew heavily upon middle class families, especially in small towns and rural areas, families willing to sacrifice to provide their children a better start in life and who generally held to the same basic values that the school did. In 1948, Mr. Dave informed the board that only one graduate did not attend college that fall and that all the graduates in 1947 "are doing well in college."

In the process, Mr. Dave did not waiver in his commitment to academics as the "overriding goal." In his report in 1950, he said, "Our percentage of failures took a big drop from the preceding year. While this percentage is still too high, there seems to be no way to lower it other than by reducing our standards. A move of that kind does not seem wise."

The Class of 1953 was to draw special praise. "It set a high scholastic pace and made things hum generally." Christ School sent that class to UNC(5), North Carolina State(2), Georgia Tech(2), and one each to Davidson, Duke, Trinity College(Conn.), Dartmouth, Rice, Sewanee, Tulane, Kentucky, Alabama, North Louisiana College, and Mars Hill.

By 1957, the applications so far exceeded space that Mr. Dave had a series of entrance and placement tests instituted. Only those who passed these examinations were to be given any consideration. "In as much as all parents send their children to us to prepare them for college," Mr. Dave said to the board, "it is only right that we accept only those capable of that type of education." The next year more than 100 boys applied for about fifteen places in the third form.

Even though he instituted a test for admissions, Mr. Dave never ceased to admit a boy whose academic work might be deficient but in whom he saw some potential as a contributor to the school and some capacity for academic growth. In general, he proved to be a good judge of character, but he did not hesitate to drop a student who proved him to be wrong. If a student could not grow to accept the Christ School way, then at some point he had to go a different way.

In 1962, Mr. Dave observed that the general scholastic average for the school year was four points above the average for the preceding year. The twenty-seven graduates attended twenty colleges, including Dartmouth, Auburn, Virginia, UNC, Washington and Lee, Yale, Trinity College, Williams College, and Carnegie Tech. The showing of the Class of 1962 demonstrated, according to Mr. Dave, that screening applicants paid off. "Naturally it eliminates some boys we would like to have for reasons other than scholastic, but after all college preparation and not athletics is our business." Five of the twenty-nine graduates in that class attended Christ School for six years and none for less than three.

The same kind of good news carried into 1963, with Mr. Dave injecting some wry humor into his remarks: "Reports of our freshmen in college indicate that one maintained a 3.9 and two others an average of 3.8. The other boys did either average or above average work with the exception of one who was dropped because of Wine, Women, and Song. There seems to be no way to avoid these tragedies." A report presented by his son in 1970 revealed that the thirty-one graduates of that class had settled in at college, with two of them receiving Moreheads to UNC and two others awarded scholarships to Washington and Lee and North Carolina State respectively.

The more visible evidence of academic success began to emerge in 1952 when Joe Robinson became the first Christ School boy both to compete for and to win an Angier B. Duke Scholarship. This was a time in which "college preparatory" meant exactly what it said, and though Christ School did not have any courses with the title "advanced placement," sixth form courses prepared students for the intellectual challenge ahead. Three of the graduates of the Class of 1951, for example, were placed in advanced standing at the University of North Carolina–Robert Eberle, Sam Emory, and David Futch. Scott Bruns, who was later to work for Reuters in London, received similar advanced standing at Tulane.

The academic awards were broad-based. In 1953, sixth formers won scholarships to Trinity College, Harvard, and Kentucky. The following year, graduates earned scholarships to Davidson (Union Carbide), Sewanee (Kemper), Trinity, and West Point. In 1955, Christ School entered the Morehead competition for the first time with three seniors competing, none of whom won but one received a scholarship to Harvard and another to Davidson. In 1956, Ian MacBryde, who was also an Angier B. Duke finalist, became the first of a series of Christ School Moreheads. The following year Christ School had three National Merit finalists, with Jerre Swann becoming our first recipient. He attended Williams College. The Class of 1958 had a Morehead, an NROTC recipient, and two other scholarship winners.

Reports from the colleges in the 1950's attested to this academic surge. For example, an article in the November 1954 *News* revealed that junior Joe Robinson '52 was initiated into Phi Beta Kappa at Duke, that Ross Smyth '54 had an A-average at Davidson, and that Dean Spurrill of UNC praised Mitchell Borden, Steve Stout, and Lionel King for advanced placement. Later in the year, Warren Myers '53 (Harvard), Loren Johnson '53 (UNC), Andrew Hamilton '53 (Harvard), and Jim Agnew '53 (Wofford) were all on the Dean's List. In the October 1957 *News*, another scholastic item read: "Warren Myers entered his junior year at Harvard, where he is among five Christ School graduates currently there. The others are Andrew Hamilton '53, Tom Robinson '57, Jim Fawcett '57, and George Terrell '57." In addition Moreland Hogan '53 had just entered graduate school in English at Harvard upon completing honors undergraduate work at Rice. That same article also revealed that Christ School had three students currently enrolled at Trinity College in Hartford, Conn., and all were making honors. They were Joel Kidder '54, Fred Boynton '54, and Jack Thrower '57.

The academic success continued deep into the 1960's, rising from "best" to "even better." The June 1961 *News* contained an article about four seniors who had received $40,000 in scholarship awards to seven different colleges. Their dilemma was where to go. All members of the Class of 1961, they were Scott Shaffer (Williams and Trinity), Robert Phifer (Presbyterian College), Albert Sneed (UNC Morehead and NROTC), and Halcott Green (Washington and Lee, Dartmouth, and Yale), who was also accepted at UNC and Columbia but was turned down as an applicant at Princeton and Davidson. Scholarship and athletics did mix at Christ School, with Shaffer and Phifer towering tackles on a Greenie football team that lost only one game.

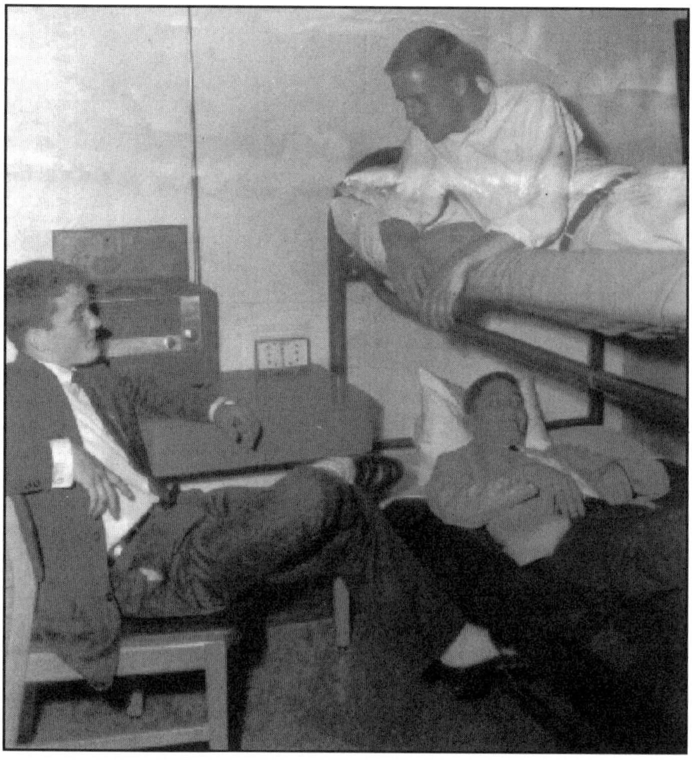

Reliving the moment and creating tomorrow's legends were happy times in the dorms. Thinking up tomorrow's mischief were (left to right) Billy Taylor, Bill Cobb (top bunk) and Art Carlson.

The Board

Until Mr. Dave retired in 1967, the Christ School Board of Directors met once a year, usually in the summer, except on that rare occasion when a special meeting might be called. Such a rare occasion occurred in December 1919 when Thompson Hall (the original Old Dorm) burned to the ground. In the early years, the board met generally at an office in a downtown bank, except on special occasions like the 1925 Jubilee, when the members gathered at Christ School to meet in the library. Later the meetings were moved permanently to the campus and most frequently the site was the living room at the headmaster's house. In general, the board, including the members of the corporation, seldom exceeded twelve in number. Recalling the meetings that he attended while Mr. Dave was headmaster, one alumnus and former board member described the sessions as "Mrs. Dave's Tea." The meetings themselves were never lengthy, with Mr. Dave making his report and suggestions for the next year and the future. Afterwards Mrs. Dave, who was a member of the board, served tea and cookies to end the day on a congenial basis.

This is not to say that the board was a useless appendage or a rubber stamp. Far from it. Rather during those first sixty-plus years, the board and the headmasters found themselves in near unanimous agreement on goals, objectives, philosophy, purpose, and methods. And the results spoke for themselves.

There were occasions when the board engaged in stern debate–though infrequently–and when the board either overrode a proposal or provided the leaven of discussion which would modify it. There were embers burning when Mrs. Wetmore and Bishop Horner, both of strong-willed determination, clashed over the dispensation of the Holt legacy to the Diocese. The Bishop wanted to divide the legacy equally among the parochial schools rather than to follow the stipulation of the will. Strong feelings were expressed when Fr. Harris proposed to end the admission of day students, as the new county schools were absorbing the mountain children. One board member, a minister and alumnus, directed curt criticism at the proposal. He was the same member who had fought each of the previous cut-offs as Fr. Harris eliminated the elementary grades in progressive stages. Another flurry came in the late 1960's over the plan for building a new headmaster's house for Mr. Dave's successor. Both Mr. Dave and Fr. Harris lived in the Old Rectory built around 1909, a cedar shingled, two-story house which evoked fine memories of the simple, unpretentious life which Christ School exemplified. At a time when the cost of building faculty homes had crept up to about $18,000, debated simmered, spilling over into faculty, about building a replacement that would cost around $65,000. What aggravated the discussion was that the original estimate was much lower than the final cost. It was evident to those who lived on campus at the time that at least one member chose to leave the board.

On occasion, the board acted as a restraint which prevented the headmaster from pursuing an objective he might later learn to regret. Such restraint exhibited itself in the early 1950's when Mr. Dave was pushing the board hard to build a new dormitory to replace the five cottages that remained. He saw in this proposal an opportunity to complete the modernization of living facilities on campus by removing the last of the cedar-shingle frame cottages that remained on campus and required increasingly frequent repair. In addition, Mr. Dave saw a new dormitory as a way to increase the student body size to 155 and yet keep the number in bounds so that the school building, dining hall, and chapel would not be overtaxed. Hastened by a desire to push the project along as quickly as possible and to provide the board a building which would be of minimal cost, Mr. Dave, at one juncture, proposed extending an unbroken, barracks-like building from Boyd to an area just beyond the Fourth Cottage. It would accommodate about seventy-five boys. The absence of funds to support the building of this dorm immediately on a pay-as-you-go basis plus the enormity of the problems of maintenance and discipline such a dormitory might create enabled the board to keep alive the discussion for several years while the more manageable solution of the Harris Dorm, sectioned into three distinct parts, emerged.

There can be little doubt that the board had deep respect for and even stood in awe of Fr. Harris and Mr. Dave. Both were beloved and respected by the boys whose lives they so skillfully molded; both had a way of taking the sting out of the problems of life which every growing boy must encounter to reach manhood, not by pampering them or letting them get by or by giving into their endless gripes but rather by requiring them to stand up to their own mistakes and thereby develop self-respect and, at the same time, earn the respect and love of others. The value of such living, even apart from the growing academic improvements, was not lost on the members of the board.

Because the board had an almost unquestioning faith in the leadership of Fr. Harris and Mr. Dave, it permitted them a full range of freedom in exercising their responsibilities. Hence the board stood behind Fr. Harris in his efforts to upgrade academics and to move the school into a boarding only situation in 1924. It supported Mr. Dave fully in his program to modernize the campus into a first rate boarding school whose mission remained unchanged–to provide the best of education for the children of families who did not have the means to send their children to college preparatory schools where tuitions rivaled those of colleges like Harvard and Cornell. There were times when Mr. Dave sought board approval after the fact. This was especially true after World War II when it became more difficult to hire single men to teach and Mr. Dave would build a house for a newly married one and obtain post facto authorization from the board. Disciplinary problems–involving faculty and students alike–were dealt with in-house, and the attention of the board was involved rarely and then only in matters of extreme concern. In fact, there is no evidence to suggest that members of the board ever tried to influence Mr. Dave on matters of discipline. Mr. Dave held each student to be of equal concern and was impervious to exceptionalism. Each student crumbed, swept his room, did various jobs about campus, attended chapel, dressed properly, and left campus only at prescribed times. The only exceptions were those caused by emergency. The policy saved many headaches, for parents, gratified by the regularity, were able to deny their children unwise exceptions in the full knowledge that school and parents were acting hand-in-hand.

Perhaps the most significant role played by the board was that it became a forum through which the goals and ambitions of Fr. Harris and Mr. Dave were hewn into practical proportions. The school lived happily on the cutting edge of solvency for these seven decades. For the first thirty-five years, Mrs. Wetmore raised the funds necessary to keep the school growing and to provide the scholarship support for the mountain children. The next thirty-five years (which included the Great Depression and great inflation) saw the school remain solvent because of the skillful management of Mr. Dave plus the support of a board deeply committed to fiscal responsibility and restraint. Seldom did the school end the year in debt, principally because it pursued a pay-as-you-go approach for capital improvement. Dreams there were but they did not outrun reality. It was a period of time when funds went into operating costs, maintenance, and capital improvements as needed and justified. It required taut budgets. For example, the athletic department, even as late as the 1960's, was operating a successful program on several thousand dollars a year. New uniforms were not used as incentives to play; doing their best for

Christ School was the primary motivation. Extra curriculars had a few dollars to work with, but after World War II the newspaper and the yearbook and the drama club and the choir and several other activities offered excellent outlets for the students and they took on a more professional hue.

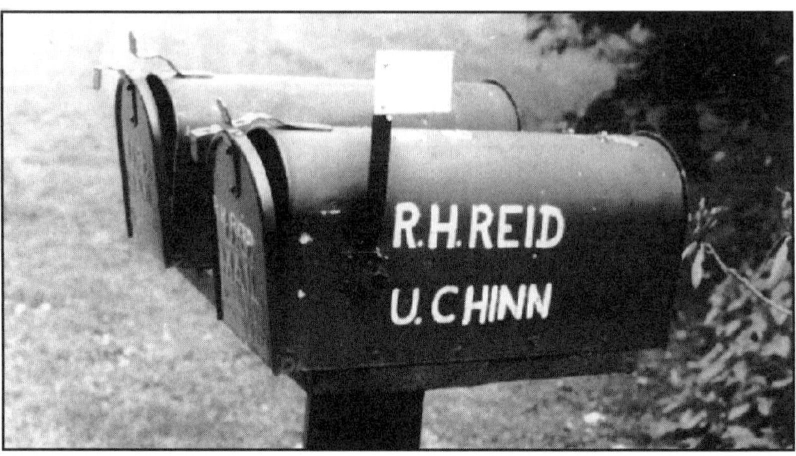

(Below left) Warren Myers engages in the traditional run to the stage as a new prefect. (Below right) Elizabeth Edgerton scratch cooked some 2,000,000 biscuits for Christ School boys.

IX: Other Things

Extra Curriculars

After World War II, extracurriculars began to assume a more important role in school life. The programs begun under the efforts of Fr. Boynton continued during the war years and became a more intrinsic part of the curriculum, with a special seventh period set aside four days a week for these activities.

But even having a seventh period did not insure that the extra-curricular activities would have smooth sailing. For one thing, little money was available so that interest, enthusiasm, and a willingness to make-do determined the success of each activity. Second, there were inevitably some conflicts between the extracurricular programs, each of which was allotted two afternoons a week. When a boy participated in more than two or in two activities that met on the same day, conflict was inevitable. Generally, the choir took precedence and other activities worked around the problem. And two seventh periods a week hardly provided the time necessary to prepare publications (the school newspaper and yearbook) or to put on a play, so that the newspaper and the Drama Club utilized nights, especially on the weekends. When roomstudy was extended to all students who earned honors, such students were free to work at nights. This weekend work often meant that a student had to sacrifice a trip to town, but he found his reward in accomplishment, camaraderie, and food provided by a faculty member's wife. The *News* staff, for example, which worked for many years in the basement of the sponsor's home, always found an ample supply of cupcakes, doughnuts, coffee, and milk available to stimulate their mental juices.

Extracurricular activies were experiences which enabled many students to find a niche where they gained recognition and applause from their classmates–a success that would have otherwise escaped them. They also produced a kind of well-roundedness among the boys, whether as a participant or a participating onlooker. In a small school, an activity must have the support of a cross section of students who play multiple roles. Thus the Drama Club was not limited to an artistic or sensitive few but might also include as lead actor in *Brother Orchid* that physics-flunking tackle who was the mainstay on the football team. And what could be more awe inspiring, especially to parents, than to see that brute of a fullback standing in the choir, from whose cherubic face came a falsetto voice that still kept him in soprano range. A play was an event which attracted the interest of all the student body for weeks on end as it was being prepared, even with changes in cast that might occur only a day or two before the curtain went up. The adventures and mishaps of practice were the conversation that kept laughter alive and spirits higher. A choir trip provided many memorable moments–most of which were conjured up in anticipation. The school newspaper recorded what was going on on campus, including the names of the participants and the successes and disasters that came in their wake. Things like the sketch class and the science class and nature study and the model airplane club came and went–according to the dynamics and interests of the students and faculty at a given time. Other activities–the newspaper, the yearbook, the choir, and the Drama Club–were perennials. All were the leaven which helped raise morale and enabled students to put behind them the routine of academic and athletics and provided them another stage to strut on. These were activities of particular special interest where a mistake was to be laughed at and enjoyed.

Like all aspects of school life, extracurricular actitities got off to a quick start at the beginning of each school year. By the second day (before 1967, the seniors alone came a day early) classes were in full swing, boys reported to varsity football and other athletics, chapel services were begun, and extracurriculars were organized. Mr. Dave, it appeared, believed that the best way to learn to adapt to a new life and to handle homesickness was to begin the school routine immediately. It worked. During the post-war years, the school's extracurricular program grew and improved as pride and professionalism manifested themselves. Each activity began to play a more definable role in the life of the school.

The Christ School News began to evolve into a publication that became more journalistic in content, make-up, and style. Changes were made in typography, headlines, make-up, and photography to give the paper a more professional look. Editorials became shorter and dealt with an ever-expanding variety of subjects. Articles became more crisp and concise, following newspaper style. The name plate was changed on occasions, but it always retained the Christ School seal drawn by Fr. Boynton. Student interest in the school paper grew from a handful to 30 or more workers, including even first and second formers. To increase the writing opportunity for the younger boys, the *News* began to publish programs for athletic contests–programs which provided an in-depth look into the schools and athletic relationships. This experience provided valuable training for future *News* staffers. The *News* entered the Columbia Scholastic Press Association contest and after an initial second place rating, finished first for about the next fifteen years. For a while, the sponsor of the *News* was a CSPA competition judge. During this period, many of the boys who worked on the school paper carried their experience with them, either to work on and edit college newspapers or to become career journalists. For example, Bob Reid, who was the first student to become a staff member while a first former, has pursued a newspaper career which has found him in charge of the *Associated Press* desk in Bonn, Beruit, Cairo, and Manila. For a number of years Rocky Hendrick was the publisher and editor of a weekly, finding time to become mayor of Rutherfordton for several terms in the process. Two current career men are Robert Wasson, who works on the city desk of the *Richmond News Leader* and Gerald Adams, who covers government beats for *The State* in Columbia, S.C. Jim McCullough, who wrote many feature articles for the school paper, did not make journalism a career, but in his junior year he edited the *Duke Chronicle*. As a moderate conservative, he had to keep together a staff of fifty reporters and specialists whose political leanings at the time were like that of a steak, pink to bleeding.

Although the *News* carried out its mission to inform the alumni and parents of what school life was like at any given moment, and though the editorials sometimes carried a bite, the paper provided a record of school life (warts and all) as it unfolded and seldom was embroiled in controversy. A major exception came in the fall of 1969, when the editor devoted half of the paper to the drug forum which the *Christ School News* sponsored at school. To insure accuracy both for the newspaper and for possible discussion in the classroom, the program was openly recorded. Much of the newspaper account simply involved verbatim comments of various speakers and respondents. The December story in the *News* provoked many letters from alumni and friends, most expressing strong approval of the drug forum and expressing alarm that the school might not be taking abuse seriously enough. Letters and comments from different views appeared in subsequent issues of the school paper and in the newly founded *Alumni Reporter*, a quarterly publication. In the spring, the school newspaper was told to discontinue publication of any more comments on the forum and the subsequent controversy.

The Drama Club seldom received the credit it deserved. It was a creative outlet which enabled many students to discover themselves in a new light. It was the magic of the Christ School stage that brought together unbelievable acting combinations to produce laughter and tears and memory lapses and prolonged cheers.

Although the Drama Club did not become a continuous, unbroken operation until it was revamped by foreign language teacher Henry Sutherland in the fall of 1956, the concept was there almost from the beginning of Christ School. During the first three decades, plays were an occasional thing usually instituted because of the interest of a group of seniors or a faculty member. Sometimes, these plays were put on by a sophomore or junior English class, whose Master wanted his students to have some experience requiring stage presence. Generally, these were short one-act plays presented as part of an assembly program. On other occasions, a group of upper classmen would put on a play to raise funds to purchase class rings or to go to the athletic department to help pay for equipment. In the spring of 1924, Dorothy Harris directed a senior class play which included the last female day student to attend Christ School (Ruth Cochrane) and a graduate (Zach Alden) who was to return here to teach and in effect became the first Drama Club director. The budget for such productions was nearly nonexistent, but costuming and makeup were provided by ladies on-and-off campus. During the late 1930's, Mr. Alden managed to direct several plays plus a number of minstrel shows, which included individual talent (singing, dancing, playing musical instruments), group singing, skits and short plays. It was a time when Fr. Boynton (who earned passage back-and-forth to Europe on the *Queen Mary* by playing the piano) made the piano dance, when Bill Shouse and Louis Cutlar gave virtuoso performances on the violin, and countless seniors rose to the occasion as end men, in the minstrel shows.

When Mr. Alden was drafted into the Air Force in 1942, the Drama Club was rescued for a year by Fr. Ralph Webster, who assisted Fr. Webbe in 1943-44 while learning about the operations of a boys school. A three-act drama almost failed to make its appearance on the stage when a boy playing a key role quit school two days before the dress rehearsal. The play must go on and did when scatback Jimmy Crary, who had to tape the football plays on his hand to remember them, replaced the vagrant and gave an Oscar-like performance. Vocally helping out off stage was English teacher Frank Read, whose booming voice could occasionally be heard giving Jimmy the support he needed.

The Drama Club reemerged when Mr. Alden returned to campus following his discharge and the club, which had about twenty members, put on several productions over the next three year, including an all-faculty presentation of *Arsenic and Old Lace* in 1949. The club was continued the next two years–first by Hal Hale and then by James Milling–before going into an hiatus from 1953-56.

With the arrival of Henry Sutherland in 1957, the Drama Club was stimulated to new growth. Within a year, more than thirty students were involved in production and in 1961 it was divided into two separate groups (upper and lower formers), with each producing its own plays. At that time, Sutherland was assisted by John David Richardson, who was to become director from 1962-65. That first year, Sutherland's group pitched in to help morale in several ways. Besides putting on *The Hasty Heart* (staring Converse Bright and Pat Darsie), the group led the pre-Asheville School game pep rally and put on a national election debate. From that point on, the number of productions increased to three or four each year and the quality and difficulty of scripts increased. A committee of club members took over the task of selecting plays in 1958 and that group (Tim Scobie, George Hudnor, and Stan Gibson) chose *The Devil and Daniel Webster*, *The Doctor in Spite of Himself*, and *The Home of the Brave*. In 1959, the Drama Club was divided into Sixth and Fifth form divisions, with each group putting on separate plays. The members combined to put on the year's smash hit, *Mr. Roberts*.

When Richardson took over the Drama Club in 1962, he began to involve the students in the directing process as well. For example, in the winter the Drama Club presented scenes from four plays: "Ross", "J.B.", "Paths of Glory", and "The Importance of Being Earnest," with students directing the first three. The next year, sixth former George Brine directed a five-act play he had written (*The Lonely One*) and Henry Barrow and Robin Douglas had charge of selections from *Dear Wormwood* and *Androcles and the Lion*. That same year, Richardson introduced Christ School to theater-in-the-round in study hall with *The Curious Savage*, a three act comedy involving inmates of a mental hospital. Cited in the *Christ School News* for exceptional performances were Robin Boylan "as the whimsical Mrs. Savage" and Ned Matheny as Mrs. Savage's daughter who "oozes outstanding feminine charms." Others in an outstanding cast were Tom Pritchard, Jim Pressly, Lyston Peebles, Charles Sneed, Richard Hudgins, Chip Webster, Bob Henry, and Tolar Bryan. In 1965, the Drama Club became known as the Playboys, and two of the major productions were *Ten Little Indians* and *The Comedy of Errors*.

For the next four years (1966-70), the Drama Club added to the depth and quality of presentations and Tom Britt brought in some locals for the plays. The first year he directed *Stalag 17* on the school building stage and T.S. Elliot's *Murder in the Cathedral* in Christ School Chapel. The next year, the terrace in front of Harris Dorm was used for *The Tempest* while earlier in the year several girls (Irven Myer, Gail McConnely and Cathy Betty) were imported from St. Genevieve's to participate in *See How They Run*. This occasion marked the first time in many years that girls had been brought in from off campus to take part in a Christ School play. In 1968, the feature performance was *Arsenic and Old Lace*, with Miss McConnely, Brenda Lansford, and Lisa Tribble of St. Genevieve's playing the female roles. In 1949, when the Christ School faculty put on the same play, several teachers from Fassifern joined the cast. No plays were forthcoming in 1969, and the choir did not formally organize. Lack of practice time and a general student malaise disrupted these two extracurriculars.

Fr. Webster and an acolcyte crew dedicate a new faculty home.

IX: Other Things

Mr. Dave Remembered

1967 was a watershed. The board began to involve itself in closer oversight of the school. Mr. Dave retired that summer, though his retirement was set in motion several years earlier when, after an operation, he turned the disciplinary duties over to others. Between then and 1970, the board became more and more concerned about the direction of academics, discipline, philosophy, and life of the school in general. One sign of this involvement was the institution of four board meetings a year rather than one, with several committees meeting between those four sessions. Partly this increased activity was the result of growing financial complexities; partly it was the result of previously mentioned concerns, one of which was highlighted by the controversy created by the *News*-sponsored drug forum held in St. Thomas Dining Hall in November 1969. In part, the death of Mr. Dave the following month added to the fears and uncertainty of the future as the steadying hand of this one-of-a-kind went to his rest.

Perhaps the greatest contribution Mr. Dave brought to Christ School was a sense of stability, a sense of certainty that bred confidence in boys turning into manhood. You were never uncertain where he stood and how he would get where he was going. You were never uncertain as to which was the right way. There were no short-cuts from values, habits, and practices that had been the Christ School character since its inception in 1900. The areas of gray did not diminish the values in life which should be held on to.

From the fiscal standpoint, Mr. Dave might be called an economic magician. He was not a trained economist, but he was a man of great common wisdom who knew that the future of the school depended upon its living within its means. This meant frills were sacrificed and the school focused on what was essential to academic growth and a healthy life. New uniforms were not necessary each year if one learned to take care of what he had. New textbooks did not need to be purchased each year when good used ones were available. The quality lay in what the school did with what it had within the philosophy it cherished.

Because Mr. Dave felt it a matter of trust and integrity for him to make every nickel do the work of a dime if those students deserving of a Christ School education were to have that opportunity, he became that magician. During his last twenty-two years as headmaster (1946-67), Mr. Dave reported black ink to the board of directors on nineteen occasions. There were no years in the red after 1949. Basically, the school lived within the receipts it obtained from room, board, and tuition–$450 per student in 1940 and $2,000 per student in 1968. During this period, the school showed a net gain of $190,184 (averaging $8,641 per year) which was used for scholarships, capital improvements, building funds, or general maintenance expenses.

For sixteen of those twenty-two years, these charges covered the total cost of operation, and they provided for ninety-four percent or more of the expenditures during the other six years. Fees from room, board, and tuition exceeded expenditures in 1944 and 1945 and covered eighty-five percent of the outlay for the other war years (1939-43), except for 1942, when enrollment declined appreciably because of the draft and the fees met only two-thirds of the operational costs.

There was no person more outspoken than Mr. Dave about the burden he hated most–raising money. In the prewar years, that task was carried out by Mrs. Wetmore but always within the framework of the school's purpose and philosophy. Always the aim of endowment had been to raise enough money to provide scholarship assistance for those in need but not a large endowment for capital or operating expenses. Mr. Dave handled the scholarship problem by operating the school at a low cost without precluding consistent improvement in academics, athletics, and the quality of life on campus.

He accomplished this by persuading parents who could afford to pay more than the average fee to do so. Enough did so that generally thirty or forty boys would pay less than the average fee. In either case, all grew up in the Christ School system which required work from all and a system which denied privilege or favor to any simply because they could afford to pay more. Small wonder that alumni who knew him have repeated independently and without exception that a quality which they admired in Mr. Dave was that he was "firm but fair." Perhaps the expression would be better put "firm and fair," because standing up for sound values in no way contradicts being fair.

One other characteristic of Mr. Dave stood out. To some his demeanor seemed gruff. Yet hardly was there a man of more gentle nature. Almost always Mr. Dave taught an invaluable lesson in a way laced with good-natured humor. The boys learned about life without realizing they were learning. These lessons could occur anywhere, more frequently outside than inside the classroom.

Bobby Moore, who remembers his years at Christ School much like Mark Twain remembered life along the Mississippi River, recalls one of those lessons Mr. Dave imparted during a meal in the dining hall. Sunday dinner was always a special occasion. Not because of the fried chicken but because ice cream always accompanied the meal. During the war and just after, ice cream was in short supply, and the Biltmore Dairy began to make more sherbet, which the school bought in Dixie cups. There was one problem. Somehow the sherbet seemed to melt some and refreeze, with most of the color and sweet stuff crystallizing at the bottom of the cup. As a result, the sherbet always looked like a pale imitation of something else.

One Sunday, when Bobby was sitting at the Headmaster's table, a second former (Bobby believed it was David Ramsey) was sitting next to The Man. When the Dixie cups were passed around, David opened his and peered into a kind of green that had lost its color. He hesitated. Mr. Dave turned to him and said, "David, you're not going to eat that nasty stuff, are you?"

"No, sir," David quickly responded. "I'm certainly not going to eat that stuff."

"Good," said Mr. Dave, the corner of his eyes crinkling. "Then you won't mind me eating it." And Mr. Dave ate the nasty stuff with obvious glee.

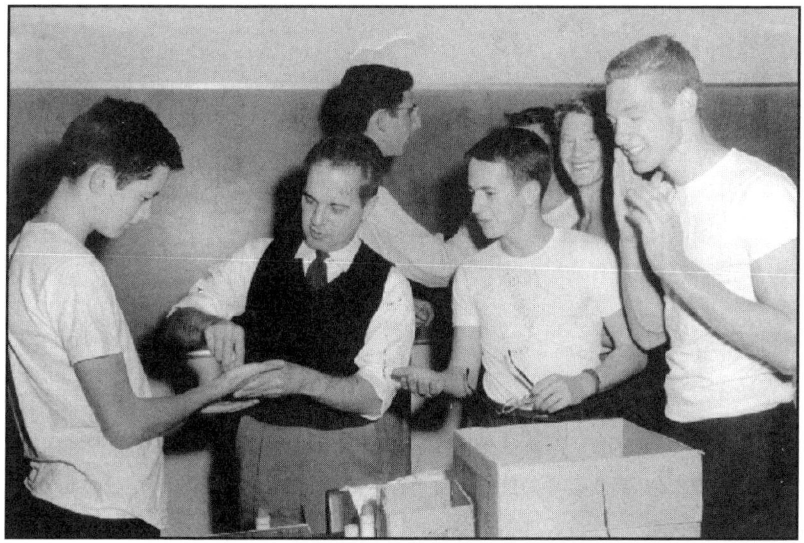

Drama instructor and French teacher Carroll Mason helps make up the cast before a Christ School production in the study hall.

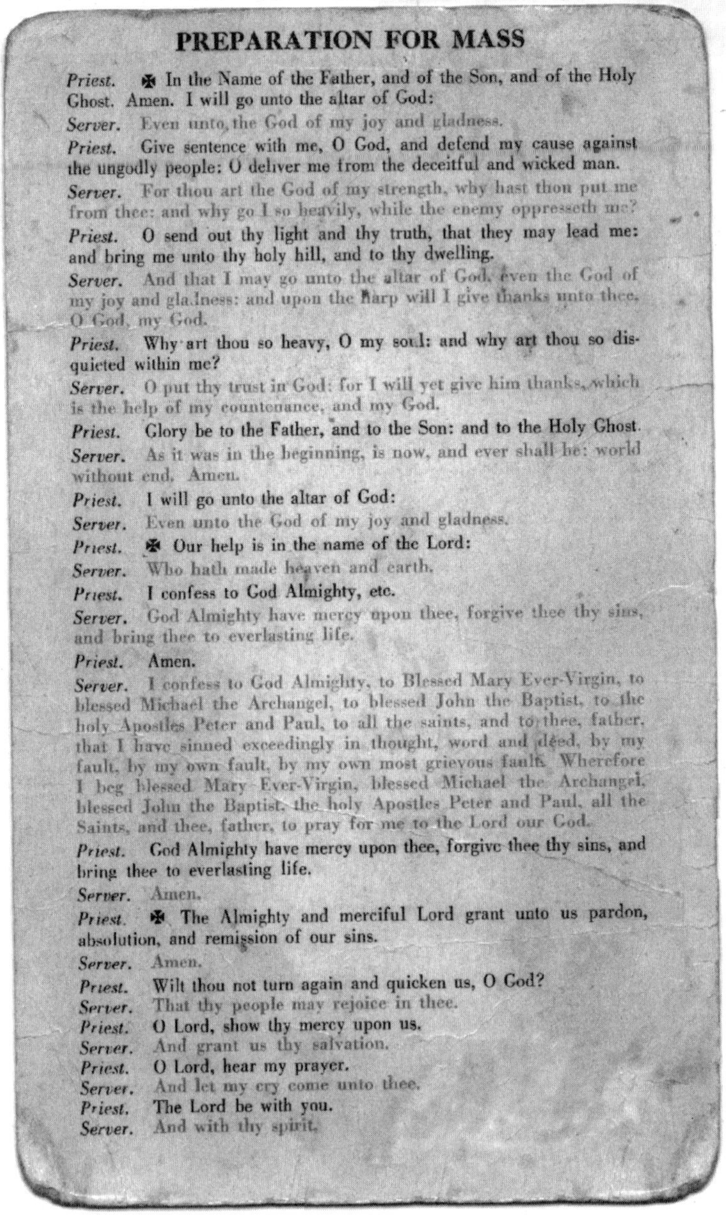

PREPARATION FOR MASS

Priest. ✠ In the Name of the Father, and of the Son, and of the Holy Ghost. Amen. I will go unto the altar of God:

Server. Even unto the God of my joy and gladness.

Priest. Give sentence with me, O God, and defend my cause against the ungodly people: O deliver me from the deceitful and wicked man.

Server. For thou art the God of my strength, why hast thou put me from thee: and why go I so heavily, while the enemy oppresseth me?

Priest. O send out thy light and thy truth, that they may lead me: and bring me unto thy holy hill, and to thy dwelling.

Server. And that I may go unto the altar of God, even the God of my joy and gladness: and upon the harp will I give thanks unto thee, O God, my God.

Priest. Why art thou so heavy, O my soul: and why art thou so disquieted within me?

Server. O put thy trust in God: for I will yet give him thanks, which is the help of my countenance, and my God.

Priest. Glory be to the Father, and to the Son: and to the Holy Ghost.

Server. As it was in the beginning, is now, and ever shall be: world without end. Amen.

Priest. I will go unto the altar of God:

Server. Even unto the God of my joy and gladness.

Priest. ✠ Our help is in the name of the Lord:

Server. Who hath made heaven and earth.

Priest. I confess to God Almighty, etc.

Server. God Almighty have mercy upon thee, forgive thee thy sins, and bring thee to everlasting life.

Priest. Amen.

Server. I confess to God Almighty, to Blessed Mary Ever-Virgin, to blessed Michael the Archangel, to blessed John the Baptist, to the holy Apostles Peter and Paul, to all the saints, and to thee, father, that I have sinned exceedingly in thought, word and deed, by my fault, by my own fault, by my own most grievous fault. Wherefore I beg blessed Mary Ever-Virgin, blessed Michael the Archangel, blessed John the Baptist, the holy Apostles Peter and Paul, all the Saints, and thee, father, to pray for me to the Lord our God.

Priest. God Almighty have mercy upon thee, forgive thee thy sins, and bring thee to everlasting life.

Server. Amen.

Priest. ✠ The Almighty and merciful Lord grant unto us pardon, absolution, and remission of our sins.

Server. Amen.

Priest. Wilt thou not turn again and quicken us, O God?
Server. That thy people may rejoice in thee.
Priest. O Lord, show thy mercy upon us.
Server. And grant us thy salvation.
Priest. O Lord, hear my prayer.
Server. And let my cry come unto thee.
Priest. The Lord be with you.
Server. And with thy spirit.

Acolcyte's preparation for serving

The Answer

Why was Christ School so remarkably successful during those first seven decades? The answer is remarkably simple:

The Rev. Mr. Wetmore.
Fr. Harris.
Mr. Dave.
And dedicated faculty.

The Man with his boys.

THE VICTORY HYMN (265)

Sing Alleluia forth in duteous praise,
O citizens of heaven: and sweetly raise
An endless Alleluia.

Ye next, who stand before the Eternal Light,
In hymning choirs re-echo to the heighth
An endless Alleluia.

The holy city shall take up your strain,
And with glad song resounding wake again
An endless Alleluia.

In blissful antiphons ye thus rejoice
To render to the Lord with thankful voice,
An endless Alleluia.

Ye who have gained at length you palms in bliss,
Victorious ones, your chant shall still be this,
An endless Alleluia.

There, in one grand acclaim, for ever ring
The strains which tell the honor of your King,
An endless Alleluia.

This is the rest for weary ones brought back.
This is the food and drink which none shall lack,
An endless Alleluia.

While thee, by whom were all things made, we praise
For ever, and tell out in sweetest lays
An endless Alleluia.

Almighty Christ, to thee our voices sing
Glory for evermore; to thee we bring
An endless Alleluia.

Postscripts

There is no greater pleasure than talking to Christ School graduates about their times on campus. This section is a transcription of what some of them had to say about their experiences and memories. As Tiny Tim so eloquently expressed it in Dickens' *Christmas Carol.* "God bless us everyone."

THE REV. NORVIN DUNCAN '07

(The Rev. Norvin Duncan enjoyed a unique vantage point in his relationship with Christ School. He attended Christ School near the beginning–from 1903-07. He was in the third graduating class. His marriage to Olivia Butt, whose brother was a graduate in the Class of 1914, was the first to be conducted in Christ Chapel––on June 28, 1911. He was greatly influenced by Mr. and Mrs. Wetmore to go into the ministry. He almost never missed a Christ School Alumni Reunion and became what he would not want to become–an icon to the alumni, a man whose appearance at the annual meetings was always accompanied by a thunderous, standing ovation. His memories of Christ School are rich in meaning.)

THE FIRST SERVICES: The services in the Red School House were beautiful, especially during Lent. They were held on the stage where Mr. Wetmore would have evening prayer and make a short talk. The boys were devoted to Mr. Wetmore. Several of us planned to go into the ministry, and the Wetmores invited us down once a week to have a talk.

FUND RAISING: On a trip to a New York parish to raise money for the building of a chapel, Mr. Wetmore was greeted by a terrific snow storm which cut both attendance and the purse. The offering was quite small. The next morning, a lady who came to the services called Mr. Wetmore to come over to her house. She gave him a check for $800.

A DREAM: One of Mrs. Wetmore's dreams was that the Chapel would be the center of an associate mission involving two or three priests, who would live here and establish missions all around the mountains. This part of her Christ School Dream did not materialize.

OFF-CAMPUS MISSION: Three of the years Cortez Cody and I walked over seven miles to Pinner's Cove, held a morning service in a home there, and crossed over a mountain to hold an afternoon service, and then back to school. It was a happy and rewarding experience, and a great help in our preparation for the ministry.

HANDS OFF: Once when there was some talk about doing something to the Chapel, I wrote Mr. Dave: "For heaven sake, don't you touch that Chapel. The Chapel is the heart of Christ School. It ties all the generations together."

COTTAGE HILL. I remember that for a couple of years some girls stayed on Cottage Hill. My wife-to-be (Olivia Butt) was of the Christ School people teaching there.

OLD RED SCHOOL: House Attic. I lived in the attic room of the school house and taught small children on the second floor. Among them were Sam Cathey (who was to become a judge) and Doc Johnson.

FR. HARRIS: He was a wonderful man. He and I sometimes disagreed on churchmanship. I happened to be on the evangelical side, you know, and he was on the high churchman side.

LEARNING A LESSON: One day a boy sneaked some eggs and hid them under the hat he was wearing. Fr. Harris, passing by, squashed the hat. He was a strict schoolmaster, but the boys were devoted to him.

TRANSPORTATION: (Uncle Van Allen, with his team of a mule and ox, was not the only source of locomotion.) Providing transportation (also) was Mrs. (Agnes) Pressley, who worked for Mrs. Wetmore. She had a two-horse wagon. It was a long trip anywhere you went.

THE STAFF 1906-1907: A key man of the teaching staff was Prof. Huske, who extended his stay at Christ School for a year following the death of Mr. Wetmore so as to be of service to Mrs. Wetmore. I took Latin and Bible under Mrs. Wetmore. The only one hundred I made was in Bible, and Mrs. Wetmore gave a 99.6, saying she didn't believe any one was perfect. Others on the staff were Mrs. (Celestine) McCullough, daughter of an outstanding clergyman from South Carolina, and Mrs. Thurston Stone, sister of Bishop Thurston.

STAINED GLASS WINDOW: In 1911, there was one stained glass window in Christ Chapel, the one over the altar. I think the one dedicated to young Tom Wetmore, who died in 1927, was the next one to be put in.

TWO FAITHFUL SERVANTS: Uncle Van Allen and Agnes Pressley were among those humble folks who are almost indispensable. Van Allen, a former slave, was faithful in all his jobs, being here from the day Christ School was founded in 1900. Agnes Pressley, who was a cook and maid for Mrs. Wetmore, was a tower of strength to her, not only in her domestic duties but as a sort of advisor /companion.

OVERSEEING THE GANG: We had the best baseball team the school ever had, but I could not play. Any extras I had consisted of "overseeing the road gang," and I did receive a medal in debating and was class valedictorian.

BOB HARRIS

HOMESICK AT KENT: Mr. Dave got so homesick Fr. Sill thought they would have to send him home. Instead Don came over from Williams College to cheer him up. Isn't that amazing?

THE TRAPPERS: One year Mr. Dave joined me in the trapping business at Christ School. We'd catch a lot of rabbits and sell them to boarding students for ten cents each. They would take them down into the woods and roast them.

TALK ABOUT THE FUTURE: I never heard Mr. Dave say he wanted to work at Christ School. My father tried to get me interested in the school one time at vacation. I felt like he wanted me to take an interest in carrying on. I was neither interested nor the type.

GOING OFF TO SCHOOL: I think Mother and Father sent all of us off to school because they were teaching at Christ School.

ASHEVILLE CONTACTS: Mr. Dave was a long time friend of Harvey Heywood who became treasurer of the board of directors. Mrs.

Dave was the daughter of the prominent Merrimon family. Mr. Dave did not socialize much; he was too much wrapped up in Christ School. His recreation was hunting and fishing.

KENT OFFER: Around 1940, Kent offered him the position of headmaster. It must have been a tough decision because of more money and prestige. In 1938, Christ School was still relatively primitive, but Dave felt his loyalty to Christ School.

RELATIONSHIP WITH FR. HARRIS: There was never any friction between Dave and Fr. Harris. I think Fr. Harris was tickled to death to see Dave take over, for his health was beginning to break down.

THE BOARD: I think Mr. Dave ruled the board rather than the other way around. The board meetings were held in the living room of the Old Rectory and Mrs. Dave would serve tea. The board would hear what happened. I think Mr. Dave put it this way: "Don't ask me what's going to happen to the money; just give it to me." It's a wonder they'd put up with him.

BRYAN WARREN '16

(In an accompanying letter some years ago, Dr. Warren said this donation should pay for the hen, including interest.)

Fr. Harris had some chickens which roosted in the pine trees near his house. One bright moonlight night, I decided to get a hen. As I climbed the tree, I could see the hen, its head tucked under its wing. The trouble was that I couldn't tell the head from the tail. Finally I grabbed the hen by, as it turned out, the tail. There was a loud squawk which set off a relay of dogs barking around the countryside. Now I grabbed the hen's neck, slid down the tree, and ran to the branch (across the road from what is now Boyd Dorm) where I killed, cleaned, and cooked the hen. For some reason, it didn't taste too good. To this day I can't decide if I did this for meat or excitement.

(That chicken escapade was to pay an unexpected dividend later while Dr. Warren was a student at Duke University. The paper he wrote for English class on the "chicken episode" earned him an "A.")

ARLENE CLAYTON HOLDERLY '20

Activities for girls were very few. Mrs. Elsie Beale Hemphill taught cooking and sewing. Mrs. R.R. Harris organized the Girls Friendly Society. Piano and voice lessons were available at times.

My home was beside Cane Creek at the foot of Burney Mountain. The Christ School boys were welcome to visit our large apple orchard and fill their pillow cases. Those who were fond of climbing came over on Saturdays and Sundays to climb Burney.

When it was apple cider time in the fall, boys came over to enjoy cider and ginger cookies that my mother made. Dr. Grove (founder of Grove Park Inn) bought our farm and it has changed hands several times since. The orchard and the garden were ploughed under and acres of timber cut down. Our big brown shingled house is now empty and deteriorating.

CLAIR R. THAIN '20

No history of Christ School could be complete without information concerning two teachers who labored faithfully along with Fr. Harris and Mrs. Harris to mold the minds and bodies of the boys and girls during the period from 1915-20.

First, Miss Frederica Edmunds, daughter and sister of an Episcopal clergyman, taught Latin and history for a number of years at Christ School. Miss Edmunds was a highly cultured person, speaking several foreign languages fluently. She took a great interest in her work and extended a kindly affection to her pupils that included such diverse activities as sewing buttons on trousers to encouraging religious development. She spent her last years in New York City and Philadelphia, still corresponding with many of her former pupils who held her in the highest esteem and love.

Second, Professor David Owl, a Cherokee Indian, nephew of the Cherokee who was chief of the tribe in North Carolina around 1920. Professor Owl taught classes and coached the football and baseball teams in 1919-1920. He was a remarkable athlete and a man with a brilliant mind who later became a missionary to various Indian tribes in the United States.

ZACH ALDEN '24

Zach Alden, who was to teach at Christ School for many years, was orphaned at about age eight. His twin brother (Mac) and he attended Christ School for several years, worked here for a couple of years after graduation, and came back to teach after completing their courses at the University of North Carolina.

THE PEOPLE: Fr. Harris had declining health. I don't see how he survived. He never slept; he tried to do everything; he ran the school on a shoestring.

Two or three wealthy people (like Mrs. E. V. Lane) helped sponsor the school. It was started to help mountain children and was not expected to become a first class college preparatory school.

Another dedicated lady was Mrs. (Elsie) Hemphill. She was very gifted – teaching carving, painting, domestic science, dancing, and so forth. A lot of the boys enjoyed her class. She also taught the mountain ladies how to weave (make rugs and other things which they could sell in a cottage industry format).

MY FIRST YEAR (1921): We had seventy boarders and over 100 mountain children. They came on horseback, in wagons, by foot; most of them wore clothes that came from the Mission House run by Mrs. Wetmore. Sometimes a package might contain beautiful silk curtains that graced a New York stage or a tuxedo worn to a grand ball. More often, though, the items were more practical.

FR. BOYNTON: He was like a breath of fresh air. He was cosmopolitan and Christ School had become ingrown. His father had been a seminary teacher, well-traveled. Fr. Boynton had a broad outlook, was attractive, knew music and history, was academic, and worked in advertising for *Vogue* magazine before entering the ministry. He had charisma. The church had quite an advantage during his six years. As some teachers will improve the faculty, by his presence he improved the outlook of the school.

CHAPEL SERVICES: The service was not sung before Boynton came, but there was already healthy, joyful singing (if not always in tune). For a while our organist was a student, Clyde Sorrels, who was admitted here on his ability to play. Each Saturday night (before Boynton came) we had quite a practice. Mother Harris would come down. I don't think she knew too much about music, but we all had a great time singing. All the boys really enjoyed it. Getting back to Sorrels, our organist. After he finished here, he went back to New York and married. Tragically, he and his wife died in the famous Cotton Club fire in New York.

ROOMMATES: Several of them stand out vividly. Nathaniel Orr was one of five of us who roomed together in the Old Dorm. He was brilliant and went on to Harvard. Wilson Cuningham went on to become a major benefactor and chairman of the board. Antonio Bass, our beloved Cuban, was sent here on scholarship by an Episcopal lady. He returned to Cuba and died, probably of tuberculosis.

THE HARRISES: You have to appeal to boys in several ways. Dave appealed to boys by his understanding of them. He had been pretty mischievous himself. He had enough of his father's moral teachings and discipline to know how far he could go with the boys and stop. Fr. Harris never stopped. I've seen him so tired that he would come up to his house, sit down, and fall asleep before he was settled in the chair. When Fr. Harris walked by, temptation disappeared; not because boys were afraid of him – it was respect.

BILL FULTON '25

CLASSWORK: I'd been a good student when I entered the tenth grade English class of Dorothy Harris (Thomson). She asked me about a term I had never heard of. I was a little smart in my answer. She said, "Bill, you're a little bit pert." I didn't pass that first month but I learned to do a lot better later on.

GOLF: We did not have a team but I played golf on Wetmore Hill in the fall and spring.

CAVES: Some of us dug a cave on Dairy Ridge, a huge one eight to ten feet deep. No one knew about it until we took some of Fr. Harris's chickens one day. That evening, after the snow had stopped falling, we went to the cave to prepare a feast. Unfortunately, we really didn't enjoy it, for Fr. Harris tracked us in the snow and we got caught.

CLASS RINGS: Spending money was scarce and class rings cost ten dollars or so. The seniors set up a little store and sold candy and other stuff to raise money for class rings. I was the clerk, since I had experience in clerking at a store back home.

AWOL: Only once did I leave campus illegally. There was a fair in Biltmore and I sneaked to the highway to hitchhike to town. I caught a ride with a big Negro man who was driving an even bigger limousine. He drove like a crazy man. I was so scared I didn't have any fun at the fair.

GEOMETRY: I was good in Fr. Harris's geometry class. He gave us two problems to solve over the holidays with the promise to reward a half-day bonus day in town for those who solved them. I worked on them as the train brought me to school after Christmas vacation . Just before the train reached the Biltmore depot, the answers finally hit me. I got that free half-day.

JOHN DOUGHERTY '25

GETTING TO CHRIST SCHOOL: The only way to get there was on a sand road running by the Shufords. (At that time, Sweeten Creek road had not been constructed). Sweeten Creek road was built during the days of the boom (1927-29).

TUITION: It was $75 a semester. Fr. Harris/Mr. Dave allowed you to come if you didn't have any money and repay it the best way you could before the next year began. (Often it was never repaid).

WHY I WENT TO CHRIST SCHOOL: I was doing well at school in Asheville. My mother was a devout Episcopalian and wanted to see that I got better instruction relative to the church.

SENIOR CLASS: It contained 13 members and was an unusual group. We started the first Jigger Shop at Christ School (sanctioned by Fr. Harris; Mr. Dave also thought it a good idea). The money gained from sales was turned over to the athletic association to help buy equipment. Bucket Fulton and I used to go to Hendersonville in the old Ford Model-T truck with the wooden bed to a wholesale grocery to get supplies about once every two weeks. The first Jigger Shop was a log cabin that stood by a big old tree almost directly behind the Chapel. (It was later built of sandstone).

LIVING QUARTERS/GYMNASIUM: There was one dormitory where the young fellows lived; other boys lived in six log huts to the east side of the first gym. The gym had a tin roof. When it rained, the noise was so great you couldn't hear the ball bounce on the floor.

WORK PROGRAM: The work program was fundamental. Everybody had a new job each week; sweeping study hall or working in the laundry or working with Mr. Boyd (a genius with woodwork). Christ School was built from its own natural resources. The stonework was done by the Boyds and students under the supervision of Mr. Boyd and Mr. Dave.

THE WETMORE HOUSE: The old house was beautiful. It was guarded by vines and looked down to planted pines. There was a beautiful view into the valley then. The area was guarded by white pines and hemlock. To build another house, the school just had to cut down a couple of pines.

CLASSES: Mr. Dave taught chemistry and math; Mrs. Harris taught

English; and Dorothy Harris taught English and directed a senior play. We loved her!

DAY-TO-DAY RUNNING OF THE SCHOOL: It was a wonderful operation. We were often mischievous and often did things that were foolish and embarrassing, but we were on a fresh water stream that carried us to shores we could never have anticipated. We never realized what we were experiencing until it was all over.

BUCKET FULTON: Fr. Harris loved him, for he had such a humorous turn about him. He was a shrewd fellow and used his grocery experience in Walnut Cove to run the Jigger Shop.

DODD BONNER: He was another fellow we loved very much. He weighed about 300 pounds and was the mainstay on the football team. Nobody could run over him. He was easily hurt, but Fessor would give him a strong talking too and stick him back in to play.

THE CAVE: We played football in the Wetmore pasture. One day Dodd Bonner, Bucket Fulton, two other boys and I decided to dig a cave in the woods above Wetmore Field. We dug away and built a big room which you entered through a shoot covered with pine poles, burlap and dirt. It was a place where we could go to cook a rabbit or do something mischievous or against the rules. What we didn't know when we completed it was that Fr. Harris and Mr. Dave knew from the beginning what we were doing. After it was finished, Mr. Dave showed up to inspect it, saying it didn't meet state standards and we got busy filling it in.

PREFECT: I was fortunate to be a prefect. Being a prefect teaches a boy the first elements of leadership– compassion, friendliness, support, and guidance to younger boys.

THE ANGELUS. I get goose bumps whenever I hear it ring.

ON MAKING MASH: Several of us had a full proof scheme for making some beer, but Fr. Harris's keen sense of smell overcame our best plans. When he detected the operation, Fr. Harris made us pour the mash out cup by cup and then smash the crock. We got claims. I think we dug rocks out in a quarry for a building that was being erected (probably the Jigger Shop).

FREDERICK KRAUSS '26

BACKGROUND: Attended Christ School one year. Had gone to

St. Barnard's in New Jersey for several years. Working there at the time was Harold Nichols, who introduced organized football to Christ School in 1915. Coach Nichols went north because of a malarial condition.

COTTAGES: There were four then and I lived in the Third Cottage. Perpendicular to the Fourth Cottage was the Log Frat House. I lived with Mark Carmen and Charles Dudley.

Each cottage had a central hot-air furnace with a vent in the middle. One boy fired it up as a permanent job. There were separate buildings for showers and toilet. There were no back porches then.

SCHOOLWORK: Academics were well organized. The teachers were Fr. Harris, Mr. Dave, Mac and Zach Alden, Fessor, and Oscar Kafer (student teacher). There were some girls: the Mallory girl who married Floyd Finch, Ruth Cochrane (nee Pinner), Aileen David (nee Pinner), Katherine Cole (nee Pinner), and the Shuford girls.

FREE TIME: Mostly spent at school. Walked to Arden to catch the bus to Asheville. Smoking: sneaking around and at the Frat. Radio was just coming in and several boys owned sets. At Christ School I put together several one-tube sets purchased at Kress Store in Asheville. Warren Redd brought with him a little ready-made RCA. Another boy had a ready-made 2 tube Crossley. A big thing was to listen after lights.

WORKLIST: Dug a lot of stumps and moved a lot of rocks while helping to build the athletic field.

KITCHEN-COOKS: Breakfast favorites: square of white margarine mixed with peanut butter and molasses. Biscuits. Would trade for cereal or sausage cake. Ed Freas did the milking. Ma Pressley was the cook.

CHAPEL. We stood still for the Angelus.

SPORTS: Not everybody participated. A few had trap lines they checked in the afternoons. Others just messed around.

DUNCAN MACBRYDE '28

FATHER HARRIS was a legend/hero. The fact that he had been able until recently to "chin the bar" with one hand was accepted without question. As far as we were concerned he was a saint only awaiting canonization.

MR. DAVE was close to the same heroic stature. We loved him even when he chastised us with "Black Mariah," his leather belt used on occasion to "take off" a couple of punitive hours against us so that we would be free, maybe to go somewhere for the weekend. Gentle but rock firm; an incredible role model!

FESSOR FAYSSOUX was equally legendary in his way. Years after I left CS he recalled to me how, as basketball manager in 1929 (I stayed on in 1929 at Mr. Dave's invitation, and among many other things served as basketball manager). In a key and crucial game, I was timekeeper and precipitated great controversy. In a closing instant of the game, one of our CS Warriors shot a field goal to win the game, but the opposition said I waited an instant too long in blowing the final whistle. Fessor was on my side...well we were on the same side...we were credited with the game, and I still think we earned it!

PERCY WISE was perhaps my most influential teacher. I admired the way he spoke French rather than English in French class, even in including such instructions as "Please turn to page 23." It seemed to me that he lived and breathed French, and it was quite an inspiration. I have loved the study of foreign languages ever since (became fluent in German; fairly fluent in French and Spanish; fair in Arabic; even amassed a couple of hundred words/phrases in Chinese during a month in the People's Republic).

AMONG UNFORGETTABLE MEMORIES: The way Mr. Dave would get up each Sunday morning and personally cook pancakes for one and all.

GRATITUDE AND RECOLLECTION: Two Spanish-speaking students came to CS and communication was difficult. Between Mr. Dave and Percy Wise, both of whom knew my interest in foreign languages, I was relieved from all study hall attendance if I would take up with these two students (one from Spain, the other from Cuba), and teach them English while they taught me Spanish. Such insight and imagination resulted in a great linguistic adventure...I still remember discussing, in faltering half-English, half-Spanish, the candidacy of Al Smith for the presidency of the United States!

LEGENDS-IN-THE-MAKING: Charles Charleton, a student from Alaska, supposedly would go out mornings to the small mountain lake (Grove Lake) nearby, break the ice of winter, and have a swim before breakfast. I'm not sure whether this was true but legend doesn't require actuality.

GENE JOHNSTON '29

Christ School in 1922. What was it like? Gene Johnston '29, sums up the things of his first year here that have stuck in his mind.

1. School Slogan: "The School that makes manly boys."

2. Tuition was $90 for the year.

3. Students were allowed fifty cents a week to spend as they liked. Some parents would slip in a dollar a weekthrough the mail unbeknownst to the school.

4. You had to be seventeen years or older before you were allowed to smoke. Smoking was allowed only on the bleachers at the basefield field. It was a sad day if you were caught smoking off limits.

5. Every boy owned a broom and every boy had a number which was painted on the broom (the number given to you by Mr.Dave). When broom inspection was called and the number called out, each boy would hold his broom up and the number was checked by a prefect. You had better have the right broom.

6. One penalty I remember was that we had to walk around the Bullring from 5:30 to 6:30 in the morning for one to two weeks every day (except Sunday), with a wooden rifle on our shoulder. If we missed one morning, our time was doubled. We walked rain or snow.

DILLION COBB '32

ARRIVING BY TRAIN: The trip to Arden from Williamston cost about $15. Usually Algae Brumbeloe met us.

CAMPUS: The buildings consisted of six cabins, one dormitory, the Carolina Club, the Gamma Lambda Sigma House. The Old Dorm contained big rooms with four to six boys in each. Mac and Zach Alden were the dorm leaders.

HAZING: Mostly new boys were taken on a snipe hunt. There was very little physical hazing.

CAROLINA CLUB: It was located to the side of the Old Gym and up toward the school building. There was no initiation and membership was decided by vote. It was a place where fellows could gather and listen to music and shoot the breeze. You could listen to the radio, play ping pong, recline in a few chairs and sofas, or play cards. Grades were a consideration for membership.

FATHER HARRIS: He was a great guy, very conscientious about everything. He checked on the boys night and day. I remember his expression, "Whoa, whoa, whoa, wait a minute, wait a minute." (This served as a warning to stop what you were doing and think about it.) You might see him pop into the dormitory at anytime...and at the clubs he'd catch boys coming in late.

BOUNDARIES AND PUNISHMENT: The railroad tracks were the boundaries. If you were late coming back, there was a first time warning. Next time, you got a claim on the ballfield. You also received a claim for leaving the campus without permission. Mr. Dave laid out the claims; sometimes he also laid out the belt.

WORKING OFF A CLAIM: This did not keep you from athletic practice. You were given a certain length of time to work the claim off. You dug in your free time: early morning, late at night, Monday afternoon, and so forth. Sometimes others helped you but at the risk of getting a claim themselves if they were caught. But the claims didn't keep people from playing in sports.

MR. DAVE: I had biology under him. He was all business in class. He was firm and fair. He might use the belt if you were late for study hall. Whenever he did this, it was always done openly and with humor.

EXTRACURRICULARS: There were none. The athletic period was longer.

ATHLETIC PARTICIPATION: Only those who wanted to participated in varsity athletics. Others took hikes through the woods over to Mr. Burney, played tennis, fished, or trapped. Sometimes there was intramural basketball and football.

JOBS/INSPECTING: The prefects did the inspecting and kept study halls. The other seniors had regular jobs.

BATHHOUSE: It was behind the Old Dorm and it had five showers. The cottages each had a toilet and a sink.

JOBS: I was fortunate. I got a regular job in the dining room and kitchen. First thing in the morning I went and started a fire in the stove in the dining room and did chores around the kitchen. The stove was a big coal one.

CHURCH SERVICES: We only sang the hymns but the service involved incense and the acolytes were robed. There was no formal choir but we had choral practice under Mrs. Cohen and Mother Harris.

MISCONDUCT: The main things were being AWOL or coming back late. Mainly we'd get into trouble crossing the railroad tracks to buy something in Arden. There were no girls around.

WORKLIST: We usually worked on Monday or other special occasions.

FOOD: If you got any, you could keep it in your room.

SMOKING: Cigarettes with parent's permission, subject to age requirement.

DRINKING: There was no drinking whatsoever back in those days. We were fortunate we didn't have to contend with that. Very rarely someone would get some malt and make some brew...but it wasn't worth drinking.

EXPULSIONS: There were a few, possibly because they came back drinking.

THE FARM: There was Laz Allen and three or four cows. We used to get a lot of powdered milk.

FOOD: Sinkers for breakfast. We had eggs once a day. There was not much meat. Sunday we would have peaches and pears, figs and grapes, and other fruit.

PREFECTS: They were respected. Mr. Dave stood behind them.

DAILY CHAPEL: There were no complaints. These services were a natural part of growing up.

FATHER HARRIS: He wore red suspenders, sometimes to the embarrassment of his daughter.

DRESS: We wore khaki pants, corduroy, and plaid shirts. We didn't wear coat and tie in the evenings. Clothes had to be neat and clean.

HAIRCUTS: You could get them in Arden or Fletcher. Sometimes a barber came to campus.

FUN IN ASHEVILLE: We went to movies, walked up and down the streets, and went shopping. There were no fights in town.

VACATIONS: You went home only for Christmas.

AMUSEMENT: Self-made. There were no programs or plays. You walked up Burney, went to the airport, or played ball.

ACADEMICS: A person who graduated from Christ School made good grades in college.

WHAT YOU LEARNED: Responsibility.

CHAPIN MCKENZIE '32

SINKERS: Ma and Etta, the cooks, hated having their cornbread muffins called sinkers. We would send new boys back to the kitchen to ask for sinkers. Ma would take dead aim. We would bore a hole in the center of the sinkers and pour in syrup. They were delicious to eat and superb as a weapon.

NIGHTLIGHTS: The Rumfeldts were from Canada. They had a Model-T. Once they got a claim, and they converted their Model-T into a pick-up. They would drive it out to the claim late at night, park it, turn on the headlights to permit digging, and haul off the dirt afterwards.

CAUGHT: I got involved with a claim once when several of us agreed to get a couple of Fr. Harris's chickens over beyond the Chapel. We seized two hens and cleaned the feathers. What we plucked we dumped into the cottage furnace. With the smell of burning feathers floating across the campus, Fr. Harris easily caught us.

CAMPING OUT: One of the fun things was camping out at Grove Lake in Fairview, a couple of miles from school, where we could go swimming. Mr. Dave would give us pork-n-beans and a slab of bacon for camping out there. What eating!

APPLES AT BURNEY: We would climb the mountain, collect apples, and bring them back to the cottage. Then we would mash them up in an old time ice cream container. The result was fresh apple cider.

INITIATION: Gamma Lambda Sigma. The members swung the paddle with authority.

ART ARMSTRONG '33

A CHAUFFEUR: I was considerably older than the balance of the students. I was born in Canada and shuffled between Chicago, Des Moines and Detroit and was set back two years in school. When I arrived at Christ School, I had my own car and was selected to drive David and Betsy to school (St. Genevieve's). I also used to drive Mother Harris to South Carolina (Union) to visit friends and family. Once in a while I would drive Mrs. Dave to various places. Driving for the school gave me a chance to get off campus legally rather than to slip off in the middle of the night, which we did once in a while.

ATHLETIC FIELD: I know that I did my share in expanding the athletic field in the form of claims. When you did something wrong that required some remedial action, the headmaster gave you a claim, which was a section of the mountain that you had to dig up and transport by wheelbarrow from one point to another in order to level off the field.

COTTAGES: There were four rooms, eight boys, and a back porch. We would sleep on the back porch, sharing all the blankets we had. Many mornings we woke up covered by frost or snow. That was lots of fun! Every once in a while some of us would climb over the back rail and head in toward Asheville.

TOM DAVALL '34

BACKGROUND: Attended Christ School four years. Served as chauffeur for Fr. Harris.

DRIVING ANECDOTE: I was driving Fr. Harris and a student who had an acute attack of appendicitis to Asheville. Fr. Harris kept on saying, "Step on it." As we approached the tracks in Biltmore, the train was coming full throttle. Fr. Harris said, "Step on it. You can make it." Whew! We did.

ON CAMPUS: Before coming to Christ School, I was an electrician, but no work was available during the depression. I came here for $150 a year and was a student and the school electrician. I wired the old infirmary, which burned down in 1938. It looked bad for me. Actually, I understand that a smoker's ashes burned it down.

ATHLETICS: I played all the sports and two on the football team were older than I was. Nobody knew how old Country Jamison was, but I think he was 20 when I entered. Country Jamison broke his arm one afternoon but he asked Fessor to "button it up" and played the next day.

TIGHT BUDGET: Mr. Dave handled the school's finances. By Thanksgiving the whole pile of coal for heating the Old Dorm had been used up. Mr. Dave said there was no more money available for coal. He put a wood stove in the basement of the Old Dorm. Everybody would race down to the basement to put on pajamas or get dressed around the fire. There was a big flu epidemic that year but the only ones to get the flu were those who lived in the 30 Dorm where there was heat in every room.

A FRIEND: There were several students here from Chicago and New York and three from Michigan. Van Bunting's father was the owner of a newspaper that folded during the depression. Van had been in a couple of other schools and bounced around. His father told him that this was a "make-or-break" situation – the last chance. It worked.

ROBERT J. SWARTOUT '35

BACKGROUND: Attended Christ School for two years from Michigan. Heard of the school from a teacher friend of his mother in Detroit. The teacher's son went here.

EXPULSIONS: Christ School played Asheville High in football and won for the first time. The school had a six day week then and Mr. Dave declared Monday a holiday. Two students got back Tuesday and were on their way home. (Normally if you were late returning from town, you dug a 6x6x6 claim.)

TOWN: Seldom went to Asheville. Generally walked to Fletcher.

CHRIST SCHOOL EDUCATION: A personification of Mr. Dave. He had a brilliant, marvelous wife.

The teachers were exceptional people. Fr. Boynton was single my first year and he assisted Fessor in football. He was tough. Others included Mac and Zach Alden, the Major (who knew Mandrin Chinese, German, and so forth).

JOBS: I used to deliver milk to Mrs. Wetmore at her home every day. She told stories about the Civil War and how her family acquired the land. Later she moved to an old house in Biltmore. Girls coming to the final dance would stay at Struan.

DRINKING: Almost none.

SURROUNDING MOUNTAIN AREA: Contained thriving moonshine industry. Lots of old shacks and stills and Christ School boys found the men there eager to tell stories. The moonshiners did not bother Christ School boys. The school was still educating many of these mountain children.

MOONSHINE EXPERIENCE: During my senior year, Mr. Dave had brought one of these mountaineer sons to school, one whose father, grandfather, and greatgrandfather were bootleggers. After I bugged him a long time, he took me to a still. It was not hidden; it was located in a valley clearing. Two brothers were working on mash. Some girls were standing there watching the copper still operate. They made two kinds of corn whisky–one they sold, the other they drank. (What they drank was aged). They used special kinds of wood which would char the caskets they had built. Once I got a sample and it tasted like a fall day of snow in the Smoky Mountains.

THE GRAY GHOST: Mr. Dave had pure instinct. He remembered the things he would do as a boy and then be prepared to head you off.

FASSIFERN (embarrassing moment): I went to Fassifern to a dance-buffet and formal. There were a dozen card dances and the girls wore long dresses, the boys dark suits. At intermission we came down the stairs to the landing where the stairs split off into two directions. As I started down the stairs, the young lady with me stopped. I stepped on her skirt. She tripped and I grabbed her, both of us falling to the bottom of the stairs. Her dress was up to her neck. I looked down, jumped up embarrassed, and made my exit. The chaperones observed.

MR. DAVE: A real leader. Had total adulation.

FESSOR: A legend in his time. He built character.

FR. BOYNTON: A driving force in Chapel, football, everywhere.

EVENSONG: At choir rehearsal on Saturday night, Fr. Boynton could pick out a false note in the back like a symphony director.

MORE ON POP: In college Fr. Boynton had a band. He could play the piano with boxing gloves on. At his Sunday afternoon teas, you learned to balance a cup on one hand and a plate on the other. These provided social training and conservation.

EARLY COMMUNION: Usually ten to twelve boys there each day.

SUNDAY: Free from 1 to 5 p.m. You did what you wanted to. We used to climb to top of Burney Mountain, jump off into space and catch the top of a limber tree and swing on to the next one. You would go from tree to tree. If you missed, you might get some bruised ribs.

OLD TRUCK: Used to haul gravel to repair roads, to haul coal to school, to haul athletic teams to various places, and to haul the boys to Fassifern.

TENNIS COURTS: There were three, the main one next to the school building. Bill Tilden came to Christ School in search of tennis talent at Mr. Dave's behest. (I think Mr. Dave hit some with him.)

BETSY HARRIS: Pigtails.

THE SCHOOL: Totally competitive. It was a school to make men. The important things were required chapel, the work system, tough academics, Mr. Dave. The school required total participation and there was total response.

FINAL EXAMS: They were tough. It took you hours to write out an exam. You didn't have to worry about what would be asked; they asked everything. The benches in Chapel before exams gave you a fresh outlook and a good feeling.

GETTING THERE EARLY: By getting to school early, you could get the best furniture and the bunk you wanted. I went back two days early my second year to claim the dresser I coveted. My life was complete: the simple pleasures were important.

E. ALLEN BROWN '36

BACKGROUND: Entered as a sophomore in 1933 at age thirteen. Professor of literature.

REASON FOR GOING TO CS: My mother, a widow in Durham, was making $85 a month. Bishop Penick got me half a scholarship to Christ School ($150). My mother paid the rest at $15 a month. She couldn't keep me at home that inexpensively. My mother also felt that I needed strong male leadership and the kind of companionship to be found at Christ School.

ARRIVING ON CAMPUS: I entered the front door of the school building and Mrs. Dave was standing there. I was so glad to see a kind, friendly face. She knew I was confused and was so kind and gracious. Somehow I got installed in the 1930 (St. Edmund's) Dorm.

BIGGEST FIRST YEAR INFLUENCE: Fr. Boynton. He lived in the apartment at the south end of St. Edmund's. He was not married then. He was the kind of person you could level with.

CHURCHMANSHIP: I was low church – confirmed in St. Phillips (Charleston, S.C.) and attended the "Church by the Bus Station" (Durham). We practiced the service which Fr. Boynton told us he had written. It took us a while to learn it since there was no choir then. Fr. Boynton would come to the middle aisle in his surplice and beat time to the music. He walked up and down the aisle saying, "Faster, faster. Let's have some life to this." Mrs. Pearce was at the organ. Finally, we got it down for the All Saints Service.

HOLIDAYS: The thing I remember was that we had church holidays rather than legal holidays. For example, our first holiday was on Michalemas (Sept. 29) and we would have three classes, a communion service, and the rest of the day off. After the service, you could go to town unless you had a claim to dig or worklists. It was nice to have a special day which the others did not have.

TRANSPORTATION TO TOWN: Mrs. Pearce (the nurse and organist) had a beautiful blue 1928 Essex. She would pile as many as she could into the car and would drop us off at Pack Square where we would assemble for the return trip. She charged us a nickle or dime each.

CHURCH SERVICES: What impressed me was fifteen services a

week! (Students had to attend eight) Morning communion was not required. Fr. Boynton would knock you out of bed ringing the angelus. There was no communion for the congregation at the 10:30 Sunday morning service. While I was there, there was no Candlelight Service, but Easter was a big service, including the sunrise communion. During Lent, Fr. Boynton encouraged boys to take on vows and at least one year we had a big wooden cross on which to put those vows in sealed envelopes. We had to write on cards what we pledged to do or not to do during Lent.

THE ORGAN: It was a two-manual old pipe. The pump organ was no more; it had been electrified.

ACADEMIC PREPARATION: I didn't fully appreciate the excellence of the education at Christ School until I saw what other incoming students at UNC lacked. I was very well prepared: Zach Alden (English/French), J. Gray McAlister (Math-excellent), Fr. Boynton (History), Mr. Dave (Science). More than academics, Mr. Dave taught us values.

THE STUDENT BODY: Socially, economically, academically we were quite an assortment. A large number were country boys–good, solid. There was quite an assortment from Detroit – well-to-do families. There was a good group from New Orleans but none from Charleston until Jack Clark came. Several came from Tennessee (Norris Dam area) and from Greensboro. In the 1930's not many had a lot of money. Christ School was a treat-all-alike school. I remember that I was upset (for him) when a Jewish boy from Asheville had to go to Chapel, but he and the Rabbi didn't mind.

GIRLS: The only girl on campus was Betsy Harris.

RECREATION: Athletics. I read a lot. There was no lack of excitement. Some boys hiked up Burney; I climbed the school building and took pictures with a baby box Brownie camera. I came with a radio (one of the few) and a little wind-up portable phonograph. I used to visit the faculty homes (the Boyntons had tea every Sunday afternoon for any students who wanted to drop in) and the Harrises did too from time-to-time. We used to go to Asheville to the movies (*Flying Down to Rio*, *Love in Bloom*, and Bing Crosby films). I remember that the drug store on Pack Square had a special on banana splits - ten cents each. Six of us cleaned them out. I ate five and was going on the sixth when I said, "I can't take anymore."

STUDENT GOVERNMENT: Prefects (they inspected jobs). There was no council. Mr. Dave dealt with troublemakers.

MUSIC: The one thing I missed at CS was music, except for church music. There were no records or music appreciation classes. Mrs. Pearce taught piano and occasionally she would take us to a concert in Asheville. I heard Joseph Hoffman there (a great experience!).

ZACH ALDEN: He influenced me to be a teacher. His depth of knowledge, presentation, material was fascinating. He explained *Macbeth* so that it was clear and alive. (Dr. Brown taught Shakespeare for over thirty years).

THE BLIZZARD: It came on St. Patrick's Day 1936 but it didn't stop school. We dug out and life moved on. Boy, it was cold in those days. I woke up on the porch one morning and my hair was frozen to the pillow for it had sleeted during the night.

THE COTTAGES: Since there was no bathroom, we had to go to the shower room behind the Old Dorm. To keep warm we huddled around the pot-bellied stove and rotated banking the fire and getting up early in the morning to get the fire going again. We had wash basins in the rooms. I never recall hearing Mr. Dave behind the cottages but you knew he was everywhere. When you least expected it, his voice would emerge from somewhere. I don't remember anyone sneaking off at night. Mostly we were too tired from a long day of work.

HAZING: I didn't experience any in my initiation into the Gamma Lamba Sigma Fraternity. I had to make a speech one Sunday afternoon. They loved the one I did on Mae West.

DANCES: We had some in the gymnasium and we always prayed that it wouldn't rain. Fassifern would come over in their bus–strictly chaperoned. The girls were escorted into the gym to meet us–all dressed up. Once we went to a May Day at Fassifern where the girls presented an abbreviated *Mid-Summer Night's Dream.*

GRADUATION DANCE: Our graduation dance was in the lobby of the Grove Park Inn. We really had arrived. Girls from Fassifern were our dates. I fell in love with a beautiful girl whom I never saw again.

EXTRACURRICULARS: I was editor of *The Warrior.* I worked mainly in Mr. Zach's classroom in the afternoons. I got on the paper because Mr. Zach was impressed by a composition I wrote in the fourth form. Working on the paper was good fun and comradeship. There was no Drama Club. For a while, there were faculty/student basketball games but we had to cut those out because Fr. Boynton played so rough. We were proud of our undefeated football team, of which I was an assistant manager.

THE SNACK: Every day we had a mid-morning snack of jelly and peanut butter sandwiches on the school building steps. Trays of sandwiches were piled high and you marched past and took one. You washed it down with water from the old well.

HAIRCUT: The barber came over from Fletcher every other week. His chair was in the Bath House. If you didn't sign up, Mr. Dave made you go. I remember that one student showed up in assembly one Monday night with a Mohawk. Mr. Dave couldn't believe it; he shaved the rest of the boy's hair off.

TABLES: You were assigned a seat by the numbers. You received a number as you went in the dining hall door Sunday night. We sang the blessing, led by Fr. Boynton.

> **Fr. B.**: The eyes of all wait upon thee, O Lord.
> **Students**: And thou givest them meat in due season.
> **Fr. B.** : Thou openest thine hands.
> **Students**: And Bless all these living with plentousness.
> **Fr. B.** : O Lord, Bless to our use all these thy gifts which we receive through thy great bounty, through Jesus Christ Our Lord.

JACK CLARK '36

CHRIST SCHOOL WAY OF LIFE: It taught me sound values and gave me the strength and faith to have a satisfying career through many tough times and lots of good ones.

MR. DAVE: He was a born leader–honest, straight-forward, fair at all times, firm at all time, a gentleman whom I think invented the word integrity.

A RECORD: I came back at age sixteen for a post graduate year, and I got to play quarterback. The year before I had been an understudy to my roommate Jimmy Ewin. In one game we played a junior college in Asheville and they barely beat us. I was fortunate enough to intercept five passes that day. After the game, Mrs. Dave came up and hugged me, saying, "Jack, you really played a fine game." The Dave's were an inspiration.

FESSOR: He taught us hard work, hard play, and clean living. He set an example to follow. I remember one practice I was calling signals and Fessor was leaning into the huddle to listen. I called a certain play and said "Let's try this." The play didn't work. After the practice was over, Fessor called me aside and said, "Jack, I don't want to ever...ever hear you call a play again and say, 'Let's try this' You have absolutely got to be positive and believe in your heart that it's going to work. You don't say 'Let's try it. You say let's do it." That lesson has stuck with me all my life.

Late one afternoon a number of us were in the shower building after practice. The bath house had an open top and the side had windows screened over. Anyone walking past could hear the conversation inside. One of the boys in the group that day used some dirty words. It wasn't long before Fessor stuck his head around the corner and shouted, "All of you get out of there." We stopped showering and listened to a good lecture about bad language. He made all of us take a bite out of a cake of soap. None of us swallowed any but we all came out a lot cleaner.

FATHER BOYNTON: I learned a lot about living life from Fr. Boynton both on the football field and in Chapel. I took religion classes under him, was confirmed there, and was an acolyte. He taught by leading, by example. He was an inspiration.

THE EGG MAN: Classmate Jake Justice was a strong mountain boy who ran fullback like a train – throttle wide open. He lived a couple of miles from school and frequently he would slip home and bring back some fresh eggs and a couple of loaves of bread. He roomed in one of the cottages and had a little cook stove. He would fry the eggs and make delicious sandwiches which he sold for a nickle or dime each. One day I traded him something (I forget what it was) and it must have been quite valuable for he gave me about fifty fried egg sandwiches in return, which I ate over a period of a month or so.

WILLARD E. CALDWELL '37

BACKGROUND: Attended Christ School three years. Graduated at age fifteen, attended University of Florida. Got his PhD at Cornell at age twenty-three but school officials made him remain in graduate work before granting degree to him at age twenty-five. He earned his way through college.

EDUCATION: Christ School taught me to be a man, to learn to improvise, get by, and make do. I feel sorry for those who can't do without.

KIND OF EDUCATION AT CHRIST SCHOOL: Absolutely fabulous. Excellent academic discipline. Extremely thorough.

The courses were tough. We got grades every week, and parents as well as school kept you on your toes.

MR. McALISTER: I had geometry under him. The way he taught made math very pleasant.

MRS. DAVE: Quiet. Dignified. Gracious. Mother-image.

FR. BOYNTON: I served as an acolyte for him for three years carrying the incense. I switched from Low Church to High Church. What participation! The Christ School Chapel did things to you.

URQ CHINN: Organist/choirmaster. A real professional.

CLAIM BANK: Had one claim. Think my grades were below expectations and Mr. Dave jacked me up.

RECREATION: We had the Frat House, cigarettes, listened to the Lucky Strike program, played bridge, had dance parties at Frat and with Fassifern. Rode truck to the dances. Also attended a formal dance at Biltmore Forest or Grove Park Inn each year.

BAD STUFF: Some smoking; very, very little drinking. Once I went to Arden and had wine with a meal.

MR. DAVE: Always at work. Would never ask us to do things he wouldn't do. Worked with his hands, head, and heart.

MR. BOYD: Worked incessantly.

BUILDING GOING ON: Fr. Harris Memorial Chapel under construction. I helped haul rock for that. 38 Dorm being talked about.

LIVING QUARTERS: The cottages. Had to walk to Shower Room to take a bath. The cottages had small back porches. We used to oil the floors.

SNOWS: Every now and then we had an immense snow storm.

PREVENTIVE MEDICINE: When a health threat existed, Mr. Dave would line up the whole school and mop throats with silver nitrate.

STUDY HALL: Kept by the prefects.

INSPECTORS: Prefects and a few seniors.

CHAPEL: Early communion daily! I went frequently.

EVENSONG: the choir was magnificent.

KIND OF STUDENTS AT CS: Mountain poor to very wealthy. Pure democracy: everybody was treated (disciplined) alike. If you were late getting back on campus, you got a claim – no matter who or what the alibi. Prefects were not immune.

SPENDING MONEY: $2 a week. Same amount for everyone. Mrs. Dave issued it and ran the bank.

THE SAWBELL: Clang! Clang! Clang!

ENDURING THINGS FROM CHRIST SCHOOL: Work system, participation, Chapel: (mind, labor, and spirit).

FEELINGS: I hated it at the time, that is my first year. But Christ School taught me to do things by hand in conjunction with head and not to be too proud to try. I have a spot on the Chesepeake Bay. I planned and built a 3-room house there by myself. It was my own work – manual labor and all. This is part of what Christ School taught me. In this lies immense satisfaction.

JACK ROBINSON '38

Jack Robinson had been injured in practice but traveled with the Christ School football team to Anderson S.C. in October 1936 to watch the Greenies lose to Boys High 7-2 in ankle deep mud. His New Orleans teammate Dough McIlhenny played in the game. "We were in a stadium filled with rednecks. They looked mighty angry. I can remember hoping we'd lose so we would get out of there alive."

JOHNNY MOORE '40

OVERCOMING FEAR: When I went out for baseball in the spring of 1938, I was scared of curveballs. Fessor, who had one good eye (most students didn't know which one was bad), saw potential in me and said he was going to throw curveballs at me until I overcame that phobia. Later in the year, centerfielder Pat Murphy got a claim (returning late from town) and couldn't make the trip to Asheville School. Luckily, the Asheville School pitcher threw nothing but curveballs. Thanks to Fessor, I hit three home runs over the bank.

THE RIGHT KIND OF PRAISE: Fr. Boynton was strong, intelligent, and inspirational. The first week my job was to clean up Pop's yard. I did a rotten job. Pop told me I didn't do a good job. He said, "A job worth doing is worth doing well." I learned the lesson. I didn't want Fessor, Mr. Dave, etc. getting on me.

CHOIR GARMENTS: The choir got vestments in 1939-40 for the first time in some years. I made the choir singing falsetto (alto); that's how Michael Jackson makes a million. Earl Jackson and I sang and had a million in fun. I still know the things we sang.

BETSY: Everybody was in love with Betsy. What a pretty little girl. At age fourteen to fifteen we were scared of girls. We all thought we were her favorite. Half of us wrote to her at Chatham Hall. She was a champion on the tennis courts.

JOE: I knew him well. I used to beat on him some. But he got the girl. He's a great guy.

MRS. DAVE: She was beautiful, sweet, understanding. An extraordinary, sensitive person. She was love!

SPORTS: We had the Big 3 (football, basketball, baseball), an embryonic tennis team, and intramural basketball. Football was the centerpiece. The head coach was Fessor; the defensive coach was Fessor; the offensive coach was Fessor; the end coach was Fessor; the backfield coach was Fr. Boynton (a scatback dressed in his habit: collar on, black shirt and pants). The Cherokee Indians were tough in the pile-up, you would come out with teeth marks on your ankles.

TRIPS: We rode in the rear end of the school's dump truck. There was a canvas cover in case of rain. The two-and-one-half ton truck hauled players and coal. I don't ever remember riding in a car or on a bus.

BASKETBALL: Fessor coached everything. My first two years we jumped center after every basket. Lots of low scoring games. After we left Brevard one night, Fr. Boynton was following the truck in his car. At one point, the police came up and arrested us for speeding (Bennett Clark was driving). I listened to Pop Boynton (in habit) talk to the police officer. Fr. Boynton accused the officer of crossing the yellow line. Looking at this man of the cloth, the policeman tore up the ticket and drove off.

THE OLD GYM: How cold was it in the Old Gym? The ball felt like circular concrete.

THE BIRDS AND THE BEES.: My fourth form year, something happened to the curriculum. Fessor was instructed to give us a sex lecture in the gym. We had never heard him say more than "gol darn". We were more embarrassed than he was as he tried to explain what made babies. We were embarrassed that this "old man" (he was around 38) had to give us this lecture.

FR. BOYNTON: He was a dynamic man. I remember him with awe. He was a strong personality with an aura, a glow. When he talked, we listened. When it was time to kneel, you knelt. Most of my corduroys had no knees left by the end of the year. We got religion from that man. I did not come to Christ School a confirmed Episcopalian. I loved the service and Fr. Boynton. His sermons were brief, poignant, forceful. He never used notes. He developed the musical aspects of the service. When I go back to Christ School, I know the words, the music, and when to kneel.

THE CHOIR: It was just beginning to be in demand when we got choir robes my senior year. Urq Chinn was an unsung hero.

A BOY'S DREAM: One of my early goals (I discussed it with Mr. Dave) was the prospect of coming back as a teacher. Many of us felt this way. You just wanted to be a part of the program. Fr. Boynton caused much of this feeling.

EASTER MORNING FIRE: The infirmary burned down my fourth year (Spring 1938). It leaped out...a firey blaze. Everyone was safe. There was no wind so it didn't spread. The Sunrise service was a mixture of smoke and incense. Fr. Boynton's talk at the service was an inspiration: "Out of the ashes will grow a new beginning...Keep spirits up...new and better infirmary will follow." You left the service feeling tragedy would lead to something better. The whole service seemed to be dedicated to the new infirmary.

ROBERT BRADHAM *'41*

FESSOR: I saw him mad only once, at the best basketball player we had. At the time, this player was sitting on the bench when one of the boys on the court did something crazy. The player on the bench said, "For Christ's sake, J––." That was all for the best basketball player. Fessor kicked him off the squad. Fessor wouldn't put up with any foolishness from anyone. I was devoted to Fessor. In fact, I don't know anyone at Christ School that I didn't like. I loved the masters; I hated to leave the place.

THE OLD GYM: There wasn't much to it, I'll tell you. There was no heat. You had to keep moving during basketball season to keep warm...It served its purpose and at our age who cared. Fessor kept the floor perfect because he never let us walk on the court with anything except clean basketball shoes. We hung the uniforms on racks around the gym.

MR. DAVE: I respected him more than any man I've ever met in my life. He was stern but he was fair.

ACADEMICS: After I left Christ School, I just floated through the first year of college.

CHAPEL: I wrote my father and asked him why they sent me to a Catholic Church. I had never before knelt or heard a chant. I caught on...and joined in the singing. By the time I finished, I had memorized most of the hymns.

ATHLETIC TRIPS: We traveled to games in an old truck with a canvas cover over it. We took the bus to Columbia but rode in cars belonging to Fessor and Mr. Hurst when going to basketball games. They took about eight players. What I liked about the trips was that we always stopped on the way back to get a soda.

FREE MONDAYS: I always had something to do. I never remember being bored. I shot basketball, hiked, walked to Arden or the airport, and so forth. I took a girl to the movies in Asheville once in three years. I didn't care for girls in those days, anyway. I went over to Fassifern to dances a couple of times; they had a chaperone for each girl.

MRS. DAVE/BETSY: Mrs. Dave was a little more sophisticated, a very sweet, kind person. We all had a crush on her daughter, Betsy. She was off at Chatham Hall but would be here on vacations. Betsy and I corresponded. I thought she was writing only to me.

TROUBLES: There was very little trouble requiring serious discipline. In part, economic times were different. We didn't have all the stuff and spending money that is available now. The temptations to do wrong weren't readily available. Everybody was in the same boat, and you didn't miss what you didn't see. Mr. Dave's presence was a steadying influence, and he made sure we didn't find any temptations around. There were no girls and girls were what caused troubles.

STUDENT GRIPES: Everybody griped all the time but none of them were serious and no one took them seriously. You would gripe about worklists...food...and going to chapel every day. Speaking of Chapel, I got so I looked forward to it, which involved rushing to get showered after athletics and doing your job before going. I don't remember anyone seriously objecting to going. And, besides, Mr. Dave and Fessor went nearly every day.

JULY WATERS

(Mrs. Waters, who was from New Orleans, had three sons graduate from Christ School)

We went up to Fletcher to visit the Robinsons and Westfeldts. We saw Christ School and instantly liked Mr. Dave. Times were hard but we wanted to send Arthur to Christ School (he had a scholarship to Taft.) Once there, he was horribly homesick and constantly complained in his letters about how Mr. Dave ran things. He wanted to come home. We got him to stay until Christmas. When he got home, we mentioned several things he had criticized Mr. Dave about. He bristled: "So you think you can run the school better than Mr. Dave?" He went back. The next year he was head perfect.

BLANCHE BRUNS

(Mrs. Bruns was a New Orleans mother whose son was a perfect at Christ School. She writes about his first year.)

His first year there, Harry developed facial paralysis and had to come home for treatment. These were hard times. There was not much money around. We called to ask Mr. Dave about the possibility of Harry's returning without payment at that time. "What," he said, "you mean Harry's not back? Put him on the train tomorrow." Mr. Dave met Harry in Arden. There was no question about money. There was no question of Mr. Dave's love for his boys.

MRS. GALE D. WEBBE

Fessor and Pop (Fr. Webbe) went to officiate a football game and I went along. On the way back we had a flat tire. Streams of football traffic were coming along Sweeten Creek Road. Cars slowed down, saw the "convict" type shirts, and sped on. Finally, I sent Gale and Fessor into the woods and the next car stopped. I told the driver and his companion not to be frightened when two men wearing convicts shirts came out of the woods. We all enjoyed a big laugh.

It was summer during the war and Pop was working in Oak Ridge. I had to kill a chicken for dinner without any knowledge of what I was doing. I took a couple of whacks at the chicken but only offended and injured the bird in the wing. I was in a state of tears as Fessor came by. He showed me how to kill a chicken painlessly for both parties–by wringing its neck. Fessor showed compassion (for me) but the chicken might have been harder to convince.

ANDREW CALHOUN '43

CLAIM BANK: I don't remember if I ever received one but remember helping (dig) some of the real estate assigned to good friends and classmates including Jim Francis (roommate) and his brother Bob and also Richard Hutson. The "collective" digging generally took place before Christmas and Spring vacations to assure that the claimholders got to leave Arden on time.

UNUSUAL EVENTS: Pisgah Forest Fire near Brevard. I volunteered to fight fires to get out of class for several days. Seniors who participated dug fire breaks and cut brush and trees. We were later rewarded at a banquet with some small blocks of wood which had the name, date, and so forth burned into the wood. There was a big story in the Asheville newspaper.

AGRICULTURAL EDUCATION: Several of us were called upon one night and dispatched to the school farm or barn to assist the farmer (name forgotten) in delivering a calf. During the difficult birth we tied a rope around the hooves and literally (tug-of-war fashion) brought the calf forth into the world. Somehow everybody survived the ordeal.

A PEPSI FLOAT: The reward at the end of the hike through the woods to the Fletcher truck stop was a big Pepsi float, which was a large Pepsi Cola mixed with a cup of vanilla ice cream. Also for a nickel you could hear the juke box big band sounds of Glen Miller, Tommy Dorsey, et al. A few guys might take a chew of tobacco on occasion.

TOM DICKINSON '43

TEACHERS: What a group of men we had for teachers! Mr. Dave, Pop Boynton, Mr. Chinn, Mac and Zach Alden, Fessor, and Mr. Carr to name a few of my favorites. Nothing has come close to (them) as a fine group of men.

THINGS THAT WERE FUN (and didn't cost much money):

1. Not just the sermons but all the fun we had with Pop Boynton. Also the different forms were invited to his house on Sunday afternoons for tea and cookies. This was really a fun occasion.

2. In those days we went to school on Saturday. Monday was the day off for either worklist or town. A bus came from Asheville and most everyone went to town for the afternoon. Only 50 cents was needed for a movie, candy, and soda after the movie. "Gone with the Wind" came out in 1939 and all those who could get together the unheard of movie price of $2.50 attended.

3. Airplanes were coming into their own about this time. It was about two or three miles to the local airport and on Sunday afternoons we would either walk or ride our bicycles over. There were many exciting air shows. Brightly colored planes doing loops and barrel rolls, stunt men jumping out in parachutes, riding on the wings of the plane, and so forth. What more could a twelve year old boy ask for?

4. We also spent many a fun-filled afternoon on Wetmore Hill sliding down the hill on our sleds and trying to avoid ending up in the icy waters of the creek at the bottom. The same stream served as the boundary line when we played "Capture the Flag." It seems we had a lot more snow back in those days than we do now. We were dressed for it though. I had the warmest corduroy knickers, longest warm socks, and highest top boots that you could find. Can't you see a boy in knickers today?

5. Playing marbles was one of the big things back then. All of the young boys at school had a big bag of marbles and a few games would be squeezed in every day. I guess the best marble player of my day was J.C. McDuffie. Boy, was he good! He had the best voice in Mr. Chinn's choir

too. I don't recall a lot of names of the boys but I certainly remember J.C. Seems to me Jimmy Stickney was pretty good at marbles too.

6. Building a model airplane was a big thing too. All the young boys built models and flew them on the football practice field. We did have to be careful to stay off the "gol dern infield" however. While attending one of the Christ School home football games , I took my son and showed him the exact spot where I had a claim. It's a part of the baseball diamond now (an area covered by the new basketball gym). Just about where the right fielder stands. I was given the claim for reporting back to school about two hours late following a free weekend.

FESSOR: I remember Fessor being able to stand on one end of the basketball court in the old gym (built in 1922) and shoot the ball through the rafters and make a basket on the other end of the court. He could do this five or six times in a row. I understand that seven was his record.

RUSTY LOVIN '45

FIRST DAY: The first day I arrived at Christ School, my Uncle Bill (Fulton), who attended here in the 1920's, and my mother brought me up in a car and stopped on the bridge over the railroad track in Arden. I asked Uncle Bill why he stopped and he said, "I think I hear a train coming and I want to make sure you see and hear it, because this will be the last thing in civilization you'll see or hear for a long time."

GROAN: In my first year, the two hardest things for me were (1) getting up in the dark so early to serve as an acolyte and (2) running from the Sixth Cottage to the Old Dorm to take a shower.

THE GRAY GHOST: I can't forget sleeping on the porch of the cottage and have Mr. Dave remind us the next day of what we were talking bout before we went to sleep.

KEEPING OUT OF TROUBLE: I got in a little trouble every now and then, but watching those boys dig their claims kept me out of any serious trouble.

AN ENGRAVED MEMORY: One of my fondest memories was Mr. Dave taking some of us boys down to the old Rock House in the pasture in front of the Wetmore House and cooking out and generally shooting the bull. The first time he took me, I thought to myself I had finally arrived.

FESSOR: I have many fond memories of Fessor. All the great help he gave me with his coaching. The many times he chewed me out and everybody for throwing a rock on his "gol dern" football field. The only time I ever saw him so mad he was almost physical was the time we were tossing some boy on a blanket in his back yard.

FIREFIGHTING: I'll never forget the time Mr. Dave put us in a truck and took us to some mountain in Weaverville to help fight a forest fire, with him leading us down the mountain in pitch black with a hand on the shoulder of the guy in front of you.

*BASKETBALL:*The time I finally got into a basketball game and Mr. Dave gave me hell because I hadn't been doing that all year.

SCHOOLWORK: In my senior year, I was taking chemistry under Mr. Dave and doing poorly in it, knowing I didn't need the credit to graduate. He came up to me one day after class, grabbed my collar in his right hand, balled up his fist and said, "Rusty, I know you don't need this course to graduate, but if you don't pass it the two of us are going out in the woods and only one of us is coming back." Not only did I know who was coming back, but I think I made the best grade on chemistry that year of any course I took.

LITTLE THINGS THAT MEAN A LOT: Like the first time I sat at the headmaster's table. Mr. Dave made me sit by him to his left. About half way through the meal his left hand came over and pinched the stuffings out of me. With that I jumped straight up and I said, "Unaccustomed as I am to public speaking..." I guess that was the first speech I ever made.

JOHN NEVILLE *'45*

A GREAT CHASE: One day Jack Catlin was sounding off to Fessor and in the heat of words, Fessor roared, "Are you calling me a liar?" Well, Jack took off. He ran into the Old Dorm, up the stairs and into his room, slamming the door and pushing his bureau against it. Fessor was in close pursuit. While Fessor was trying to open the door, Jack climbed out the back window and got away...for the moment.

OPENING REMARKS: On this occasion (something a trifle off center had apparently occurred), Mr. Dave set the tone of who was boss. "I want you to know," he told the students at assembly, "that I'm the Boss. If you don't agree with that, let's just roll up our sleeves and step out onto the ball field." I was convinced. So was everyone else.

SCOTTY ROOT '45

In the long run, who loves a school more – the boy who bucks the system or the one who sticks close to the rules. Only God can answer that question and when He does it will not matter anymore. Scotty Root attended Christ School for nearly four years. His path was a bumpy one. His memories of Christ School are poignant and convey much of what the school meant to us all. In the next few pages, Scotty lets us see the years 1938-42 through his eyes. These are some of the things he remembers:

THE ROAD TO HEAVEN: Lordy I remember Lazarus used to come up and pick up the slop at the porch off the dining room and he always let us sit on the back of the wagon and ride back to the barn with him. There were usually two or three of us and that was a great thrill in those days to ride on the garbage wagon and watch Lazarus slop the pigs. Then we would run like mad to get back before it was time to do the jobs and go to assembly and Chapel.

PLAYING FOR KEEPS: I remember every year there came a time when Mr. Dave said, "Well, it's o.k. not to wear your shoes any more." So all the little boys would go barefoot. It was also marble time and Stricker Mays and J.C. McDuffie made the best marble players. Within a week they had won all the marbles in the dorm and then they would sell them back to us so they could win them again.

HE IS RISEN INDEED, ALLELUIA: About 5 a.m. on Easter, the Chaplain used to hurry around the campus and knock on each door, saying, "Alleluia, the Lord is risen." Sleepily we would reply, "He is risen indeed, alleluia." One year I could hardly wait for Easter to arrive. Bobby Newell, a deft left-handed pitcher renown for raising knots on brats' heads with his senior ring, had a bat break on him in baseball practice. He gave the hand end of the bat to me and I began to whittle on it, cut at it, sand it down and polish it. When the work was done, I put a little bow on it and gave it to Fr. Boynton. I think one of the proudest moments of my life was when he knocked on my door that Easter morning (I roomed in the first room on the corner of the 30 Dorm) and opened it and said, "I'm using your knocker. He is risen indeed."

SNOW DAYS AT WETMORE HILL: I think the greatest thing that ever came down the pike were the days when it snowed and Mr. Dave would show up at morning assembly. Everybody would be looking out the window and he would say, "Boys, let's take the day off!" I remember going down to Wetmore Hill where we went sliding and sledding and had those great snowball fights, with armies of kids on one side and the other. That was great fun!

A CURE THAT WORKED: I will never forget Mr. Dave "the doctor." First time he heard somebody cough, he would look into the throat with one of those little pallets from the infirmary. If coughing persisted, he and the nurse (Maude Watkins) would come to study hall and paint our throats with silver nitrate. If you ate too much candy in town on Monday, Mrs. Watkins relied heavily on a huge dose of castor oil as the cure.

THOSE BOXING NIGHTS: Right after the outbreak of WW II, we had to build an obstacle course and I remember doing calisthenics in front of what is now Boyd Dorm. One of the fitness things Fessor instigated was boxing. We had not had boxing in my memory. He knew that Billy Meekins and I were suitors for the same girl – Betty Sumner. Fessor knew that I had Billy kind of cowed but I think he knew more about Billy's boxing ability than I did. He put us together and Billy just whipped me good. I never boxed again.

FR. WEBBE THE GYMNAST: Fr. Webbe was one of those who helped turn boys into men. I remember that the first time I played football I hurt my knee, and I decided I would leave football glory to others. Somehow Fr. Webbe got some gymnastic equipment. We had a horizontal bar and parallel bars and some mats. Fr. Webbe had been a gymnast in college and taught us some techniques. I became fairly proficient on the horizontal bar and later made the Plebe gymnastic team at Annapolis.

FATHER FIGURES: Among my fondest memories of Christ School and the forces that most influenced me later in life were the Chaplains there. My father died when I was five and these men provided a father figure for me and influenced my decision to enter the ministry. The three were Fr. Boynton, Fr. Webbe, and Fr. Hammond. I'm very thankful for their lives at Christ School.

TOM YARDLEY '46

MR. DAVE was many things:

He had a reputation of being a stern disciplinarian; I think it was perhaps more illusion, like a legend that he perpetuated. I don't know if he was nearly as stern as people made you think he was. Or if the stories told about him made you think he was.

He was a large part of what Christ School was. He knew the boys well and how to motivate them. He was a leader, an extremely unique person.

He took the sting out of worklists because he would work with you. He helped you pull the stump...he supervised...he taught hands on. He had a knack of communicating with us– a difficult thing to do.

From the stage he would bark out occasionally, probably just enough to keep us quiet for a couple of weeks. Mr. Black: I remember hearing about Mr. Black the two years I was there but I never remember seeing him use it.

Mr. Dave was the Ghost. We used to talk about his being about at night. Perhaps once or twice while I was there he caught someone up after hours doing something, but the legend was longer than the reality. I don't think he wandered around every night.

TROUBLEMAKING: There wasn't much breaking of rules. There weren't large numbers of worklists. We had a couple of runaways. Basically the discipline system worked; it really did. You were brought up through the system and realized that the prefects and the senior class ran the school. By the time you became a senior, it was pretty much instilled in you who ran things. Seniors keeping discipline kept a lot of problems from happening.

DRINKING/SMOKING/SLIPPING OFF TO TOWN: These were rare occurrences. Most weekends no one was doing any of these things. Pipe smoking was permitted at the grandstand and frat house. The Grandstand was a great place. We ran out there to smoke between classes. Usually at night ten or fifteen people would be there. We sat on the same places (you had rank) and you could go there legally four or five times a day.

DOING JOBS: I think Christ School was the most efficient organization I've ever been associated with. Prefects and seniors did the inspecting. The jobs had been developed over the years and they were done with precision. The only non-student working personnel on campus were the cooks and two women in the laundry. Student work kept the place clean and maintenance costs low.

GOING TO TOWN: There was an illusion that this was a big thing. You got all ready and you had all these big plans and then you walked around the streets of Asheville and then came back to school. Or perhaps you sneaked off somewhere and smoked a cigarette. You occasionally went to a movie.

THE FACULTY: The faculty presented a manly model. Mr. Dave,

Fessor, and Fr. Webbe were three very strong characters. The other faculty were above average in this area.

Classes were small (fifteen or less) and teachers knew you in every area of life. You couldn't fool anybody. There was no thought of going to class unprepared; you might as well go ahead and be prepared. A lot of boys studied (here) who wouldn't have otherwise.

WEEDIE FERGUSON: Weedie and I did the class prophecy in the school paper. He was an athlete so he stayed off the claim bank. He didn't play football (banged up knee) but played basketball and baseball. It was worth the price of admission to watch him pitch.

JULIUS AND ELIZABETH: The meals were very good...There were plenty of biscuits. There was lots of protocol on who went up to get a refill on biscuits. Julius was irascible; nobody fooled with him. Elizabeth did all the work.

ATHLETICS: Played a big role. We had a good program – brats, junior varsity, varsity. The school turned out good football teams at all levels with only sixty or seventy boys to choose from. It was remarkable what Fessor did. The program provided a chance for boys who could not play elsewhere. We were taught and motivated to be overachievers by the junior and senior years. Thus we beat schools we shouldn't have. Everybody went to the home games. It wasn't compulsory to do so but there was no question that everybody went.

GIRLS: We had dances but not a lot of running contact with girls. They came from Asheville and elsewhere for dances. We went to Fassifern and St. Genevieve's. The transportation to dances was often the coal truck, which seemed normal and caused no embarrassment. You would haul coal Saturday afternoon, sweep out the truck, and be ready to ride to Fassifern that night.

LUXURY ITEMS: When you came to Christ School, you brought your clothes and perhaps one person in a cottage might have a guitar. That was about it. Perhaps there were two radios in a cottage.

PHYSICS: Mr. Dave taught me a lot of things in physics, some of which were in the text. I was not renowned for having a high energy level. In class he used to say, "What is the specific gravity of lead?" (He would look right at me and say, "Lead-butt?") I think he knew everybody pretty well.

LEWIS BERKELEY '46

FESSOR'S CLASS: My brother warned me not to mess around. I probably got most of my education right there in Fessor's room, because I paid attention, did everything I was supposed to do, and I did it right. My brother had told me, "When his lips get swollen, look out."

*FESSOR AS COACH:*The best baseball man I ever had...in all sports he did a good job on the fundamentals.

THE SMALL MINORITY: Mr. Dave gave a talk in school one day (1946) about the "small minority" undermining the school. This group called themselves the small minority and they went out in the woods and were drinking wine and smoking cigarettes. They had a cabin out there. Soon we no longer had the small minority with us.

GRADES: Frank Read always put his themes on his window sill when they were graded. You could go up and get your theme. I'd always get a B. No matter what I wrote, I got a B. Dave always got A. I was always jealous because I couldn't get an A. Then I got to college and I got E's. I found out Mr. Read had been doing me a favor by pushing me.

THE HUNGRY INDIAN: He used to take his oatmeal and slice oranges into it. The kids couldn't believe that.

MR. DAVE: Once I trembled for a week. I came to class and Mr. Dave blew his stack at me for losing fifty-five points on the dish-washing machine to the health inspector.

WRONGDOINGS: There was an occasional six-pack as well as some smoking in the woods or cabins. When I was in the second form, a boy from Asheville pulled out a bag filled with beer and stored it in the pond to chill.

TOM LAROSE '50

BACKGROUND: Tom Garden (development director) said Tom LaRose was a little concerned about "how fancy" Christ School was getting – judging by all the solicitous letters, circulars, pamphlets, and so on. LaRose then recalled an experience he had in helping to raise money for Memorial Gymnasium in 1949, just before he returned for his sixth form year.

–When I went home for the summer, I went around Greensboro to call on all my friends and my father's friends, asking for money to help Christ School build a new gymnasium. I walked from house to house, getting $5 here and $10 there, which I collected in two athletic socks. When I returned to campus early in September, I presented the socks to Fessor, which contained between $500 and $600. Fessor thanked me, but that wasn't quite the end of the story. Two days later, he returned my socks – washed and ironed. (Fessor did everything right. . . and then some.)

DAVID FUTCH '50

ACADEMICS: Christ School prepared us well for college work. I almost got into trouble my first year because UNC was almost too easy. I was taking advanced courses but the material was basically what I had covered here, especially in English and Algebra. And the theme writing (especially in Mr. Read's class) was a real help. While at Christ School I learned how to study and how to write.

*CAPT. REID:*He was a unique teacher. I took Latin and history under him. You couldn't help but feel the excitement that he had for these things. I can remember him, while we went through Caesar, diagramming battles on the blackboard and giving a blow-by-blow account with comparisons to the Civil War.

STUDY HALL: The prefects and seniors kept study halls, and there was no noise or rowdiness. Letter-writers had to be pretty clever to avoid worklists. The prefects were able to keep such good order because they had authority from Mr. Dave and Mr. Dave and the faculty backed them up. If one of them (prefects, seniors) told you not to talk or whatever, not too many students were going to argue with them. Mr. Dave never undercut a senior unless something was totally wrong. He did not undercut a judgment call.

SENIOR YEAR: Seniors were not above the law when it came to doing their rooms and so on. They were inspected too. Seniors would give other seniors worklists for shoddy rooms. Prefects would provide overall inspection and so did Mr. Dave. There was no attitude that the seniors no longer had to uphold the rules. Mr. Darsie or Fessor or some other teacher might be wandering around and turn up.

MONDAY LETTERS: My letters were usually short. It was a nuisance but it insured us getting mail in return. We sent grades home every week and wrote about things we were proud of.

JIGGER SHOP: You were permitted to withdraw a dollar a week. (If a student withdrew more than one dollar a week, he had to get Mr. Dave to countersign the check.) One day a senior went to Mr. Dave and took with him a pair of shoes he wanted repaired and requested additional money. Mr. Dave said, "No dice, son. That's the third time I've seen that same pair of shoes today."

FRONT DOOR: No one except faculty and seniors were permitted to enter the front door of the school building. This was a big thing.

CLASS RING: Cost $18. We got them after Christmas of our senior year and had to wear them with the Chapel facing in until graduation. These rings did raise a few lumps on heads while seniors kept order.

FINAL EXAMS: Counted 1/3 of the year's grade.

HOMEWORK: All the teachers required daily homework. There were math problems and a several page theme each week in Frank Read's class. Mr. Zach required a short story and long research paper. Capt. Reid required lots of notes. In Latin, we did much translation at the board.

CHAPEL: Not much grumbling about going to chapel. Most of the griping centered on having to have shoes shined and wearing a tie. After a football victory there was a great clamor to get to Chapel to sing 265. The singing in Chapel was good and strong; other churches were a let down.

ILLNESSES: One boy went down with spinal meningitis. We were quarantined for several weeks and had to take sulphur tablets and drink soda water. Then a flu epidemic closed the campus for a week. Mr. Dave converted the 38 Dorm into a hospital. Miss Mac took care of the infirmary. She ran a tight ship (where I was) and so did Mr. Dave (I heard).

MR. DAVE: He was an impressive man and he could do almost anything with success. He had a strong personality. When he said something, he meant it and you knew he meant it. When he said something that was a joke, you knew that. A twinkle in his eyes made the difference. He had a great sense of humor, even when he was very tired or upset. He could bring out a laugh.

MR. DAVE's MOODS: His moods affected faculty and students. You knew if he was upset; in assembly you could read his face. After a good football game, he would loosen up. His feelings were open.

At other times you could see the distress–especially when he had to ship a boy whom he was particularly fond of despite the boy's record of mistakes. Boys liked and respected him because they always knew where he stood.

He stood by his boys. I remember one Sunday afternoon a group had gone to Fletcher in the truck. They encountered some local boys who had been drinking. The locals gave pursuit back to school. These same locals were sent reeling back by Mr. Dave with a short- sleeved, "Get the hell out of here!" They didn't want to mess around with him either.

FACULTY AT CHAPEL: Mr. Dave went regularly. Fessor went to many early communions (three times a week). Frank Read and Zach Alden went to most services. All went on Sundays. All athletic teams made it back for Chapel except on rare occasions.

FESSOR: His values were those that taught you how to live a clean life. He was competitive but within the framework of sportsmanship.

SPORTSMANSHIP: Officials really liked to work games at Christ School. Fessor would even silence the grandstand if anyone criticized the officials. If your conduct was not proper, you'd get it from Fessor and then later from Mr. Dave. Everybody knew that CS teams did not argue with referees and played the game as cleanly as possible. Many coaches talk sportsmanship and leadership; Fessor lived both.

TABLE CHANGING: We ran over from Chapel Sunday night to get the best seats. The senior was the only one who had a set seat–to the left of the master.

CRUMBING STRATEGY: Bring in chicken, dump it on table, and rush back for more. This strategy didn't apply to Fessor's table.

DISHROOM/DINING HALL RECORDS: There was lively competition as to who could crumb the fastest or get out of the dish room quickest. A good man could complete his crumb before Mr. Dave rang the bell. A fast slopper in the dishroom would assure a record pace in getting through the dishes.

SEVENTH AND EIGHTH GRADE MISCHIEF: Mainly bedeviling the Hungry Indian. The lower formers went to bed half an hour before the rest of the school. Lot of rough-housing. Playing ghosts on

Wetmore Hill (especially on Saturday nights). Yo-yo fad. Hunting knives. Sterno stoves used while exploring in the woods. Built huts. Wore short pants. Allowed to go barefooted in fall and spring.

CLASS PICNICS: Had them at Pisgah, Mills River, and Wetmore Hill. Mr. Dave had a senior picnic at the beginning of the year–steaks, smoking lamp lit, etc. You had to like steaks a little on the raw side.

RICHIE MEECH '50

SHORT END OF THE STICK: My first roommate was Jack Russell and we were together for three years. I was pretty naive and Jack, who was a second year student, filled me in on what to do. So for the first two weeks I cleaned up the room before I realized that he was supposed to help.

HOMESICKNESS: One thing that held me steady those first few months was the work system. Coming off the farm, I had chores to do so I didn't mind jumping into the work about campus. In fact, instead of going into town on a Monday afternoon, I would go out and help with the worklist, just to have something to do.

What really kept you going the first six weeks was Mr. Dave. That first night, when he dismissed the old boys from the meeting after supper, he gave the new boys a pep talk on what was expected of them. Living up to those expectations kept your mind occupied. He also requested (translated "ordered") parents not to come up to school for at least six weeks to give their sons time to adjust.

FESSOR'S CLASS: My first impression of classes came in Fessor's room. I dropped my pencil on the floor. That was a no-no. I went to pick it up and was instructed to leave it there and was informed that "we don't do that in this class." Those first few weeks I don't know whether I was taking math or history in that class but I remember those times when Fessor would soften class up with his pep talk on character-building and things like that, about becoming a man. Things like that stuck with you through the years.

ROLL CALL: Being late to assembly after a vacation was an automatic claim. It was fun at these assemblies to watch somebody try to answer for a friend who was late when Mr. Dave called the roll. But Mr. Dave was pretty sharp on things like that. You could shove the desks together and hide a chair so that it didn't look like someone was missing. But Mr. Dave looked down over his nose through his glasses and marked every absence. I believe he could have spotted an empty seat with his eyes closed.

DINING HALL MISHAP: One night Donald (I can't recall his last name) was crumbing on the stage. The step down from the stage was always a potential danger point. Well, Donald overloaded his tray and misstepped on the way down. The crash was breathtaking. Everybody got as quiet as quiet can be. I looked at Mr. Dave to see what his judgment was. Then Robert McDonald's voice wafted out of the dishroom. He said, "My, my, what a catastrophe." That was all Mr. Dave needed. He jumped up from his chair and charged toward the dishroom door, saying on the way, "You'll know what a catastrophe is when I get through with you."

MR. DAVE IN CLASS: Mr. Dave knew those geometry theorems backward-and-forward. When he sent you to the board to prove one, he would stand and look outside the window. Then when you tried to explain what you were doing, he corrected your mistakes without looking at the board.

Lights were always out at 10 p.m. except the night each week that you had chemistry lab under Mr. Dave. After you finished the experiments, he would make you stay right there and write them up, sometimes long into the night. This guaranteed that you did your own lab write-ups.

He had a way of dealing with those who were unprepared that almost always worked – at least in encouraging preparation for the next session. When he asked you a question and you didn't know the answer, he would let that awful silence settle in for a while. Then, a hand cupped to his ear, he would say, "Well, say that again. I didn't hear you."

WRONGDOINGS: Smoking was the major problem. You could smoke pipes (if sixteen or over with parents' permission) but even then you wanted to catch a drag occasionally on the back porches of the cottages after lights. One time a group had lit the smoking lamp on the back porch after lights when Douglas Jarnigan flashed a picture. Everybody took off in pursuit of Jarnigan who fled to safety in the darkness. A few days later he showed the boys the print. The evidence was quite clear. The boys grabbed the picture and tore it up, but Jarnigan, who got some nice treatment after that, simply smiled and reminded them that he had hidden the negative.

CHESTERFIELDS: The man always smoked Chesterfields. Sometimes, especially in the Spring, when you walked around to the back of the cottage you would see two or three Chesterfield stubs. Mr. Dave knew an awful lot about what was going on.

WORKING A CLAIM: Working on a claim was a spare time thing, Monday afternoon or early in the mornings if you were in a big hurry. It did not interfere with your doing your regular duties. You went to football or basketball practice though usually, depending on events, Fesser wouldn't let you play or start until your claim was finished.

THE UNEXPECTED: Mr. Dave was a master of the unexpected. Late in the year, the weather sometimes became sultry, like the dog days of August. In assembly he would bark out in a rather gruff voice, "Don't let me see you with those chokerags on." Then, while the heat wave lasted, it was no coats and ties for Chapel and supper.

Or that first snowfall of the year, we'd all be looking out of the window from assembly (a lot of the boys had never seen snow before), and he would say, "Oh, hell, let's go have some fun." And the snowballs would fly and the sledding would begin.

And on another occasion, a Sunday night, after everybody had filed into assembly, he would say, "What the heck are you doing in here– supper's on Wetmore hill." And it's amazing how much better cold baked beans and apple sauce on paper plates tasted in a new location.

BARBEQUING: It was in 1957 that I got the assignment of barbequing the pigs for the annual reunion. In 1956, things had gotten out of hand and the alumni who were doing the barbecue partook too much of refreshments and five pigs turned pretty much to charcoal. But worse, a group of students, mostly fifth formers, took their cue from the visitors and had their own party down at the lake. They were caught, but Mr. Dave did not ship them. Though there were isolated instances of drinking before, this was the first sizeable affront. Claims were handed out. Mr. Dave revealed later that this blatant violation of school rules hurt him deeply.

SAM EMORY '51

GRADES: At Christ School, you earned your grades the old fashioned way – by hard work. Report cards were handed out weekly either at Saturday assembly after supper or at Sunday morning assembly before Chapel. Seventy was passing and it was the only school I had ever been to where you could earn a zero. Parents learned of your weekly grades in your Monday letter home. The frequency of the grades kept you aware of where you stood (as it did your parents) and your parents helped to provide motivation for improved effort.

PUNISHMENT: I don't recall any serious punishments while I was at Christ School but someone was expelled the year before. The claim bank went out of existence, replaced by cutting down trees and digging up stumps. I got a stump once for having food in my room. After a long struggle I finally got the tree to fall down. This put me on the wrong side of Mr. Dave for a while, because the tree fell across a power line running into the fraternity.

Failing a lot of school work brought a different kind of punishment. If you failed a course for a week, you automatically lost room study. Failing a couple of courses would put you in Monday afternoon study hall and prevent you from going to town.

I remember one boy who couldn't pass Spanish. He stayed until he was about twenty-one, trying. The last day before the final examination in 1951, he joined the Air Force for the U.S. was involved in the Korean War. His ambition was to be an undertaker.

THE FOOD: I didn't complain much at the time about the cooking of Julius and Elizabeth. Probably, I would be less happy eating school food now. I remember Lenten Fridays: beans, bread, and water. But you didn't complain because it was part of the church season. One thing, though, I stopped being a finicky eater.

MR. DAVE: He understood how to deal with boys. He knew when to be a tyrant and when to be a friend. He could do both. He could intimidate, scare you when he wanted to – with his voice, a look, a scowl. He could also be very friendly and encouraging when he thought you were trying. A smile put you on a cloud. He just projected himself. Looking back, I think he often stage-acted his anger, though I didn't feel this at the time.

GOING TO CONCERTS: Once I remember another boy and I were late getting back to our front row seats at the community concert. A famous Puerto Rican cello player glared at us as we moved into our squeaky seats. Suddenly, he gave us a bow. I felt about six inches tall. Neither one of us told anyone that we were from Christ School.

SCHOOL SPIRIT: School spirit was very good. It came from quite a few people. Mr. Dave was a part of it. It was a group thing. I don't know how it was achieved. I think things like the worklists and jobs did part of it. These made you feel as if you were a part of the school because you were doing some worthwhile work.

MAC STONHAM '53

GYM CONSTRUCTION (1952-53): I was skinny, small, non-athletic. Had the option of working on gym construction instead of participating in athletics. One job I had was catching bricks on the scaffolding. There were no hard hats then. Down below, a student would put brick on a wooden paddle and toss it skyward. You reached out to grab it – if too far, down you fell. FUN!

THREE CHAPLAINS: Fr. Dahl here one year. Fr. Rossmaessler was here two years. He was called Batman (wore long robes, which flowed in the air with his long, fast stride or while he was riding his bike). He created some resentment among students by refusing to be called "Pop" instead of Father. When it snowed, students used to get up early and collect snow off the Old Dorm roof and toss it at Fr. R. as he went to early chapel. He never acknowledge anyone throwing snowballs, even when he got hit. Fr. Webster– a great guy. He had an easier time because he followed the two who had followed Harris-Boynton-Hammond-Webbe. His wife was nice too. His house was open all the time to talk out problems. He did not overpower you on religion. I told him one day I couldn't accept the whole thing (Christianity). He wasn't terribly concerned. He said I was liable to change my mind one of these days; said it didn't matter what one felt at a particular time but how he grew over a period of time.

CHOIR PRACTICE: This came during seventh period. You could participate in two or more extra-curriculars (usually two days a week for each) or go to study hall. Urq was a master at his trade. He knew how far to let kids go. He was a pretty good actor, permitting a reasonable amount of cutting up but keeping you under control.

JOBS: Mr. Dave assigned everybody a job. You looked for your assignment early Monday morning. Teachers had report boys– to dump trash, clean-up, etc. When older boys were assigned to Urq, they would find that from time to time he would leave a pack of cigarettes out, and you could slip one or two out. I think he did so on purpose.

STUDY HALLS: They were kept by the prefects and some seniors. They did an excellent job. A rap on the head with a senior ring quelled any talking. Older kids were placed in the rear of study hall but not by form. You knew when a senior spoke, he carried Mr. Dave's voice.

*WRONG DOING:*The main "bad thing" was illegal smoking, mostly in the woods (caves, cabins, huts) and sometimes on the back porches of the cottages. Drinking was an occasional thing, and generally in the caves, huts, and cabins.

ACADEMICS: I don't think they could have been better.

RICHARD ARNOLD '56

MR. DAVE: The thing that struck me most about Christ School was Mr. Dave. His presence was overwhelming. He assumed an almost god-like hold, not only over our actions but (over) our thoughts and feelings themselves. A few things brought him down to earth. One was the sight of him being chewed out by Mrs. Dave for having lost a pair of hedge-clippers; another was the frequent sight of him carefully watering the plants on his parents' graves. All in all, however, his authority was such that many of us looked for his approval over and above that of our parents.

TEACHERS: A good thing I remember was the accessibility of teachers to students, especially to you and Urq Chinn. Harris Jr. would invite us over to his house to listen to records. Urq was everybody's friend. You had us in to your rather humble digs and gave us encouragement concerning the newspaper. And Fogle Clark even lent out his classical records to some of us.

A STRONG IMPRESSION: If I could name one student who dominated my impressions of Christ School, it would be Warren Jordan Myers '55. No athlete, Porky Myers brooked no nonsense from anyone. He was the only student able to read Milton aloud in front of an open window without provoking derision. Myers stimulated all of his friends to greater academic efforts. Even those who weren't his friends felt his approval or disapproval strongly. When Myers was selected prefect, gasps were followed by wild cheering – even tears were shed. It was Myers' example that drove me toward admission to Harvard Graduate School.

LEARNING I: Teachers were my bete nori, simply because I was an obnoxious kid. You got through to me by the simple expedients of some sarcasm, an occasional smack up the side of the head, and praise when deserved. My English grades rose from sixty to eighty-five within six weeks (and rose even higher). Other teachers had no such luck as I shall explain.

LEARNING II: Mr. Darsie tried to teach me Algebra. His intent was sincere but he was soft-spoken and relied upon gentle persuasion except for the time he grabbed Frank Hudnor by the scruff of the neck and ejected him for some ill-timed remarks. I wish he had leaned upon me a little bit too. It was only after I had graduated that I learned what a civilized and cultivated man Mr. Darise was.

LEARNING III: Captain Reid was a marvel. He slapped himself on the forehead and thighs while prefacing every important historical point with: "Can you imagine!" I ran afoul of Captain by not having a lead pencil for several daily tests. The resulting roar subdued me for the rest of the year. I'm only sorry I was such a callow youth. Captain Reid was first-rate.

LEARNING IV: Phil Croft was an inspiring biology teacher. He conveyed an excitement about the ideas he was concerned with. He called me "Livingston" because of my interest in explorations. However, he lost me in Fifth Form chemistry. I simply refused to memorize valence numbers.

LEARNING V: Giles Taggert was an interesting man but not strong as a Spanish teacher. He told fascinating stories about his travels but turned a blind eye to work in class. He cultivated the absent-minded professor image while still striking the pose of the buccaneer.

LEARNING VI: Alexander Mays was as peculiar a man as ever taught at Christ School. He would place a lounge chair on top of his desk, climb up on the desk and recline in the chair, take off his shoes, stick a cigarette in his mouth, then call someone up – usually Mama Willis, to give him a light. From then on it was pure magic. He made us write and rewrite and rewrite.

LEARNING VII: Mr Dave's geometry class was a baptism in fire. He sent you to the board with a problem– and nailed you there if you were not prepared to handle the task at hand....Geometry was not an easy subject for me but the experience of having to think on my feet was one of the best I have ever had.

PREPARATION FOR COLLEGE: On the whole Christ School prepared me for college very well. Having survived your and Mays' English courses, I found freshman composition in college a snap. The rigors of geometry helped me in a number of courses at the University of Pennsylvania, including logic and linguistics. Math was never my subject in high school or college so I can't say much about it. Foreign language at Christ School then was inadequate because of a lack of laboratory equipment and intensive courses. Christ School's biology course was too easy to be of much help with the course taught at Davidson. Captain Reid's history course was more than adequate preparation for a similar one I took at Pennsylvania. His course was also generally valuable because of the training he provided in accurate note-taking.

INTANGIBLES: The intangible benefits of Christ School education were several. They consisted mainly in teaching you:

1. To take responsibility for your own and others' actions.
2. Not to manufacture excuses, feel sorry for yourself, or take yourself too seriously.
3. To stick up for your friends.
4. And, above all, to maintain a sense of humor.

With these intangibles behind me, I was easily able to handle Davidson College, the University of Pennsylvania, and Airbourne and Special Forces training.

JOHN HOPE '58

FORT NICOTINE: Bill Barnwell and I cut down a number of white pines near the lake to build Fort Nicotine. While we were preparing to build the log hut, down came Mr. Dave and out came Mr. Black.

STUMPS: I had an affinity for stumps. Three of them came from having a single bar of candy in the room on different occasions. I dug them up near the site of the Hand House (east of the gym).

LESENSE'S STUMP: Lesense Smith was about 6'1" tall. He had to dig through six feet of fill to get to the surface of the roots. Hence his head was below the level of the trench. You couldn't see him digging; you could only hear him.

MCCULLOUGH'S MARINES: My bad football knee didn't like exercise. (Neither did the rest of me.) Mr. McCullough had great fun exercising a group of not-so-athletic boys on the site where the Old Gym stood.

SOLO: I was scheduled to sing my first solo in Chapel. Scared, I froze up and nothing came out of my mouth. Urq Chinn did an impromptu solo on the organ. Fr. Webster didn't fuss but told me that I would have to do it again next week and that the next time I would do it right. I did. (Pop wouldn't let a person fail; he made you see it through.)

IMPORTANT THINGS: What I remember vividly about Christ School are the tough things. The easy aren't worth remembering.

MAKING CHOICES: My allowance then was small. I remember not going to town three straight times in order to save up enough money to buy a toy.

ATHLETICS: I had one pair of tennis shoes – for all sports seasons.

THE CHAIR: In the cottage, each room had two chairs with wooden slats. In his room, Kells Hogan ran copper wiring along the slats. He would invite you into his room for coffee and a bite to eat. When you sat down, he would turn on the juice. The current carried a real wallop.

KITCHEN HELP: I made friends with the Kitchen help (Elizabeth, Julius, Pete–philosopher, cook, dishwasher, friend). Pete used to let me slip in and get some cold biscuits, cover them with peanut butter, and then drown them with molasses.

JOE PRESSLY '60

DORM LIFE: I moved into Harris Dorm in 1960 from the Fifth Cottage, which was finally quarantined or washed off to the sand-filter. Wilton Lynch and I were in charge of the middle section. It was a fairly close-knit group of folks who probably needed maids but we didn't have any, so we set about to do the best we could. We were a hair above health department standards....

MR. HAND: I was in several of his classes. I don't know if I repeated one several times or was in different courses. We had a communications problem for he was from the Northeast. His view of the South was not the same as mine. I remember his saying "if you built a bridge from Massachusetts to Savannah, there would be nothing underneath except wasteland."

RUNAWAYS.: I lost several good friends who were not permitted to return after they ran away. One pair, Chuck Middleton and Will Kennedy, went down the French Broad River and were not picked up until they reached Columbia. When the police located Middleton, he was mistaken for a leper. It was said that he had the worst case of poison ivy in the history of the Palmetto State.

COOT HOOPER: After supper, a large group of seniors would gather in his apartment (Lower 38 Dorm) to listen to rock or have some heavy religious discussions. Despite what some faculty may have thought, there was no drinking going on and very little smoking. After about twenty minutes of heavy talk, Teddy (Wagner) and I would head to the woods for a quick smoke.

A SLOW LEARNER: I was always a slow learner. Somebody had told me early in life, "early ripe, early rot," so I was determined not to grow up until my senior year. Actually I finally managed to do so, but it was my senior year in college. By then I had two children and a wife.

MR. BLACK: I traded licks for worklists once after being on campus for nine straight Mondays. I felt like I had to see daylight. My only trip before the Student Council involved some licks. Julius Swann and I were living on the back porch of the Fifth Cottage. There was no heat and only a caveman could exist in that kind of environment. We were talking after lights when Bill Freeman said, "Quieten down out there." Swann, who was smarter than I was, said to me, "Joe, you're not going to take that, are you?" I shouted "hell no" and added a couple of obscenities. I got a worklist. Coached to even more aggressive responses by Julius, I soon had six more worklists and a trip before the Council.

BEER: In 1960, beer drinking was an occasional thing. We'd take a beer occasionally and go to the movie and sit in total darkness and drink the thing.

GEOMETRY: Teddy (Wagner) and I were on Mr. Dave's 60-team (60 was passing). He would always ask us to go to the board to solve the problem, which we could never do. After a while, there was a ready made audience waiting for our appearance. I loved to take my position in front of the audience and show off. Mr. Dave provided the stage for me. One time when he returned my paper he said, "The work was poor but the acting was excellent."

IMPORTANT LESSON: Mr. Dave used to say, "No man is completely worthless – he can always serve as a bad example." That might have been how he felt about me. He and I were good friends, or at least I always felt that way. I had adopted him whether he had adopted me or not. I spent a lot of time hanging around the front porch (of the school building) to wait for him to get through with dinner and come up and sit there and talk to anybody about sundry things.

FESSOR: He was a great no-nonsense guy. He didn't just teach you to win but that it was necessary to discipline your mind and body to win. He was that way when my Dad was there (1925-29), and I guess he never changed his position.

FACULTY: I was never intimidated by Mr. Dave or any of the other Masters. They were good men. They demanded that we be men instead of boys.

FR. WEBSTER: He was an inspiration to us all. His Sacred Studies class was open discussion. You went through different periods, from being an atheist to an evangelist, but Pop let you develop your religion in a personal way. Being from the Presbyterian Church, I thought, at the time, that Fr. Webster was a Roman Catholic wearing an Episcopal cloak.

MORE ON THE FACULTY: They were good men, very well trained and educated. We all looked up to them. There wasn't a single Master I had whom I didn't respect and look up to and feel that he was providing a quality education. Of course, at that particular time I was fighting them tooth and nail.

MOLDING THE FACULTY: While Mr. Dave was moulding the students, the faculty were being moulded too. His philosophy rubbed off on them. The toughest faculty to work for were those who had been Christ School students. There was a degree of excellence that faculty-former students demanded which the other teachers did not know about. The new ones didn't know the qualities of excellence you were striving for.

THE INFIRMARY: It was run by a lady with real thick glasses (Mrs. Virginia Klose). She was a kind lady and occasionally I went over there to help her out. Woe be unto you if her glasses were out of place or fogged up; the thermometer might land in your ear. The infirmary was a nice facility but I would not have wanted to undergo brain surgery or triple by-pass there.

A BIG LESSON: I think the biggest thing I learned from Mr. Dave was that we all had something to contribute. He wanted us to do what we could to the best of our ability. He expected no more of us than our best.

TOLAR BRYAN '64

Art Carlson meeting J.B. Herring in the stairwell, bumping him up against the wall, thinking he was a new brat. (Mr. Herring was an English teacher.)

Chuck Norlander grabbing me by the shirt in the Jigger Shop and lifting me up against the wall – his amusement when I said he handled me as easily as he catches football passes.

Mrs. Root running the Jigger Shop.

As a second former, how I looked up to the seniors, especially John L. and Tom Currie, Bill Robertson, etc.

And how gullible I was about the stories that Phil Middleton, Bubba Lesemann, Ed Souther, et al told me about their girl friends and girls in general.

How lonely Sunday afternoon could be – but how amusing Bob Link was in his fantasy world playing imaginary baseball and other games.

The constant conflict between McKellar and Moffat/Warren/Mitchell.

The one time I did something bad and really got in trouble with Mr. Dave. He caught my brother Tom, Ned Matheny, and me swimming down at the lake after the faculty lifeguard had already left. Boy, was he mad!!!

The fun time playing soccer in the mud, snow, and bitter cold. How grubby and gross everyone was in the locker room with practice uniforms and gym underwear that hadn't been washed in weeks. And having to make the long trek up the hill after practice down at Wetmore.

The fun of sledding and skiing down Wetmore Hill and trying to avoid going into the ice cold creek.

Ice skating on the frozen pond. Learning to skate backwards, trying to play hockey, staying away from thin ice.

Camping in the woods in the spring – having to put out several brush fires started from careless campfires.

Visiting some of the caves in the fall and encountering all the crickets.

Shovelling snow off campus roads and paths in the middle of winter.

Getting out of classes to work the coal truck (in the winter) or cut corn (in the fall).

Frank Blanton sticking a pitch fork through my hand (gloves and all) while we were working in the silo, stomping down and leveling shredded corn.

Making the long walk down to Meadow's general store to buy candy – then having to eat it all before the next food search to avoid being assigned a stump. I do remember who the stump king was – Lineberger.

Keeping look-out at the Frat while dozens of students (and men hired by Pressly's father) helped Phil Middleton and Joe Pressly dig their 300 yard ditch (claim) before graduation.

Dave McCullough's special classroom style and dry wit – especially one time emphasizing to Frank Ross the difference between "expectant" and "unsuspecting" when referring to a pregnant woman.

Mrs. McCullough's attempts to teach us how to square dance – but we did have fun!

Working late at night on the *News* in the McCullough basement.

Working on layout and trying to come up with the best headlines.

The frequent social events – dances in the gym. One year it was snowing so badly that my date from the east Carolina coast didn't arrive until nearly 10 p.m. Another year, I was set up with a blind date from Viet Nam.

Pete the dishwasher was so much fun and so friendly. I remember when Mr. Dave asked him to fill in as the barber. All the upper formers were first in line because it had been over two months since we had had haircuts. Their haircuts were a sight to behold.

Then there were the campus rumors about Pete's moonshining activities. They say Mr. Dave was a character witness.

And then there was the pen-pal relationship that Tommy Goodman established with Olympic heart-throb, Donna DeVarona. He even called her on the telephone late one evening. She was on the cover of *Sports Illustrated* one week. Even now, every time I see her on TV as a sports commentator, I think of Goodman.

The enjoyment and companionship of watching TV on Saturday and Sunday evenings at the faculty homes – especially at HJ's. Mrs. Harris was so nice and friendly.

Going downtown to Asheville on Monday afternoons with nothing better to do than go to a movie – sometimes we watched the same movie two or three times in the same afternoon.

And how could I ever forget Capt. Reid's Latin class – how he used to turn four shades of red when someone messed up. Buck Squires was a favorite target of his shake-ups.

MARNEY HENDRICK '67

HAZING: Mostly there were some broom-swats (noisy but not severe) and frog-popping that might bruise your arm. One instance sticks out in my mind. The seniors all came down to the dorm one night and we dropped water balloons on their heads. We got what was coming to us. The seniors in my dorm (Boyd) were pretty nice; they picked on everybody equally.

SENIORS: You looked up to them with respect and some fear. When I was a senior, some of the things I did were modeled after earlier ones. I thought Bob Toomey (prefect) was the greatest guy in the world but he probably didn't know who I was. And Jenks Pressly was another fine leader.

NOTE-TAKING: I remember that History VI course. That particular course was the first I went into that required a lot of notes. It paid off in college.

FOOTBALL MANAGER: Those were good years to be football manager. I managed the last two years and got to know Fessor quite well. Our record was 15-0-1. We also had excellent basketball and track teams then.

PROBLEMS: There were no drug problems. I don't even recall anybody smoking marijuana. That just didn't come into play. I'm pretty sure I would have known about it. Probably the worst thing was several runaway situations. There was occasional drinking (a little beer), especially around Thanksgiving. Smoking was not a big deal since Fifth and Sixth forms had the frat. After the Final Banquet, the Fourth Form (which waited on the tables and worked the dishroom) got to light up on the back porch and we killed ourselves consuming about a dozen packs of cigarettes.

DISCIPLINE: You knew where Mr. Dave stood. He was very consistent in the way he wanted the boys to act. You knew where he was coming from. By 1967, discipline was becoming less consistent.

THE EMPTY FEELING: In four years, I never lost that empty stomach sensation associated with the beginning of school after each vacation. There was always some uncertainty; you didn't know what to expect from new teachers and the seniors.

FOOD IN THE ROOM: The only change was that you could have food in your room on Saturday and Sunday but it had to be eaten up by six o'clock on both days. There was a lot of "pigging-out" going on about 5:30 each Saturday. The most frequent penalty in school was getting a stump for food in your room.

SOUTHER'S STORE: I remember this store was put off limits to us for a couple of years. This meant we had to walk to Wilma's, a little further down the old airport road. This came after one boy marched around the store, running his hands through a bin of rabbit pellets and impersonating Mr. Souther.

SUNDAY: Besides a day to walk to the nearby stores, ours was a time of good athletes and we spent many Sunday afternoons playing basketball, baseball, softball, volleyball, rope-climbing, and other things. Very few girls came out to campus so that we saw them only at dances or in town on Mondays.

CHAPEL: Though I was not an Episcopalian, I got involved in the services and was fascinated by the singing and chanting. There was some griping about going to Chapel every day, not about the services but rather about having to wear a necktie and keep the shoes shined.

FR. WALLACE: He was a strong – enthusiastic and hard-working – leader in the Chapel and I respected him for that. His Sacred Studies course was really interesting. He was a pretty tough teacher, about as "mean" as the rest of you.

CLASS OF 1967: We picked up four boys from the Class of 1966, a class which went through some troublesome times. At graduation that year, Mr. Dave gave the shortest commencement talk on record, about twenty-five words.

MY BIG FIGHT: I was a fifth former and senior Robin Boylan was giving out the mail. I stuck my head through the mail opening and asked if he was going to give me my mail and he threw it at me. I threw it back. He threw it back at me. I threw it back at him. He came out the door and I broke his hand on my face. Then I sucker punched him while holding him off and gave him a black eye. We laughed about this recently when he called me to raise money for the Loyalty Fund.

THING I LEARNED: The Christ School system taught me to be self-sufficient and to develop some confidence. I learned how to do things for myself. It helped me academically, though I was never a great scholar. I developed there a great appreciation for reading and I read a lot. That's probably why I went into the newspaper business.

I REMEMBER....

To many, Christ School memories flow like free verse, little strokes that create vivid metaphors, stirring both the mind and heart. **FREDERICK PARRISH** spent four years here (1953-56). His images remain vivid, as recalled in "I remember...."

Mr. Dave throwing wood on an October fire...the smell of the crosscut white pine...throwing up before my first brat football game...the strange fascination with the brat caves (soon discarded)...walking to the country store near the old airport and buying some Scalf's Indian River Medicine and wondering why Robert Wasson and Ritchie Hutchinson didn't want any...the peaceful look in Mr. Dave's eyes and his advice , his quietly considered words. He was Christ School...Father Webster's vestments and the magic regalia of the High Church ritual...Captain Reid lining up the peas on his plate to give retinal substance to his description of a Civil War battle...the smoky big city feeling of Asheville...eating lunch out with my parents and maternal grandparents in Biltmore Forest...the football game girls with pretty faces like flowers.

The World War II years brought students from everywhere to the campus, and for the children of many people going into the service, Christ School became home. **GRAHL SCHAFFERT** '45 comments:

We can all remember the outstanding events during our years at Christ School. It is the daily occurrence I like most to recall, the things that helped me most: sleeping on the back porch of the cottage until Christmas, running to the dining hall on a cold dark morning, trying to be first in the shower before the hot water disappeared, breaking the ice in the john before using, just sleeping on Sunday afternoon, looking forward to getting our dollar and spending it on Monday in Asheville, waiting for the study hall bell to ring so we could go to the football field before turning in for some lies and a smoke, the never ending task of keeping the (clay) tennis courts in shape, of Father Webbe's geometry lessons with the THUD, and on and on, but most of all Mr. Dave's fairness and quick but sure justice.

MORE I REMEMBER

PETER B. WATERS '69: Fessor's dislike of Grape "Blow Gum"– Mr.Dave's sweater – coal truck detail with Sid – the 1968 Asheville School game in sleet and snow – Captain Reid's night study hall with alarm clocks hidden in the trash can – the look in Bill Sewell's eyes when he got the chance to coach the linemen when Mr. McCullough was absent – McDonald's after a ball game off campus – Ollie Lance's ravioli – John Huffman in Bynum's biology class (or any class for that matter) – newcomers fainting in Chapel – rattling your coat buttons on the edge of the collection plate – Sunday afternoons at the Frat – Sunday afternoons with dates on Clover Hill near "The Grange" – Monday afternoons with dates in the back row of the Imperial Theatre – the first and last visit to the Jade Club – playing basketball in the Blue Ridge gym – the '38 Bathroom – washing dishes with Pete – fights on the football field after lunch – the old "Green Monster" – Wilma's and Nelson Souther's – Nelson Souther's daughter – reporting to Heno for breath tests after a senior Saturday night out – etc. etc. etc.

TAYLOR SHIPLEY '67

Winter nights in study hall...apples off the back porch of the kitchen...Elizabeth's "hard" cake for which she charged a fee... fall walks to the lower field during football season...great teachers...bus trips to places like Rosman and Old Fort for football or basketball...pick-up games in the gym on Saturday nights...assemblies with all the profs lined up along the wall...Monday morning work period...three year permanent job on milk bottle washer...walks to the store...trying to stump Tom Suiter with sports trivia...worklists with Mr. Dave...working in the gym shop with Fessor...prefect tapping...successful football and basketball seasons.

PAT ECHOLS '42

Unloading coal cars in Arden...walking through the deep snow to Arden to get bread...Julius...skinny dipping in icy water...roasting purloined chickens in the Chapel furnace...attack of measles...near exhaustion as the school fought forest fire on Hickory Top Mountain...a smile from Betsy Harris...first day in Asheville...meeting moonshiners John Docket and Dude Jones after getting separated from Mr. Zach's hiking class...getting "put in" to a football game at long last for the first time.

Most vivid and unforgettable: Sunday, December 7, 1941, standing outside Chapel after service on a beautiful clear day and hearing on a car radio under the pine trees that "Pearl" had been bombed...we military "brats" more conscious than the others that "it" had happened because we were away at school for the reason that our fathers were overseas or on the way...other service juniors Bill Bartlett (died in France), Homer Venture (his father went down on a Japanese prison ship), the Mallets (who recruited us "new boys" at Fort Sill, Oklahoma), Muddy Watters, Steve Christie, I think, and a horse calvary type who was in the Fourth Cottage, and a number of others I can't recall.

BILL COBB '61.

Mr. McCullough's Fourth Form English Class (I use the term loosely)...tobacco...the Fifth Cottage...Smoking in the woods (and getting caught)...Mr. Dave..."Coot" Hooper...Nelson Boone...a moving three years religious experience...grubby tie night...Perry Mason at Mr. Hand's...the Frat...raising chickens in the Harris Dorm closet...successful search for girl living inside the tracks...being a senior...the importance of the ring (still wear it)...graduation.

BILL HAUSER '50

Moving on to the back porch of the cottage during the February thaw and then freezing for the next couple of months because no one would be first to chicken out...smoking forbidden cigarettes in "Paradise"..stopping the bus in Skyland for fried chicken after beating Asheville School in soccer...sledding on Wetmore Hill...swimming in the old pond, icy even in September...the day I found out I'd been admitted to West Point, and Mr. Dave confiding to me that he would have gone but for a wood chopping accident to his knee.

GAYLORD SHEPHERD '47

First worklist, with two of us unloading an entire hopper car of lump coal in Arden from 6 a.m. to 7:30 p.m....breaking cinders with an iron pipe to make the track (around the present football field)...when the Frat House burned...Mrs. Dave...apple slices in pipe tobacco...folding clothes in the laundry...forbidden snacks in the room after lights...room cleaning and inspections...sleeping on the cottage porch...burying water pipe at 2 a.m. in anticipation of a freeze...Mr. Dave and night chemistry class: hydrogen release from sodium gone awry...dances at Fassifern and St. Genevive's.

AND MORE I REMEMBER

Getting to Christ School was an experience: all night train rides from Savannah to Arden via Southern Railroad with two engines to pull the mountain. (**ANDY CALHOUN** '43).

Only one illegal thing I can remember. As I recall, the potatoes used to be stored in the basement in a bin under the kitchen. Several times we would swipe a potato and take it out in the woods and cook it over a fire. What a treat! (**TOM DICKINSON** '43).

Mr. Chinn could play anything on the organ. I remember going over to the Chapel with him some nights and he would play for us. Name a sound or a situation and he could play it on the organ. Boy! Could he play a haunted house. (**DICKINSON**).

Ollie and Dot were in the kitchen. Big Pete ran the dish-washer. He had biceps muscles that didn't end. (**KING LOGAN** '70).

We put on a play to make enough money to buy our class rings. They were $9 each. The school fee was $150 per year. (**ALBERT DOUGHERTY** '23).

I think I built the first lower tennis court. (**FRANK ZIMMERMAN** '36).

No question about it, Christ School stopped me from flunking out of the school of life. (**BILL KIRKLAND** '65).

Very seldom does a day go by that I don't do something that I learned at Christ School, whether it's washing a window (with newspapers) or organizing an association involving a great number of individuals. (**DURWARD GRADY** '54).

Fr. Harris said in our classwork we should be equal to woodpeckers. They used their heads. We all respected him and we stood when he entered the classroom. (**EDWARD FREAS** '27).

One boy wanted to be baptized by immersion so Fr. Harris baptized him in the old lake. It was a little on the cool side. (**FREAS**).

The winter snows did not keep the day students from walking several miles to school. They never missed classes. People now couldn't live like they did with the few clothes they had. (**MARGARET BRUMBELOE** '27).

The girls wore "giddy" blouses (white with sailor collars), dark pleated skirts, and black satin bloomers. They wore sweaters (there were no heavy coats), black hightop shoes, and black knee stockings. (**MRS. BRUMBELOE**).

Classes were very small. The boys stood up when girls entered the room. (**MRS. BRUMBELOE**).

I'll never forget the 36 inches of snow my first year. (**TOM MCGILL**'69).

Bo Morehead was undoubtedly a brilliant comedian and a master in imitating Captain Reid in Latin class behind his back. (**ALBERT MATHENY** '68).

I sang soprano for five years in Mr. Chinn's choir. I finally made tenor in the Sixth Form. (**GEORGE KIMBERLY** '50).

A never forgotten moment occurred when we defeated Asheville School in overtime in the 1969 Prep School Tournament. (**HOKE CURRIE** '67).

Mr. McCullough led the laughter as John Huffman (from a classroom above his) jiggled a frog on a string outside his window. (**BOB BEARD** '69).

Chapel services meant so much. I remember vividly how students raised money for the construction of Fr. Harris Memorial Chapel; the envelopes we pinned on the cross in Chapel which contained our Lenten Resolutions; the beautiful Nativity scene set up in Advent; early communion on cold mornings. (**JIM PATTY** '42).

One day a week, I think it was Saturday, was set aside for taking tests in all courses – four or five, as the case might be. This meant that you had to keep up with your work. And you did. (**E. ALLAN BROWN** '36).

JACK MCDUFFIE'41: The images of Christ School never fade away; they remain a faithful part of what was received.

Mrs. Dave moving a potted plant into the sun in her living room . . Mrs. Boynton offering tea on a Sunday afternoon . . . Pete, that faithful servant whom all the boys loved, walking as pallbearer at Mrs. Dave's funeral . . . Mr. Dave kneeling at the altar rail . . . Mr. Dave noisily riding a tractor on campus during church services when he disliked the liturgical antics of a new priest . . . Mr. Dave singing "*Cumberland Gap*" at the boy's request . . . Mr. Dave standing by the old Sawbell at night.

A PLACE OF COMFORT: Few boys who go off to boarding school escape at least some homesickness. It usually strikes quickly on the first day –about sun down when parents have gone away. Here the feeling was intensified by the knowledge (until the late 1950's) that the only telephone available was in Mr. Dave's house. One Florida boy (**Harry Taylor** '53) had that empty feeling for a couple of weeks. One day, he said, things got so bad that he went to Chapel, got on his knees, and prayed: "God, what have I gotten myself into? Can you help me to get back home?" His prayer was answered swiftly and with unexpected results. "The next day I began to fit into the daily routine. My worries evaporated. Life at Christ School turned into a four year happy experience."

IMPROVING POSTURE: Much of Mr. Dave's discipline was homespun. For example, he had a practical, sure-fire remedy for improving a boy's posture in the dining hall. One thing he especially detested were boys who rocked back in their chairs. Second former Bob Carlisle succinctly described Mr. Dave's antidote in a letter he wrote to his mother: "I have the chair with the two legs that are sawed in-half and it surely is hard to sit in. I fall down an average of two times a meal." (**Bob Carlisle** '49)

AIDING THE UNDERDOG: During World War II, Saturday night boxing matches were part of a student's physical fitness training. Sometimes the spirit flowed over into the dinning hall. Harcourt Waters recalled such an incident. "I was leaving the dining hall when Bill Ellis went to aid a lower former who was being picked on. Two other boys joined in the mele against Ellis. He yelled to me and I went to his assistance. No sooner had I landed a punch than Ellis took off, leaving me one-on-three. Later, after being mussed up a bit, I asked him why he ran off and left me alone. "I went to get some help," was his lame reply. (**Harcourt Waters** '43)

WALTER HOOPER: "There were two things which made a complete conquest of me soon after my arrival at Christ School in the early 1960's. One was the nearly overwhelming beauty of the campus and its fields and woodlands. I fed on the beauty with all five senses. Who could not be forever enamored of that warm bitter-sweet smell of the boxwood Mr. Dave was forever trimming? Walk a few yards from them and the scent of a thousand pines washed over you.

"Mr. Dave was not the first there, but most of what was best about Christ School was his creation. Without his sympathy for 'country boys' he would not have attracted so many there. I think he tried to keep it from his mind that it was because the school was so successful that the 'city boys' (whose parents drove Mercedes) were trying to flock there too."

TELLING THE TRUTH: One day before World War II, Mrs. Dave was driving back to school from Arden. About half way back, she saw an older student carrying a green box on his shoulder. Obliviously, it was heavy. She stopped to offer him a ride, which he gratefully accepted. She asked him what he was carrying. He replied, "A case of beer." Both laughed. Later, the boy deposited the bottles to cool in the old spring. Not much later he was digging a claim.

MOONSHINERS: Fr. Harris loathed moonshining and the dreadful damage liquor did to many surrounding families. Illegal stills dotted the countryside, and many mountain people considered the profession an honorable one. From time to time, Fr. Harris reminded the community in chapel services that he would report anyone he saw running a still.

On one such occasion, deputies arrested two men who were operating a still on the school's property following a call from Fr. Harris. Each Sunday afternoon (while the two men were serving on the county chaingang) Fr. Harris would hitch up his carriage, pick up the wives of the two convicted men, and take them to the prison camp to visit their husbands.

On another occasion, a moonshiner threatened to kill Fr. Harris for reporting him. He came to the rectory one night, deep in drink and waving a pistol. He called for Fr. Harris to step outside and said that he was going to kill him. Fr. Harris, wearing his familiar black cossack, stepped calmly off the porch, walked up to the disturbed visitor and took the pistol from his outstretched hand. There was no bitterness, only concern for the man and what his condition did to his family. (**Bob Harris**)

SPANISH MASS: Fr. Ralph Webster, who was to be ordained a priest in Christ School Chapel on Oct. 24, 1943, introduced something new at Fr. Harris Chapel, an early morning communion said in Spanish. Nearly all the boys in the Spanish classes attended the 6:30 a.m. service, with all responses and prayers said in Spanish. After this year of teaching and learning administration here, Fr. Webster went to Puerto Rico to organize a mission school.

MEMPHIS BELLE: After landing his plane at the old Asheville-Hendersonville Airport on October 1943, Major Bob Morgan '36, visited Christ School and described his raid over Bremen, one of the twenty-five daylight raids his famous Flying Fortress made over Germany. After the successful raid in which the mission wiped out the Focke Wolfe plant, (he described the preparation and attack in detail), Morgan said the planes, on their return home, formed such close formation the wings overlapped. The altimeter read one hundred feet since German radar equipment was unable to locate a plane under a thousand feet. Morgan was a member of Christ School's first tennis team and later contributed a trophy to the most valuable player. (*Christ School News*)

JUSTICE: Strong ingredients in Mr. Dave's justice were both humor and fairness. **Deas Richardson** '39 recalled one such occasion involving a nearby mink farm. "One day my roommate and I swiped a sign at the mink farm which read, "No visitors allowed during breeding season." A couple of weeks later, we went to a dance in Hendersonville and hung the sign under the one which announced "Fassifern School for Girls." It was several days before Mrs. Woodward, the headmaster, saw it and had it taken down. She had it wrapped up and , still fuming, ordered her chauffeur to drive her to Christ School. She stormed into Mr. Dave's office for a thirty minute stay. Well, we expected the worst, but nothing was said that night in assembly and the students were dismissed for Chapel. As we started out the door, a familiar voice said, "D.R., I'd like to see you and Rommie (Nick Carter) in my office now." We walked in, two scared rats. Mr. Dave unwrapped the sign, looked at it, and broke out laughing. I'm not going to ask you if you had anything to do with putting this sign up because I know you won't lie to me. But if you ever do anything like this again, start packing."

BLANKET TOSS: It was a warm spring night and a group had gathered on Yard D in front of the First Cottage, with both blanket and victim. The unnamed Third Cottager had received a couple of good-natured tosses when a familiar voice thundered from Fessor's front porch: "What's going on over there?" What was going on over there suddenly stopped going, with the victim still on the rise. Hands and feet scattered in different directions from the glare of the cottage lights. Even so, everyone felt remorse and anguish as the classmate landed with only a blanket separating him from the terra firma. He did not lie sprawled for long. He too recognized the authority in that voice and considered the tone too strident to be helpful and he also took to flight, using the nearby woods as a place of refuge. Happily for the tossers, the victim kept the episode to himself as he hobbled to class the following morning. (**David McCullough** '45)

CONFESSION: In 1943-44, the man who would become Chaplain here in 1950, re-introduced confessional services at Christ School. Fr. Webster, who was assisting Fr. Webbe, held the confessional during Ash Wednesday in Fr. Harris Chapel. Since such relationships remain private to priest, confessor and God, no earthly measure is available as to the power of intercession. In a letter home, one student, a second former, provided some insight into the practice. "Yesterday the two priests were in the chapel so that we could confess our sins. Nearly everybody went so I did too. Although I haven't many (ha'ha')." At least not before he wrote the letter.

LAZ ALLEN was a beloved Negro who was both a minister and operator of the school farm from 1928-45 while living in the old farm house on the lower road. Three of his dozen children worked for the school. **Jim Patty** '42, a retired professor of French at Vanderbilt University, recalled Laz's impact. "Many students (it would be more accurate to say most) used to spend at least part of their free time –a Thursday, Saturday, or Sunday afternoon– down at the old barn, chatting with Laz. These students remember him as an honest, hard worker, who always had a kind remark for everyone. Not all education comes from books or the classroom. The influence these students carried from Laz was his kind, gentle manner. Most have never forgotten his favorite saying: "Have faith, the Lord will provide."

WATER PRESSURE: Water pressure was always a problem at Christ School and getting caught in the shower all soaped up was not a rare occurrence. **Bill Wells** '59, recalled one such occasion. It was a prank which required masterful timing and organization. Under the leadership of a boy who would become a prefect, we would synchronize our watches and flush all the toilets on campus at the same moment. This would have a scalding effect on bathers and send them screaming to safety.

Bill also recalled another prank which Kells Hogan '56, would pull while testing some theory. He would come up to the 30 Dorm and spread a rumor. He would set his stopwatch going and run back to his cottage. Then he would time how long it took the rumor to travel (in some form) to the cottage.

A STUMP: When you were burned for the little thing, there was not too much reason to get into big trouble. One symbol of The Man that remains etched in the mind so of many Christ School students was his axe, which usually was leaning by the front door of the dining hall every morning. **Chuck Wright** '53, a poet, translator, and now professor at the University of Virginia, remembers it well. One morning, before knowing that it belonged to The Man, Chuck liberated the axe to work on his stump, (actually an oak tree), which was located behind the Fifth Cottage. He had only been in school a few weeks of his first year when he made the mistake of having candy in his room after a trip to town. When someone asked Chuck where he had gotten his axe, he learned that he had kidnapped the one belonging to Mr. Dave. "My first instinct was to run and hide," Chuck said, "but instead I ran to my stump, took the axe and cleaned it up, and slipped it silently into its accustomed spot." The tree provided a lot of work and good deal of fun. The tree finally came down when Dennis Georgion '52 –who at that time had some size on him– climbed to the top of the tree and rode it to the ground. "The whole stump episode was a good one for me," Wright recalled. "My roommate, Bill Covin '53, helped me to get it out, and all kinds of people pitched in at the end to help me get it down. It gave a real sense of the friendship and fellowship of the place, and also taught me to do fewer dumb things in the future. No one needed to have food in his room all the time, the mice didn't need to be fed, and eating three square meals a day was better for you."

HOW THE COTTAGES WERE BUILT: In 1921 Fr. Harris obtained some money he could spare, and so he had Mr. Boyd begin construction of the first of six frame cottages, the last one being completed in 1925. By replacing the log cabins, the area would be opened up for a gymnasium. Fr. Harris had in hand $1,500 to build one cottage, but he had a plan which he hoped would lead to a second one soon thereafter. After the foundation had been laid for the first cottage along with some sub-flooring, Fr. Harris told Mr. Boyd to have the workers lay the foundation for another one next to it. To a puzzled Mr. Boyd, Fr. Harris explained why he wanted the second foundation started before the other cottage was completed, even when there was not enough money on hand to complete it. "Well, some one might come along and ask why we weren't finishing that one and I could tell them we didn't have the money." Things worked out perfectly. One day a woman friend of the school came up the road leading to the Chapel and inquired as to why the men weren't working on the other cottage. Fr. Harris told her the school just didn't have the money to finish it. The lady donated $1,500 to complete the second structure. (**David Harris Jr.**)

A BEAUTIFUL MOMENT: It was early in October 1933 when mornings were cool and the afternoons like Indian summer, and color was creeping across Burney Mountain. Classes were interrupted when thousands of Monarch butterflies appeared over the football field on their migratory flight. The swarm of big orange and black butterflies –said to be the only species of this family which survive the winter– was so large that it was hours in passing over the campus.

A PHENOMENAL MEMORY: Seldom if ever did Fessor fail to remember the name of an alumnus and something about him. One alumnus who stopped by Fessor's house in Arden thirty years after he graduated found this out in a striking fashion. He walked into the house, looked straight at Fessor and said, "I bet you don't remember who I am." Quick as a wink, Fessor shot back, "Yes, I do. You're the boy who didn't hustle in the outfield and let the ball drop in the ninth inning to cost Clay Croom a no-hitter at Asheville School."

SQUEEZING THE GRAPEFRUIT: You learned a lot of things in the dining hall when the tablehead spoke with authority. One morning Julius and Elizabeth provided grapefruit halves at breakfast. I was seated at Fessor's table when, after finishing the meaty part, I picked up the grapefruit to squeeze the remaining juice into my spoon. Things got real quiet. Immediately Fessor suggested (how strong was his power of suggestion) that I could leave the table, hence casting doubt upon my table manners. On the way out of the dining hall, I passed the head table, where The Man (Mr. Dave) was just squeezing his grapefruit juice into a spoon. I thought how lucky he was not to be sitting at Fessor's table. (**Muddy Watters** '42)

MISS MAC: Harriet McCoy was the tonic the Christ School infirmary needed. She had retired from a career as an army nurse to a small house overlooking Lake Summit in Tuxedo (NC). She could be abrupt or tender, depending on what the situation required. She could distinguish between the fake (the ones who tried to cough their way out of study hall) and those who needed a nurse's care and affection. She was not reluctant to make the necessary judgment. Her diagnostic skills were tested in 1943-44 when a lower former (Sammy Paschal) became suddenly ill, and was taken over to the infirmary. In a matter of minutes, Miss Mac ordered him sent to the hospital in Biltmore, correctly diagnosing that he had a virulent form of spinal meningitis. Within half an hour he was in the hospital and treated successfully at a time when spinal meningitis generally meant death or severe crippling. As the doctor explained later, it was Miss Mac's quick, precise diagnosis and her willingness to make decisive judgments which saved Sammy's life. In fact, her mixture of vinegar and sugar won the respect and love of all and made her leaving some years later a sad occasion.

THE ORIGINAL ORGAN: The pump organ, dedicated on All Saint's Day in 1907, was often the source of amusement until it was electrified in the 1930's. Two boys would sit in a little chamber outside the main Chapel, waiting for a tug on a string to tell them to start the pumping process which sent air into the chamber. Around 1923 that assignment belonged to **John Dougherty** '25 and Bucket Fulton '25. Dr. Dougherty tells the story:

"Bucket and I got the job as pumpers. Sometimes we would start talking or get to reading and would not notice that the string had been pulled. Thus, when Mrs. Willis would start to play, the chamber would not be full of air and the organ would wheeze like an attack of asthma. Frantically we would start pumping. Fr. Harris would glare at Mrs. Willis and Mrs. Willis, who always wore a black straw hat in church, would stare straight ahead, neither face creased by amusement. Mrs. Willis always wore a very severe black dress with black shoes, and we loved to hear her play and loved to sing when she did play. Often on Saturdays, Mother Harris would practice with us a capella. These sessions would last a long time– until we reached the perfection she expected from us at the next Sunday service."

SATURDAY NIGHTS: One answer to boredom on long winter nights were the Saturday night programs. Some were homemade, others were imported. One such example of made-at Christ School-entertainment occurred on the last Saturday of October in 1939. The entertainment was provided by the newly-established Iota Omega Club. A musical show of talent followed with Dick Read at the piano, Charles Unsworth on the drums, David Harris Jr., playing the piano, and Bill Shouse playing Bocherreni's "Minuet and Seitz Concerto" on the violin. Interspersed were some Italian monologues by James Clarke.

UNCLE VAN ALLEN: One of the early legendary characters at Christ School was Uncle Van Allen, a former slave who was about sixteen years old when President Lincoln issued the Emancipation Proclamation. He belonged to a man in Rutherfordton but was later brought into the Arden area by another man named Karnes. Uncle Van Allen worked for Christ School from day one, utilizing his wagon team of ox and a mule. His claim to starting Christ School was that he cut the trees, cut the logs, hauled the logs to the saw mill, and then hauled the lumber back to the campus which went into the building of the Red School House. Uncle Van Allen was a strong Baptist, and he might not have been comfortable with the term "Father" as applied to Fr. Harris. He was said to refer to "Pappy" Harris when not on campus.

CHAPEL TRADITIONS 1900-1970

Life at Christ School was centered around services held in the two chapels. The major services, including High Mass and Evensong, took place in the large Chapel, which was consecrated as "Christ Chapel" but was usual called The Chapel. Low Mass was observed each morning, first in the main chapel and then later (beginning in 1938) in Fr. Harris Chapel. The choice and execution of Christ School's liturgical observances were governed by the Church Year and the solemn traditions of the high church established here.

ALL SAINT'S DAY: High Mass was celebrated at 10 a.m., generally with corporate communion. It was accompanied with a holiday up to World War II.

CANDLELIGHT SERVICE: Fr. Boynton introduced the Candlelight Service of Lessons and Carols modeled after traditions in England. Celebrated the night before Christmas vacation began, this service included the Blessing of the Creche, the traditional six lessons and carols, and a candlelight procession into the night while the Choir sang and hummed *Silent Night.*

ASH WEDNESDAY: For many years, all the students attended, before classes, the service of the Imposition of Ashes and the Penitential Rite. In later years, the service was held in the evening.

LENT: The Sundays of Lent were observed with Low Mass –that is, the service was not sung. No incense was used then and the number of servers was reduced from six to two.

PALM SUNDAY: Blessing of the Palms, Procession, the Passion, and High Mass.

HOLY WEEK: The student body was always on campus during this period of time.
Monday-through-Wednesday: The Penitential Rite.
Maundy Thursday: High Mass, Stripping of the Altar.
Good Friday: Three Hour Service included Stations of the Cross, Chapel talks, bell tolled thirty-three times. Fasting encouraged. (By 1960, reduced to one hour, from 2 to 3 p.m.)
Holy Saturday: Pascal Candle lit. Mass of the Pre-Sanctified.
Easter Day Sunrise Service: At 5:30 a.m., the Chaplain rapped loudly on each door, proclaiming "Alleluia, the Lord is Risen." The boys replied, "The Lord is Risen Indeed, Alleluia."
Easter Sunday Sung Eucharist at 11 a.m.
Little Easter: Sung Eucharist with Confirmation usually held that night at Solemn Evensong.

GRADUATION: High Mass with brief talk by headmaster and the singing of "I Bind Unto Myself Today."

GENERAL SERVICES

HIGH MASS: Was sung on Sundays and major feast days.

LOW MASS: Celebrated every morning. Frequently offered in thanksgiving, or in memory of certain occasions or people, or in memory of the departed.

DAILY EVENSONG: Was sung/chanted by student body before supper. Special Intercessions.

SOLEMN EVENSONG: Every Sunday evening and also during the week to recognize one of the lesser feasts or fasts, such as The Annunciation of St. Stephen or the Conversion of St. Paul. Benediction of the Blessed Sacraments (Adoration). The chaplain/acolytes processed from Father Harris Chapel with the host. Often used in place of Solemn Evensong.

THE LITANY: Often offered on Wednesdays and/or Fridays during Lent.

SEASONAL SERVICES OF TALKS OR LECTURES: The Chaplains often elected to give a series of talks one evening each week during Advent or Lent. Guest priests or laymen were often invited to participate.

COMPLINE: Offered after study hall in Lent, during the 1950's and early 1960's. It was under the leadership and direction of the students.

THE RESERVED SACRAMENT:It was kept at all times in the Father Harris Chapel. A sanctuary light burned there continually.

SAINT VINCENT'S GUILD:Servers were admitted to the Guild only after a period of training and other commitments. Only Guild members served on Sunday acolyte crews.

OTHER EVENTS

Christ School hosted District Women's Auxiliary.

Christ School hosted 13th annual Diocesean Convention, Bishop Gribbin presiding.

Visitations, talks, and meditations led by brothers and sisters from Holy Orders.

Trinity Church Men's Bible Class attended Evensong, ate supper, and presented a program during study hall period.

Solemn Evensong with choir recital preceded the Barbecue on the day of the annual Alumni Reunion.

Armistice Day (November 11) generally observed prior to World War II with a festive half-holiday. The Angelus would toll at 11 a.m., followed by prayer and homage to those who fought to preserve freedom. Sometimes, Algae Brumbeloe, a graduate injured during the Great War, gave a talk in assembly that day.

CHAPEL MARRIAGES

Christ School Chapel was the site of many marriages involving alumni and friends of the school. The following, with ministers listed, were on the records kept in the sacristy. There may have been others not recorded.

June 28, 1911	Norvin C. Duncan to Olivia Butt	William E. Gay
Oct. 22, 1919	John Hemphill Reagan to Nellie Souther Shuford	Fr. Harris
Dec. 1 1919	Richard Fayssoux to Sarah Shuford	Fr. Harris
Sept. 7, 19--	Charles H. Moore to Edith W. Porter	Fr. Harris
Nov. 1, 1922	Donald Ryan Harris to Francis Weedon Walker	Fr. Harris
Jan. 11, 1923	David P. Harris to Elizabeth Merrimon	Fr. Harris
June 17, 1924	John Herndon Thomson to Dorothy Elizabeth Harris	Fr. Harris
Sept. 10, 1924	A. Luther Baldwin to Tempie Wilkie	Fr. Harris
Dec. 4, 1924	Hugh W. Davis to E.R. Baldwin	Fr. Harris
Sept. 1,1926	Douglas Nye to Susannah Robertson Wetmore	Fr. Harris
April 20, 1927	Austin Robbins Gordon to Edna W. Clark	Fr. Harris
Oct 8, 19--	John Peacock Brown to Susan Merrimon	Fr. Harris
Aug. 12, 1928	Jesse J. Causby to Ethel Pressly	Fr. Harris
Aug. 16, 1931	Joe S. Stroupe to Kate E. Nesbett	Fr. Harris
Oct. 25, 1936	Robert Henry Lee to Mary Francis Weeks	Fr. Boynton
Mar. 27, 1937	Ben Barger to Nell Alice Bryant	Fr. Boynton
Apr. 30, 1938	Preston Lee Campbell to Virginia Stoneham	Fr. Boynton
Nov. 6, 1938	Dunklin M. Sullivan to Cecilia C. Brown	Fr. Boynton
Dec 21, 1938	Marvin E. Nesbitt to Rebecca Shuford	Fr. Boynton
April 9, 1939	Thomas C. Davall to Fannie L. Bowles	Fr. Boynton
Nov 4. 1939	R. Ben Shuford to Betty Ledbetter	Fr. Reid Hammond
Dec. 24, 1941	Ralph S. Morgan to Ruth E. Dobb	Rufus Morgan

Dec. 24,1941	Lucius McKinney to Virginia Sprinkle	Fr. Gale D. Webbe
Apr. 5, 1942	Dillon Cobb to Margaret Griffin	Fr. Webbe
Jan 9, 1942	Lette Parker to Betty Sageser	Fr. Webbe
June 29, 1944	Fr. Ralph L. Webster to Virginia Farnsworth	Bishop Gribbin
Aug. 10, 1946	Joe McCullough to Elizabeth Ryan Harris	Bishop Gribbin
May 1, 1947	John A. Gibson to Nina Morrison	Fr. Webbe
May 27, 1948	Frank Farnham Brown to Barbara McClure	Fr. Dahl
June 12, 1951	David P. Harris Jr., to Margaret Spencer Gravatt	John Gravatt
June 11, 1955	Moss Miller Jr. to Rose Lee Cox	Fr. Webster
July 27, 1955	Peter Fulton Ordway to Particia Adams	Fr. Webster
Aug. 11, 1956	Raymond Bradley Jr. to Dollie Rae Langley	Fr. Webster
Aug. 13, 1960	David W. McCullough to Ann Woltz Currie	Fr. Webster/The Rev. Kenneth Goodson
May 28, 1961	John S. Stevens to Imogene Radeker	Fr. Webster
June 8, 1968	Ralph K. Webster Jr., to Kristina Snelling	Fr. Webster
May 31, 1969	Charles A. Hacskaylo to Maryetta Hayes	Fr. Tom Seitz

Gamma Lambda Sigma
Fraternity
Founded at Christ School Oct. 26, 1914

A PLEDGE THAT COULD NOT BE KEPT:

It was a very solemn oath. The kind that only teenagers can make at a thoughtful pause in their lives.

The time was probably near graduation of 1940. The place was the Gamma Lambda Sigma Fraternity House. The oath-takers were members from the Classes of 1940 and 1941.

What they pledged, on a letterhead bearing the names of Clay Croom and picturing the Gamma Lambda Sigma seal, was their sacred honor to gather in the Fraternity House on December 13, 1944, at 2 p.m.

Signing that resolve were Nick Carter, Clay Croom, Haynes Hunter, Ernie Boatwright, Hoyle Adams, Robert Betts, Ned Simmons, Fanny Gilman, Earl Jackson, W. A. Pratt, Jack Mears, Jim Fowler, Bennet Clark, Durward Johnson, Sam Logan, Louis "Creole" Finely, and Hubert Edney.

But this reunion of brothers was destined never to occur. For two reasons. For one thing, none of the illustrious group had anticipated America's entry into World War II, and most of them were serving in the military in 1944, some overseas.

The second reason involved an unexpected twist. Two days before the December 13, 1944 reunion was to take place, a careless faternity brother apparently spilled hot ashes from his pipe on a couch. By midnight, the Gamma Lambda Sigma House was smoldering rubble.

An. . .ge. . .lus!

An. . .ge. . .lus! In the morning and in the evening, the ring of the Angelus turned Christ School into a frieze– a still-life portrait of quietness that touched homes far beyond the campus. In the evening, when it rang, the Angelus would catch us all at our work – sweeping our room or policing the grounds. Wherever we were and no matter what we were doing, we stopped and stood in silence, bowing our heads or stifling our laughter if we were in the middle of some humorous moment. Our silence was a form of prayer directed to God, avowing (though we did not understand it) that all was right with the world. When the last peel rolled from the tower, we finished our work, stood inspection, and then went to assembly. Mr. Dave would talk to us about something that was important to him or us. The prefects would call out the names of those who had received worklist, and then we'd all walk to the Chapel for Evensong. The quiet was a part of all assemblies (you did not carry talking and banter into assembly for it was a place of efficient business), a quiet you carried into Chapel where you squeezed five into a row and seniors made sure there was no disruption on the row. The oneness with the universe came across simply as the Chaplain said, "My soul doth magnify the Lord, and my spirit hath rejoiced in God my Saviour." Later in the magnificat we would affirm in the unison, chanting "It is He who made us and not we ourselves."

(**Jack McDuffie** '41)

Postscripts Contributors

ACKNOWLEDGMENT

So many of you were generous of your time and sources in the writing of *Three Score and Ten*, I hesitate to name anyone because I know some will inadvertently be omitted. For such omissions, I beg your forgiveness.

Christ School opened its archives, publications, and alumni records to provide basic background information. In addition, the minutes of the meetings of the board of directors were available to help establish time and debates and records of growth and development.

Fifty people or more –mostly alumni– were both candid and kind in talking to a tape recorder about the Christ School inscribed in their memories. They were Dorothy Thomson, Urq Chinn, Richard Fayssoux Sr., The Rt. Rev. Charles F. Boynton, Sam Emory, Warren Redd, Lewis Berkeley, Sarah Fayssoux, Johnny Moore, Richard Hanes, Ivison Ridgway, Art Armstrong, The Rev. Scott Root, Mrs. Ruth Black, Dillon Cobb, Jimmy Ewin, G.G. Griswold, Tom Suiter, Clair Thain, Alma Shroat Thain, Don Chamberlin, Edmund Glenny, Billy Campbell, Jeff Wyman, and Dr. John Dougherty.

Also Robert Bradham, Doug McElhenny, Jack Robinson, Jack Clark, Emory Clark, Halcott Green, Marney Hendrick, Tom Curtis, Margaret Brumbeloe, Robert Harris, Charlie Shuford, Zach Alden, David Harris Jr., The Rev. Ralph Webster, the Rev Gale Webbe, Allan Brown, Tom Yardley, Richie Meech, George Durant, Ballard Tebo, Tom Favrot, John Cooper, David Futch, Steve Stout, Joe Pressly, and J.D. Jones.

More than a dozen alumni or people connected with Christ School provided a variety of pictures, including many of good quality of the earlier years. For these we are deeply indebted to Richard Fayssoux Sr., Bob Harris, Margaret Brumbeloe, Dorothy Thomson, Zach Alden, Tom and Alma Thain, Jack Starrett, Sarah Fayssoux, Richie Meech, Johnny Moore, Joe McCullough, Dabney Johnson, and Sam Logan.

Another major source was information from other alumni and friends which came through personal correspondence, alumni surveys, and telephone interviews. These included The Rev. Norvin Duncan, Gene Johnston, John Fulton, John Dougherty, Frederick Krauss, Duncan MacBryde, Chapin McKenzie, Dillon Cobb, Tom Davall, Willard Caldwell, Robert Swartout, Tom Dickinson, Andrew Calhoun, Rusty Lovin, Tom La Rose, Mac Stonham, The Rev. Jack McDuffie, and Richard Arnold.

Also John Hope, Tolar Bryan, Frederick Parrish (Dashiel), Grahl Schaffert, Peter B. Waters, Taylor Shipley, Pat Echols, Harry Taylor, Bill Cobb, Bill Hauser, Gaylord Shepherd, King Logan, Albert Dougherty, Frank Zimmerman, Bill Kirkland, Durward Grady, Edward Freas, Tom McGill, Albert Matheny, George Kimberly, Hoke Currie, Bob Beard, Jimmy Patty, The Rev. Walter Hooper, Bob Carlisle, Harcourt Waters, Deas Richardson,Bill Wells, Chuck Wright, Adair Watters, Bryan Warren, July Waters, Blanche Bruns, and Pete Webbe.

Other sources of information included the Chapel register, *Christ School News* files, *The Galax Leaf*, brochures and pamphlets, *The State Magazine*, the *Asheville Citizen-Times*, *Christ School Magazine*, *Kent School Magazine*, and *The Warrior*.

I came out of the process with something I did not think possible–an even deeper love of Christ School and appreciation of everyone who went there, taught there, and worked there.

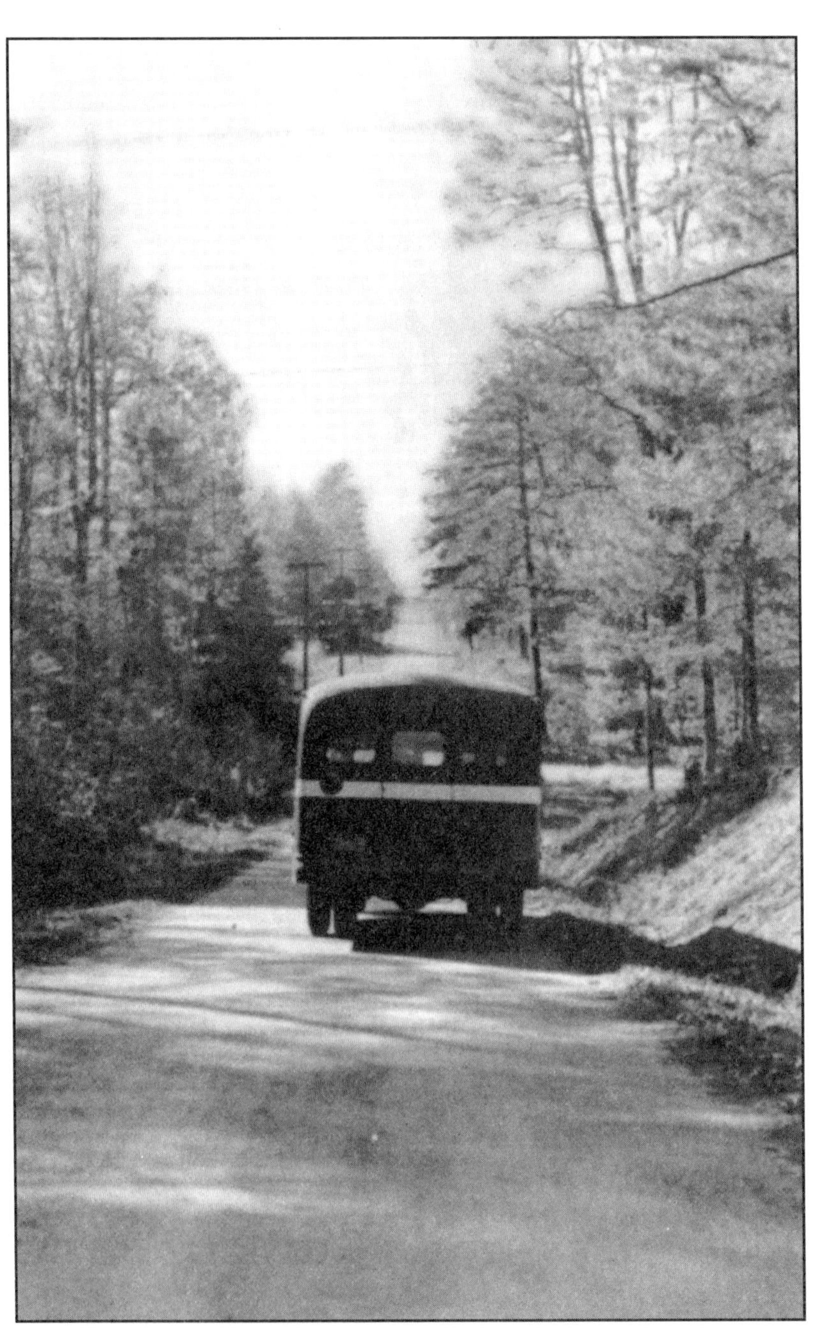